Hacking For Dummies®

Cheat Sheet

Ethical Hacking Tools You Can't Live Without

As an information security professional and ethical hacker, other than experience and common sense, your toolkit is the most critical item you can possess. Make sure you're never caught on the job without the following tools:

- An Internet connection and access to your favorite search engine such as Google
- War dialing software, such as ToneLoc or THC-Scan
- Password cracking software, such as LC4 or pwdump2 and John the Ripper
- Network scanning software, such as SuperScan and Nmap
- Network vulnerability assessment software, such as Nessus or QualysGuard
- Network analyzer, such as Ethereal or EtherPeek
- Web application assessment tool, such as Nikto or WebInspect

Common Security Weaknesses

Hackers often check the following vulnerabilities first when they try to break into networks and computers. Put these on your checklist when performing your tests:

- Gullible and overly trusting users
- Unsecured building and computer room entrances
- Discarded documents and computer disks that have not been shredded or destroyed
- Weak or no passwords
- Unsecured modems attached to network hosts
- Network perimeter with no firewall
- Poor, inappropriate, or missing access controls
- Antivirus software that's not properly updated or nonexistent
- Malware attachments in e-mails
- Unpatched systems
- Web applications with authentication or information disclosure issue
- Wireless LAN equipment running with default settings and without encryption or authentication
- SNMP-enabled network hosts with default or easily guessed community strings
- Firewalls, routers, and other dialup devices with default or easily guessed passwords

For Dummies: Bestselling Book Series for Beginners

Hacking For Dummies®

Commonly Hacked Ports

TCP ports 20 and 21 — FTP (File Transfer Protocol)

TCP port 23 — telnet

TCP port 25 — SMTP (Simple Mail Transfer Protocol)

TCP and UDP port 53 — DNS (Domain Name System)

TCP ports 80 and 443 — HTTP and HTTPS

TCP and UDP ports 1433–1434 — Microsoft SQL Server

TCP and UDP port 135 — RPC in a Microsoft environment

TCP and UDP ports 137–139 — NetBIOS over TCP/IP

TCP and UDP port 161 — SNMP

TCP port 3389 — Windows Terminal Server

Success Tips

As an information security professional, whether you're performing ethical hacking against a customer's systems or your own, these are the secrets for success:

- Get permission to perform your tests *in writing.*
- Set goals and develop a plan before you get started.
- Have access to the right tools for the task at hand.
- Test at a time that's best for the business.
- Understand that it's not possible to detect every security vulnerability.
- Study hacker behaviors and tactics. The more you know about how hackers work, the better you are at testing your systems for more realistic security vulnerabilities.
- Put as much effort into testing for nontechnical security issues as the technical ones. These are often exploited first.
- Make sure that all your testing is aboveboard.
- Treat other people's confidential information at least as well as you treat your own.
- Bring vulnerabilities you find to the attention of management and implement the appropriate countermeasures.
- Show management and customers that ethical hacking is good business. Ethical hacking is an investment to meet business goals, not silly hacker games.

Item 5784-X.
For more information about Wiley Publishing, call 1-800-762-2974.

For Dummies: Bestselling Book Series for Beginners

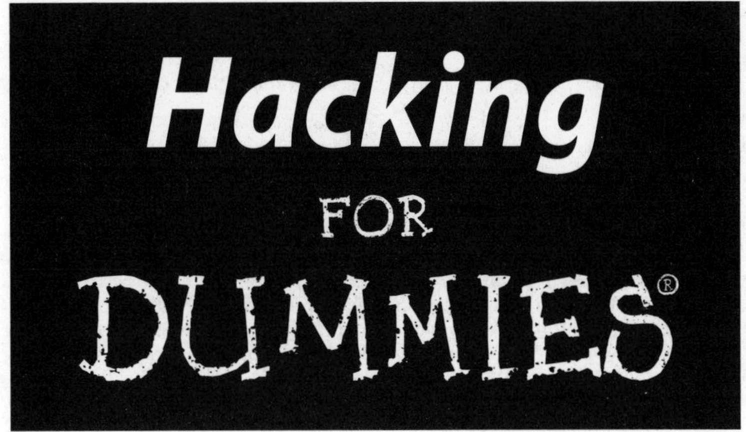

by Kevin Beaver

Foreword by Stuart McClure

Wiley Publishing, Inc.

Hacking For Dummies®

Published by
Wiley Publishing, Inc.
111 River Street
Hoboken, NJ 07030-5774

Published by Wiley Publishing, Inc., Indianapolis, Indiana

Published simultaneously in Canada

For general information on our other products and services or to obtain technical support, please contact our Customer Care Department within the U.S. at 800-762-2974, outside the U.S. at 317-572-3993, or fax 317-572-4002.

Wiley also publishes its books in a variety of electronic formats. Some content that appears in print may not be available in electronic books.

Library of Congress Control Number: 2004101971

ISBN: 0-7645-5784-X

Manufactured in the United States of America

10 9 8 7 6 5 4 3 2

1B/RV/QU/QU/IN

About the Author

As founder and principal consultant of Principle Logic, LLC, **Kevin Beaver** has over 16 years of experience in IT and specializes in information security. Before starting his own information security services business, Kevin served in various information technology and security roles for several Fortune 500 corporations and a variety of consulting, e-commerce, and educational institutions. In addition to ethical hacking, his areas of information security expertise include network and wireless network security, e-mail and instant messaging security, and incident response

Kevin is also author of the book *The Definitive Guide to Email Management and Security* by Realtimepublishers.com and co-author of the book *The Practical Guide to HIPAA Privacy and Security Compliance* by Auerbach Publications. In addition, he is technical editor of the book *Network Security For Dummies* by Wiley Publishing, and a contributing author and editor of the book *Healthcare Information Systems,* 2nd ed. by Auerbach Publications.

Kevin is a regular columnist and information security expert advisor for SearchSecurity.com and SearchMobileComputing.com and is a Security Clinic Expert for ITsecurity.com. In addition, his information security work has been published in Information Security Magazine, HIMSS Journal of Healthcare Information Management, Advance for Health Information Executives as well as on SecurityFocus.com. Kevin is an information security instructor for the Southeast Cybercrime Institute and also frequently speaks on information security at various workshops and conferences around the U.S. including TechTarget's *Decisions* conferences, CSI, and the Southeast Cybercrime Summit.

Kevin is the founder and president of the Technology Association of Georgia's Information Security Society and serves as an IT advisory board member for several universities and companies around the southeast. Kevin earned his bachelor's degree in Computer Engineering Technology from Southern Polytechnic State University and his master's degree in Management of Technology from Georgia Tech. He also holds CISSP, MCSE, Master CNE, and IT Project+ certifications. Kevin can be reached at `kbeaver@principlelogic.com`.

Dedication

For Amy, Garrett, Master, and Murphy — through thick and thicker, we did it! I couldn't have written this book without the tremendous inspiration each of you have given me. You all make the world a better place — thanks for being here for me.

Author's Acknowledgments

First, I'd like to thank Melody Layne, my acquisitions editor at Wiley, for contacting me with this book idea, providing me this great opportunity, and for being so patient with me during the acquisitions, writing, and editing processes. Also, thanks to all the other members of the acquisitions team at Wiley who helped me shape my outline and initial chapter.

I'd like to thank my project editor, Pat O'Brien, as well as Kim Darosett and the rest of the tireless editorial staff at Wiley for all of your hard work, patience, and great edits! Also, thanks to Terri Varveris for making the initial Dummies contact several years back in the Hungry Minds days and for introducing me to the team — you truly helped get this ball rolling.

Major kudos go out to the security legend, Peter T. Davis, my technical editor. Your *For Dummies* experience and seemingly never-ending technical knowledge are a great asset to this book. I really appreciate your time and effort you've put forth, and I'm truly honored that you helped me on this project.

I'd also like to thank Stuart McClure — the highly-talented security expert and phenomenal author — for writing the foreword. It's funny how this book turned out and how you still ended up being involved! Just look at what you created instead — you should be proud.

To Ira Winkler, Jack Wiles, Dr. Philippe Oechslin, David Rhoades, Laura Chappell, Matt Caldwell, Thomas Akin, Ed Skoudis, and Caleb Sima — thank you all for doing such a great job with the case studies in this book! They're a perfect fit and each of you were true professionals and great to work with. I really appreciate your time and effort.

I'd like to extend deep gratitude to Robert Dreyer — my favorite professor at Southern Poly — who piqued my technical interest in computer hardware and software and who taught me way more about computer bits and bytes than I thought I'd ever know. Also, thanks to my friend William Long — one of the smartest people I've ever known — for being the best computer and network mentor I could ever have. In addition, I'd like to thank John Cirami for showing me how to run that first DOS executable file off of that 5 1/4" floppy way back when and for helping me to get the ball rolling in my computer career.

A well-deserved thanks also goes out to all my friends and colleagues — you know who you are — who helped provide feedback and advice about the title change.

Finally, I'd like to thank Rik Emmett, Geoff Tate, Neil Peart, and *all* of their supporting band members for the awesome lyrics and melodies that inspired me to keep pushing forward with this book during the challenging times.

Publisher's Acknowledgments

We're proud of this book; please send us your comments through our online registration form located at www.dummies.com/register/.

Some of the people who helped bring this book to market include the following:

Acquisitions, Editorial, and Media Development

Project Editor: Pat O'Brien

Acquisitions Editor: Melody Layne

Senior Copy Editor: Kim Darosett

Technical Editor: Peter T. Davis

Editorial Manager: Kevin Kirschner

Media Development Manager: Laura VanWinkle

Media Development Supervisor: Richard Graves

Editorial Assistant: Amanda Foxworth

Cartoons: Rich Tennant, www.the5thwave.com

Production

Project Coordinator: Maridee Ennis

Layout and Graphics: Andrea Dahl, Denny Hager, Lynsey Osborn, Heather Ryan, Jacque Schneider

Proofreaders: Carl W. Pierce, Brian H. Walls, TECHBOOKS Production Services

Indexer: TECHBOOKS Production Services

Publishing and Editorial for Technology Dummies

Richard Swadley, Vice President and Executive Group Publisher

Andy Cummings, Vice President and Publisher

Mary C. Corder, Editorial Director

Publishing for Consumer Dummies

Diane Graves Steele, Vice President and Publisher

Joyce Pepple, Acquisitions Director

Composition Services

Gerry Fahey, Vice President of Production Services

Debbie Stailey, Director of Composition Services

Contents at a Glance

Table of Contents

Foreword

Little more than 10 years ago, security was barely a newborn in diapers. With only a handful of security professionals in 1994, few practiced security and even fewer truly understood it. Security technologies amounted to little more than anti-virus software and packet filtering routers at that time. And the concept of a "hacker" came primarily from the Hollywood movie "War Games"; or more often it referred to someone with a low golf score. As a result, just like Rodney Dangerfield it got "no respect" and no one took it seriously. IT professionals saw it largely as a nuisance, to be ignored — that is until they were impacted by it.

Today, the number of Certified Information Systems Security Professionals (CISSP) have topped 23,000 (www.isc2.org) worldwide, and there are more security companies dotting the landscape than anyone could possibly remember. Today security technologies encompass everything from authentication and authorization, to firewalls and VPNs. There are so many ways to address the security problem that it can cause more than a slight migraine simply considering the alternatives. And the term "hacker" has become a permanent part of our everyday vernacular — as defined in nearly daily headlines. The world (and its criminals) has changed dramatically.

So what does all this mean for you, the home/end user or IT/security professional that is thrust into this dangerous online world every time you hit the power button on your computer? The answer is "everything". The digital landscape is peppered with land mines that can go off with the slightest touch or, better yet, without any provocation whatsoever. Consider some simple scenarios:

- Simply plugging into the Internet without a properly configured firewall can get you hacked before the pizza is delivered, within 30 minutes or less.
- Opening an email attachment from a family member, friend, or work colleague can install a backdoor on your system allowing a hacker free access to your computer.
- Downloading and executing a file via your Internet Messaging (IM) program can turn your pristine desktop into a Centers for Disease Control (CDC) hotzone, complete with the latest alphabet soup virus.
- Browsing to an innocent (and trusted) website can completely compromise your computer, allowing a hacker to read your sensitive files or worse delete them.

Trust me when we say the likelihood of becoming an Internet drive-by statistic on the information superhighway is painfully real.

I am often asked, "Is the fear, uncertainty, and doubt (FUD) centered on cyberterrorism justified? Can cyber-terrorists really affect our computer systems and our public infrastructure as some have prognosticated like new age Nostradamus soothsayers? The answer I always give is "Unequivocally, yes". The possibility of a digital Pearl Harbor is closer than many think. Organized terrorist cells like Al Qaeda are raided almost weekly, and when computers are discovered, their drives are filled with cyber hacking plans, U.S. infrastructure blueprints, and instructions on attacking U.S. computer and infrastructure targets.

Do you believe the energy commissions report about the biggest power outage in U.S history? The one that on August 14, 2003 left 1/5th of the U.S. population without power (about 50 million people) for over 12 hours? Do you believe that it has to do with untrimmed trees and faulty control processes? If you believe in Occam's Razor, then yes, the simplest explanation is usually the correct one but remember this: the power outage hit just three days after the Microsoft Blaster worm, one of the most vicious computer worms ever unleashed on the Internet, first hit. Coincidence? Perhaps.

Some of you may be skeptical, saying "Well, if the threat is so real, why hasn't something bad happened yet?" I respond simply, "If I had come to you on Sept. 10, 2001, and said that in the near future people would use commercial airplanes as bombs to kill over 3,000 people in the matter of 5 hours, would you believe me?" I understand your skepticism. And you should be skeptical. But we are asking for your trust, and your faith, before something bad happens. Trust that we know the truth, we know what is possible, and we know the mind of the enemy. I think we can all agree on at least one thing, we cannot allow them to succeed.

Every minute of every day there are governments, organized crime, and hacker groups turning the doors on your house looking for an unlocked entry. They are rattling the windows and circling your domicile, looking for a weakness, a vulnerability, or a way into your house. Are you going to let them in? Are you going to sit idly by and watch as they ransack your belongings, make use of your facilities, and desecrate your sanctuary? Or are you going to empower yourself, educate yourself, and prevent them from winning? The actions you take today will ultimately answer that question.

Do not despair, all hope is not lost. Increasing security is more of a mindset than anything else. Security is akin to working out. If you don't do it regularly, it won't become a part of your lifestyle. And if it doesn't become a part of your lifestyle, it will quickly become something you can forego and avoid. In other words, you won't be fit. Same thing applies for security. If you don't realize that it is a process, not a goal, then you will never make it part of your everyday wellness routine, as a result it quickly becomes something you forego and avoid. And if you avoid it, you will eventually be bit by it.

The greatest gift you can give yourself is that of education. What you don't know may not kill you but it may seriously impact you or someone you care about. Knowing what you don't know is the real trick. And filling in the gaps of knowledge is paramount to preventing a significant attack. *Hacking For Dummies* can fill in those gaps. Kevin has done a remarkable job in presenting material that is valuable and unique in that it covers hacking methodologies for Windows, Novell, and Linux, as well as such little covered topics as physical security, social engineering, and malware. The varied coverage of security topics in this book is what helps you more completely understand the mind of the hacker and how they work; and it will ultimately be the singular reason you may avoid an attack in the future. Read it carefully. Learn from it. And practice what it says in every area you can.

Make no mistake; the digital battlefield is very real. It has no beginning, it has no ending, it has no boundaries, and it has no rules. Read this book, learn from it and defend yourself or we may lose this digital war.

Stuart McClure is a world-renowned information security expert, founder and co-author of the highly-popular Hacking Exposed series of books, and founder and President and Chief Technology Officer of Foundstone, Inc., experts in strategic security. He can be reached at stu@foundstone.com.

Introduction

Welcome to *Hacking For Dummies.* This book outlines computer hacker tricks and techniques — in plain English — to assess the security of your own information systems, find security vulnerabilities, and fix the vulnerabilities before malicious and criminal hackers have an opportunity to take advantage of them. This hacking is the professional, aboveboard, and legal type of security testing — which I call *ethical hacking* throughout the book.

Computer and network security is a complex subject and an ever-moving target. You must stay on top of it to ensure your information is protected from the bad guys. You can implement all the security technologies and other best practices possible, and your information systems may be secure — as far as you know. However, until you understand how hackers think and apply that knowledge to assess your systems from a hacker's-eye view, you can't get a true sense of how secure your information really is.

Ethical hacking — sometimes referred to as *penetration testing, vulnerability testing,* or *white-hat hacking* — is a necessary requirement to ensure that information systems are truly secure on an ongoing basis. This book provides you with the knowledge required to successfully implement an ethical hacking program, along with countermeasures that you can implement to keep malicious hackers out of your business.

Who Should Read This Book?

If you want to hack other people's computer systems maliciously, this book is not for you.

Disclaimer: If you choose to use the information in this book to hack or break into computer systems maliciously in an unauthorized fashion, you're on your own. Neither I, as the author, nor anyone else associated with this book shall be liable or responsible for any unethical or criminal choices that you may make and execute using the methodologies and tools that I describe. This book is intended solely for the IT professional to test information security in an authorized fashion.

Okay, now that that's out of the way, time for the good stuff! This book is for you if you're a network administrator, information-security manager, security consultant, or someone interested in finding out more about legally and ethically hacking your own or a customer's information systems to make them more secure.

As the ethical hacker performing well-intended information-security assessments, you can detect and point out security holes that may otherwise be overlooked. If you're performing these tests on your own systems, the information you uncover in your tests can help you win over management and prove that information security should be taken seriously. Likewise, if you're performing these tests for your customers, you can help find security holes that can be plugged before malicious hackers have a chance to exploit them.

The information in this book helps you stay on top of the security game and enjoy the fame and glory that comes with helping your organization and customers prevent bad things from happening to their information.

About This Book

Hacking For Dummies is a reference guide on hacking computers and network systems. The ethical hacking techniques are based on the unwritten rules of computer system penetration testing and information-security best practices. This book covers everything from establishing your hacking plan to testing your systems to managing an ongoing ethical hacking program. Realistically, for many networks, operating systems, and applications, thousands of possible hacks exist. I cover the major ones that you should be concerned about. Whether you need to assess security vulnerabilities on a small home-office network, a medium-size corporate network, or across large enterprise systems, *Hacking For Dummies* provides the information you need.

How to Use This Book

This book includes the following features:

- Various technical and nontechnical hack attacks and their detailed methodologies
- Information security testing case studies from well-known information security experts
- Specific countermeasures to protect against hack attacks

Each chapter is an individual reference on a specific ethical hacking subject. You can refer to individual chapters that pertain to the type of systems you're assessing, or you can read the book straight through.

Before you start hacking your systems, familiarize yourself with the information in Part I so you're prepared for the tasks at hand. The adage "if you fail to plan, you plan to fail" rings true for the ethical hacking process. You must get written permission and have a solid game plan.

This material is not intended to be used for unethical or illegal hacking purposes to propel you from script kiddie to mega hacker. Rather, it is designed to provide you with the knowledge you need to hack your own or your customers' systems — in an ethical and legal manner — to enhance the security of the information involved.

What You Don't Need to Read

Depending on your computer and network configurations, you may be able to skip chapters. For example, if you aren't running Linux or wireless networks, you can skip those chapters.

Foolish Assumptions

I make a few assumptions about you, aspiring information-security person:

- You're familiar with basic computer-, network-, and information-security-related concepts and terms.
- You have a basic understanding of what hackers do.
- You have access to a computer and a network on which to test these techniques.
- You have access to the Internet in order to obtain the various tools used in the ethical hacking process.
- You have permission to perform the hacking techniques in this book.

How This Book Is Organized

This book is organized into eight parts — six regular chapter parts, a Part of Tens, and a part with appendixes. These parts are modular, so you can jump around from one part to another as needed. Each chapter provides practical methodologies and best practices you can utilize as part of your ethical hacking efforts, including checklists and references to specific tools you can use, as well as resources on the Internet.

Part I: Building the Foundation for Ethical Hacking

This part covers the fundamental aspects of ethical hacking. It starts with an overview of the value of ethical hacking and what you should and shouldn't do during the process. You get inside the hacker's mindset and discover how to plan your ethical hacking efforts. This part covers the steps involved in the ethical hacking process, including how to choose the proper tools.

Part II: Putting Ethical Hacking in Motion

This part gets you rolling with the ethical hacking process. It covers several well-known hack attacks, including social engineering and cracking passwords, to get your feet wet. The techniques presented are some of the most widely used hack attacks. This part covers the human and physical elements of security, which tend to be the weakest links in any information-security program. After you plunge into these topics, you'll know the tips and tricks required to perform common general hack attacks against your systems, as well as specific countermeasures to keep your information systems secure.

Part III: Network Hacking

Starting with the larger network in mind, this part covers methods to test your systems for various well-known network infrastructure vulnerabilities. From weaknesses in the TCP/IP protocol suite to wireless network insecurities, you find out how networks are compromised using specific methods of flawed network communications, along with various countermeasures that you can implement to keep from becoming a victim. This part also includes case studies on some of the network hack attacks that are presented.

Part IV: Operating System Hacking

Practically all operating systems have well-known vulnerabilities that hackers often use. This part jumps into hacking three widely used operating systems: Windows, Linux, and NetWare. The hacking methods include scanning your operating systems for vulnerabilities and enumerating the specific hosts to gain detailed information. This part also includes information on exploiting well-known vulnerabilities in these operating systems, taking over operating systems remotely, and specific countermeasures that you can implement to make your operating systems more secure. This part also includes case studies on operating-system hack attacks.

Part V: Application Hacking

Application security is gaining more visibility in the information-security arena these days. An increasing number of attacks are aimed directly at various applications, which are often able to bypass firewalls, intrusion-detection systems, and antivirus software. This part discusses hacking specific applications, including coverage on malicious software and messaging systems, along with practical countermeasures that you can put in place to make your applications more secure.

One of the most common network attacks is on Web applications. Practically every firewall lets Web traffic into and out of the network, so most attacks are against the millions of Web applications available to almost anyone. This part covers Web application hack attacks, countermeasures, and some application hacking case studies for real-world security testing scenarios.

Part VI: Ethical Hacking Aftermath

After you've performed your ethical hack attacks, what do you do with the information you've gathered? Shelve it? Show it off? How do you move forward? This part answers all these questions and more. From developing reports for upper management to remediating the security flaws that you discover to establishing procedures for your ongoing ethical hacking efforts, this part brings the ethical hacking process full circle. This information not only ensures that your effort and time are well spent, but also is evidence that information security is as an essential element for success in any business that depends on computers and information technology.

Part VII: The Part of Tens

This part contains tips to help ensure the success of your ethical hacking program. You find out how to get upper management to buy into your ethical hacking program so you can get going and start protecting your systems. This part also includes the top ten ethical hacking mistakes to avoid and my top ten tips for ethical hacking success.

Part VIII: Appendixes

This part includes two appendixes that cover ethical hacking reference materials. This includes a one-stop reference listing of ethical hacking tools and resources, as well as information on the *Hacking For Dummies* Web site.

Icons Used in This Book

This icon points out technical information that is interesting but not vital to your understanding of the topic being discussed.

This icon points out information that is worth committing to memory.

This icon points out information that could have a negative impact on your ethical hacking efforts — so please read it!

This icon refers to advice that can help highlight or clarify an important point.

Where to Go from Here

The more you know about how hackers work and how your systems should be tested, the better you're able to secure your computer systems. This book provides the foundation that you need to develop and maintain a successful ethical-hacking program for your organization and customers. Keep in mind that the high-level concepts of ethical hacking won't change as often as the specific information-security vulnerabilities you're protecting against. The art and science of ethical hacking will always remain an art and a science — and a field that's ever-changing. You must keep up with the latest hardware and software technologies, along with the various vulnerabilities that come about year after year. No one best way to hack your systems ethically exists, so tweak this information to your heart's content. Happy (ethical) hacking!

Part I

Building the Foundation for Ethical Hacking

"Hey Philip! I think we're in. I'm gonna try linking directly to the screen, but gimme a disguise in case it works. I don't want all of New York to know Jerry DeMarco of 14 Queensberry, Bronx NY, hacked into the Times Square video screen."

In this part . . .

Your mission — should you choose to accept it — is to find the holes in your network before the bad guys do. This mission will be fun, educational, and most likely entertaining. It will certainly be an eye-opening experience. The cool part is that you can emerge as the hero, knowing that your company will be better protected against hacker attacks and less likely to have its name smeared across the headlines at any time.

If you're new to ethical hacking, this is the place to begin. The chapters in this part will get you started with information on what to do and how to do it when you're hacking your own systems. Oh, and also, you find out what *not* to do as well. This information will guide you through building the foundation for your ethical hacking program to make sure you're going down the right path so you don't veer off and end up going down a one-way dead-end street.

Chapter 1

Introduction to Ethical Hacking

In This Chapter

- Understanding hacker objectives
- Outlining the differences between ethical hackers and malicious hackers
- Examining how the ethical hacking process has come about
- Understanding the dangers that your computer systems face
- Starting the ethical hacking process

This book is about hacking ethically — the science of testing your computers and network for security vulnerabilities and plugging the holes you find before the bad guys get a chance to exploit them.

Although *ethical* is an often overused and misunderstood word, the Merriam-Webster dictionary defines *ethical* perfectly for the context of this book and the professional security testing techniques that I cover — that is, *conforming to accepted professional standards of conduct.* IT practitioners are obligated to perform all the tests covered in this book aboveboard and only after permission has been obtained by the owner(s) of the systems — hence the disclaimer in the introduction.

How Hackers Beget Ethical Hackers

We've all heard of hackers. Many of us have even suffered the consequences of hacker actions. So who are these hackers? Why is it important to know about them? The next few sections give you the lowdown on hackers.

Defining hacker

Hacker is a word that has two meanings:

- Traditionally, a hacker is someone who likes to tinker with software or electronic systems. Hackers enjoy exploring and learning how computer systems operate. They love discovering new ways to work electronically.

- Recently, *hacker* has taken on a new meaning — someone who maliciously breaks into systems for personal gain. Technically, these criminals are *crackers* (criminal hackers). Crackers break into *(crack)* systems with malicious intent. They are out for personal gain: fame, profit, and even revenge. They modify, delete, and steal critical information, often making other people miserable.

The good-guy *(white-hat)* hackers don't like being in the same category as the bad-guy *(black-hat)* hackers. (These terms come from Western movies where the good guys wore white cowboy hats and the bad guys wore black cowboy hats.) Whatever the case, most people give *hacker* a negative connotation.

Many malicious hackers claim that they don't cause damage but instead are altruistically helping others. Yeah, right. Many malicious hackers are electronic thieves.

In this book, I use the following terminology:

- *Hackers* (or *bad guys*) try to compromise computers.
- *Ethical hackers* (or *good guys*) protect computers against illicit entry.

Hackers go for almost any system they think they can compromise. Some prefer prestigious, well-protected systems, but hacking into anyone's system increases their status in hacker circles.

Ethical Hacking 101

You need protection from hacker shenanigans. An *ethical hacker* possesses the skills, mindset, and tools of a hacker but is also trustworthy. Ethical hackers perform the hacks as security tests for their systems.

If you perform ethical hacking tests for customers or simply want to add another certification to your credentials, you may want to consider the ethical hacker certification Certified Ethical Hacker, which is sponsored by EC-Council. See `www.eccouncil.org/CEH.htm` for more information.

Ethical hacking — also known as *penetration testing* or *white-hat hacking* — involves the same tools, tricks, and techniques that hackers use, but with one major difference: Ethical hacking is legal. Ethical hacking is performed with the target's permission. The intent of ethical hacking is to discover vulnerabilities from a hacker's viewpoint so systems can be better secured. It's part of an overall information risk management program that allows for ongoing security improvements. Ethical hacking can also ensure that vendors' claims about the security of their products are legitimate.

To hack your own systems like the bad guys, you must think like they think. It's absolutely critical to know your enemy; see Chapter 2 for details.

Understanding the Need to Hack Your Own Systems

To catch a thief, think like a thief. That's the basis for ethical hacking.

The law of averages works against security. With the increased numbers and expanding knowledge of hackers combined with the growing number of system vulnerabilities and other unknowns, the time will come when all computer systems are hacked or compromised in some way. Protecting your systems from the bad guys — and not just the generic vulnerabilities that everyone knows about — is absolutely critical. When you know hacker tricks, you can see how vulnerable your systems are.

Hacking preys on weak security practices and undisclosed vulnerabilities. Firewalls, encryption, and virtual private networks (VPNs) can create a false feeling of safety. These security systems often focus on high-level vulnerabilities, such as viruses and traffic through a firewall, without affecting how hackers work. Attacking your own systems to discover vulnerabilities is a step to making them more secure. This is the only proven method of greatly hardening your systems from attack. If you don't identify weaknesses, it's a matter of time before the vulnerabilities are exploited.

As hackers expand their knowledge, so should you. You must think like them to protect your systems from them. You, as the ethical hacker, must know activities hackers carry out and how to stop their efforts. You should know what to look for and how to use that information to thwart hackers' efforts.

You don't have to protect your systems from everything. You can't. The only protection against everything is to unplug your computer systems and lock them away so no one can touch them — not even you. That's not the best approach to information security. What's important is to protect your systems from known vulnerabilities and common hacker attacks.

It's impossible to buttress all possible vulnerabilities on all your systems. You can't plan for all possible attacks — especially the ones that are currently unknown. However, the more combinations you try — the more you test whole systems instead of individual units — the better your chances of discovering vulnerabilities that affect everything as a whole.

Don't take ethical hacking too far, though. It makes little sense to harden your systems from unlikely attacks. For instance, if you don't have a lot of foot traffic in your office and no internal Web server running, you may not have as much to worry about as an Internet hosting provider would have. However, don't forget about insider threats from malicious employees!

Your overall goals as an ethical hacker should be as follows:

- Hack your systems in a nondestructive fashion.
- Enumerate vulnerabilities and, if necessary, prove to upper management that vulnerabilities exist.
- Apply results to remove vulnerabilities and better secure your systems.

Understanding the Dangers Your Systems Face

It's one thing to know that your systems generally are under fire from hackers around the world. It's another to understand specific attacks against your systems that are possible. This section offers some well-known attacks but is by no means a comprehensive listing. That requires its own book: *Hack Attacks Encyclopedia,* by John Chirillo (Wiley Publishing, Inc.).

Many information-security vulnerabilities aren't critical by themselves. However, exploiting several vulnerabilities at the same time can take its toll. For example, a default Windows OS configuration, a weak SQL Server administrator password, and a server hosted on a wireless network may not be major security concerns separately. But exploiting all three of these vulnerabilities at the same time can be a serious issue.

Nontechnical attacks

Exploits that involve manipulating people — end users and even yourself — are the greatest vulnerability within any computer or network infrastructure. Humans are trusting by nature, which can lead to social-engineering exploits. *Social engineering* is defined as the exploitation of the trusting nature of human beings to gain information for malicious purposes. I cover social engineering in depth in Chapter 5.

Other common and effective attacks against information systems are physical. Hackers break into buildings, computer rooms, or other areas containing critical information or property. Physical attacks can include *dumpster diving* (rummaging through trash cans and dumpsters for intellectual property, passwords, network diagrams, and other information).

Network-infrastructure attacks

Hacker attacks against network infrastructures can be easy, because many networks can be reached from anywhere in the world via the Internet. Here are some examples of network-infrastructure attacks:

- Connecting into a network through a rogue modem attached to a computer behind a firewall
- Exploiting weaknesses in network transport mechanisms, such as TCP/IP and NetBIOS
- Flooding a network with too many requests, creating a denial of service (DoS) for legitimate requests
- Installing a network analyzer on a network and capturing every packet that travels across it, revealing confidential information in clear text
- Piggybacking onto a network through an insecure 802.11b wireless configuration

Operating-system attacks

Hacking operating systems (OSs) is a preferred method of the bad guys. OSs comprise a large portion of hacker attacks simply because every computer has one and so many well-known exploits can be used against them.

Occasionally, some operating systems that are more secure out of the box — such as Novell NetWare and the flavors of BSD UNIX — are attacked, and vulnerabilities turn up. But hackers prefer attacking operating systems like Windows and Linux because they are widely used and better known for their vulnerabilities.

Here are some examples of attacks on operating systems:

- Exploiting specific protocol implementations
- Attacking built-in authentication systems
- Breaking file-system security
- Cracking passwords and encryption mechanisms

Application and other specialized attacks

Applications take a lot of hits by hackers. Programs such as e-mail server software and Web applications often are beaten down:

- Hypertext Transfer Protocol (HTTP) and Simple Mail Transfer Protocol (SMTP) applications are frequently attacked because most firewalls and other security mechanisms are configured to allow full access to these programs from the Internet.
- Malicious software *(malware)* includes viruses, worms, Trojan horses, and spyware. Malware clogs networks and takes down systems.
- *Spam* (junk e-mail) is wreaking havoc on system availability and storage space. And it can carry malware.

Ethical hacking helps reveal such attacks against your computer systems. Parts II through V of this book cover these attacks in detail, along with specific countermeasures you can implement against attacks on your systems.

Obeying the Ethical Hacking Commandments

Every ethical hacker must abide by a few basic commandments. If not, bad things can happen. I've seen these commandments ignored or forgotten when planning or executing ethical hacking tests. The results weren't positive.

Working ethically

The word *ethical* in this context can be defined as working with high professional morals and principles. Whether you're performing ethical hacking tests against your own systems or for someone who has hired you, everything you do as an ethical hacker must be aboveboard and must support the company's goals. No hidden agendas are allowed!

Trustworthiness is the ultimate tenet. The misuse of information is absolutely forbidden. That's what the bad guys do.

Respecting privacy

Treat the information you gather with the utmost respect. All information you obtain during your testing — from Web-application log files to clear-text passwords — must be kept private. Don't use this information to snoop into confidential corporate information or private lives. If you sense that someone should know there's a problem, consider sharing that information with the appropriate manager.

Involve others in your process. This is a "watch the watcher" system that can build trust and support your ethical hacking projects.

Not crashing your systems

One of the biggest mistakes I've seen when people try to hack their own systems is inadvertently crashing their systems. The main reason for this is poor planning. These testers have not read the documentation or misunderstand the usage and power of the security tools and techniques.

You can easily create DoS conditions on your systems when testing. Running too many tests too quickly on a system causes many system lockups. I know because I've done this! Don't rush things and assume that a network or specific host can handle the beating that network scanners and vulnerability-assessment tools can dish out.

Many security-assessment tools can control how many tests are performed on a system at the same time. These tools are especially handy if you need to run the tests on production systems during regular business hours.

You can even create an account or system lockout condition by social engineering someone into changing a password, not realizing that doing so might create a system lockout condition.

The Ethical Hacking Process

Like practically any IT or security project, ethical hacking needs to be planned in advance. Strategic and tactical issues in the ethical hacking process should be determined and agreed upon. Planning is important for any amount of testing — from a simple password-cracking test to an all-out penetration test on a Web application.

Formulating your plan

Approval for ethical hacking is essential. Make what you're doing known and visible — at least to the decision makers. Obtaining *sponsorship* of the project is the first step. This could be your manager, an executive, a customer, or even yourself if you're the boss. You need someone to back you up and sign off on your plan. Otherwise, your testing may be called off unexpectedly if someone claims they never authorized you to perform the tests.

The authorization can be as simple as an internal memo from your boss if you're performing these tests on your own systems. If you're testing for a customer, have a signed contract in place, stating the customer's support and authorization. Get written approval on this sponsorship as soon as possible to ensure that none of your time or effort is wasted. This documentation is your *Get Out of Jail Free* card if anyone questions what you're doing.

You need a detailed plan, but that doesn't mean you have to have volumes of testing procedures. One slip can crash your systems — not necessarily what anyone wants. A well-defined scope includes the following information:

- Specific systems to be tested
- Risks that are involved
- When the tests are performed and your overall timeline
- How the tests are performed
- How much knowledge of the systems you have before you start testing
- What is done when a major vulnerability is discovered
- The specific deliverables — this includes security-assessment reports and a higher-level report outlining the general vulnerabilities to be addressed, along with countermeasures that should be implemented

When selecting systems to test, start with the most critical or vulnerable systems. For instance, you can test computer passwords or attempt social-engineering attacks before drilling down into more detailed systems.

It pays to have a contingency plan for your ethical hacking process in case something goes awry. What if you're assessing your firewall or Web application, and you take it down? This can cause system unavailability, which can reduce system performance or employee productivity. Even worse, it could cause loss of data integrity, loss of data, and bad publicity.

Handle social-engineering and denial-of-service attacks carefully. Determine how they can affect the systems you're testing and your entire organization.

Determining when the tests are performed is something that you must think long and hard about. Do you test during normal business hours? How about late at night or early in the morning so that production systems aren't affected? Involve others to make sure they approve of your timing.

The best approach is an unlimited attack, wherein any type of test is possible. The bad guys aren't hacking your systems within a limited scope, so why should you? Some exceptions to this approach are performing DoS, social-engineering, and physical-security tests.

Don't stop with one security hole. This can lead to a false sense of security. Keep going to see what else you can discover. I'm not saying to keep hacking until the end of time or until you crash all your systems. Simply pursue the path you're going down until you can't hack it any longer (pun intended).

One of your goals may be to perform the tests without being detected. For example, you may be performing your tests on remote systems or on a remote office, and you don't want the users to be aware of what you're doing. Otherwise, the users may be on to you and be on their best behavior.

You don't need extensive knowledge of the systems you're testing — just a basic understanding. This will help you protect the tested systems.

Understanding the systems you're testing shouldn't be difficult if you're hacking your own in-house systems. If you're hacking a customer's systems, you may have to dig deeper. In fact, I've never had a customer ask for a fully blind assessment. Most people are scared of these assessments. Base the type of test you will perform on your organization's or customer's needs.

Chapter 19 covers hiring "reformed" hackers.

Selecting tools

As with any project, if you don't have the right tools for ethical hacking, accomplishing the task effectively is difficult. Having said that, just because you use the right tools doesn't mean that you will discover all vulnerabilities.

Know the personal and technical limitations. Many security-assessment tools generate false positives and negatives (incorrectly identifying vulnerabilities). Others may miss vulnerabilities. If you're performing tests such as social-engineering or physical-security assessments, you may miss weaknesses.

Many tools focus on specific tests, but no one tool can test for everything. For the same reason that you wouldn't drive in a nail with a screwdriver, you shouldn't use a word processor to scan your network for open ports. This is why you need a set of specific tools that you can call on for the task at hand. The more tools you have, the easier your ethical hacking efforts are.

Make sure you that you're using the right tool for the task:

- To crack passwords, you need a cracking tool such as LC4, John the Ripper, or pwdump.

  A general port scanner, such as SuperScan, may not crack passwords.
- For an in-depth analysis of a Web application, a Web-application assessment tool (such as Whisker or WebInspect) is more appropriate than a network analyzer (such as Ethereal).

When selecting the right security tool for the task, ask around. Get advice from your colleagues and from other people online. A simple Groups search on Google (`www.google.com`) or perusal of security portals, such as SecurityFocus.com, SearchSecurity.com, and ITsecurity.com, often produces great feedback from other security experts.

Hundreds, if not thousands, of tools can be used for ethical hacking — from your own words and actions to software-based vulnerability-assessment programs to hardware-based network analyzers. The following list runs down some of my favorite commercial, freeware, and open-source security tools:

- Nmap
- EtherPeek
- SuperScan
- QualysGuard
- WebInspect
- Elcomsoft Proactive Windows Security Explorer
- LANguard Network Security Scanner
- Network Stumbler
- ToneLoc

Here are some other popular tools:

- Internet Scanner
- Ethereal
- Nessus
- Nikto
- Kismet
- THC-Scan

I discuss these tools and many others in Parts II through V when I go into the specific hack attacks. Appendix A contains a more comprehensive listing of these tools for your reference.

The capabilities of many security and hacking tools are often misunderstood. This misunderstanding has shed negative light on some excellent tools, such as SATAN (Security Administrator Tool for Analyzing Networks) and Nmap (Network Mapper).

Some of these tools are complex. Whichever tools you use, familiarize yourself with them before you start using them. Here are ways to do that:

- Read the readme and/or online help files for your tools.
- Study the user's guide for your commercial tools.
- Consider formal classroom training from the security-tool vendor or another third-party training provider, if available.

Look for these characteristics in tools for ethical hacking:

- Adequate documentation.
- Detailed reports on the discovered vulnerabilities, including how they may be exploited and fixed.
- Updates and support when needed.
- High-level reports that can be presented to managers or nontechie types.

These features can save you time and effort when you're writing the report.

Executing the plan

Ethical hacking can take persistence. Time and patience are important. Be careful when you're performing your ethical hacking tests. A hacker in your network or a seemingly benign employee looking over your shoulder may watch what's going on. This person could use this information against you.

It's not practical to make sure that no hackers are on your systems before you start. Just make sure you keep everything as quiet and private as possible. This is especially critical when transmitting and storing your test results. If possible, encrypt these e-mails and files using Pretty Good Privacy (PGP) or something similar. At a minimum, password-protect them.

You're now on a reconnaissance mission. Harness as much information as possible about your organization and systems, which is what malicious hackers do. Start with a broad view and narrow your focus:

1. **Search the Internet for your organization's name, your computer and network system names, and your IP addresses.**

   Google is a great place to start for this.

2. **Narrow your scope, targeting the specific systems you're testing.**

   Whether physical-security structures or Web applications, a casual assessment can turn up much information about your systems.

3. **Further narrow your focus with a more critical eye. Perform actual scans and other detailed tests on your systems.**

4. **Perform the attacks, if that's what you choose to do.**

Evaluating results

Assess your results to see what you uncovered, assuming that the vulnerabilities haven't been made obvious before now. This is where knowledge counts. Evaluating the results and correlating the specific vulnerabilities discovered is a skill that gets better with experience. You'll end up knowing your systems as well as anyone else. This makes the evaluation process much simpler moving forward.

Submit a formal report to upper management or to your customer, outlining your results. Keep these other parties in the loop to show that your efforts and their money are well spent. Chapter 17 describes this process.

Moving on

When you've finished your ethical hacking tests, you still need to implement your analysis and recommendations to make sure your systems are secure.

New security vulnerabilities continually appear. Information systems constantly change and become more complex. New hacker exploits and security vulnerabilities are regularly uncovered. You may discover new ones! Security tests are a snapshot of the security posture of your systems. At any time, everything can change, especially after software upgrades, adding computer systems, or applying patches. Plan to test regularly (for example, once a week or once a month). Chapter 19 covers managing security changes.

Chapter 2

Cracking the Hacker Mindset

In This Chapter

- Understanding the enemy
- Profiling hackers
- Understanding why hackers do what they do
- Examining how hackers go about their business

Before you start assessing the security of your own systems, it helps to know something about the enemies you're up against. Many information-security product vendors and other professionals claim that you should protect your systems from the bad guys — both internal and external. But what does this mean? How do you know how these bad guys think and work?

Knowing what hackers want helps you understand how they work. Understanding how they work helps you look at your information systems in a whole new way. In this chapter, I describe what you're up against, who's actually doing the hacking, and what their motivations and methods are so you're better prepared for your ethical hacking tests.

What You're Up Against

Thanks to sensationalism, the definition of *hacker* has transformed from harmless tinkerer to malicious criminal. Hackers often state that the general public misunderstands them, which is mostly true. It's easy to prejudge what you don't understand. Hackers can be classified by both their abilities and underlying motivations. Some are skilled, and their motivations are benign; they're merely seeking more knowledge. At the other end of the spectrum, hackers with malicious intent seek some form of personal gain. Unfortunately, the negative aspects of hacking usually overshadow the positive aspects, resulting in the stereotyping.

Historically, hackers have hacked for the pursuit of knowledge and the thrill of the challenge. Script kiddies aside, hackers are adventurous and innovative thinkers, and are always thinking about exploiting computer vulnerabilities.

(For more on script kiddies, see "Who Hacks," later in this chapter.) They see what others often overlook. They wonder what would happen if a cable were unplugged, a switch were flipped, or lines of code were changed in a program. These old-school hackers are like Tim the Toolman Taylor — Tim Allen's character on the late, great sitcom *Home Improvement* — thinking mechanical and electronic devices can be improved if they're "rewired." More recent evidence shows that many hackers are hacking for political, competitive, and even financial purposes, so times are changing.

When they were growing up, hackers' rivals were monsters and villains on video game screens. Now hackers see their electronic foes as only that — electronic. Hackers who perform malicious acts don't really think about the fact that human beings are behind the firewalls and Web applications they're attacking. They ignore that their actions often affect those human beings in negative ways, such as jeopardizing their job security.

Hackers and the act of hacking drive the advancement of security technology. After all, hackers don't create security holes; they expose and exploit existing holes in applications. Unfortunately, security technology advances don't ward off all hacker attacks, because hackers constantly search for new holes and weaknesses. The only sure-fire way to keep the bad guys at bay is to use behavior modification to change them into productive, well-adjusted members of society. Good luck with that.

However you view the stereotypical hacker, one thing is certain: Some people always will try to take down your computer systems through manual hacking or by creating and launching automated worms and other malware. You must take the appropriate steps to protect your systems against them.

Who Hacks

Computer hackers have been around for decades. Since the Internet became widely used in the late 1990s, we've started to hear more and more about hacking. Only a few hackers, such as John Draper (also known as Captain Crunch) and Kevin Mitnick, are well known. Gobs more unknown hackers are looking to make a name for themselves. They're the ones to look out for.

In a world of black and white, it's easy to describe the typical hacker. A general stereotype of a typical hacker is an antisocial, pimple-faced teenage boy. But the world has many shades of gray and, therefore, many types of hackers. Hackers are human like the rest of us and are, therefore, unique individuals, so an exact profile is hard to outline. The best broad description of hackers is that all hackers *aren't* equal. Each hacker has motives, methods, and skills. But some general characteristics can help you understand them.

Not all hackers are antisocial, pimple-faced teenagers. Regardless, hackers possess curiosity, bravado, and often very sharp minds.

Is the government hacking?

While in a conflict with another country, some governments will wage war via the Internet and other computer systems. For example, the U.S. government reportedly has launched cyberattacks against its adversaries — such as Yugoslavia during the Milosevic crisis in the late 1990s and in the recent war in Iraq.

Are we headed toward a digital Pearl Harbor? I'm not convinced that we are, but this method of waging war is becoming more common as technology progresses. Many folks are skeptical about this as well, and the U.S. government denies most of its involvement. However, because the world increasingly relies on computer and network technology, PCs, and the Internet, those avenues may become the launching pads or battlegrounds for future conflicts.

Just like anyone can become a thief, an arsonist, or a robber, anyone can become a hacker, regardless of age, gender, or race. Given this diverse profile, skills vary widely from one malicious hacker to the next. Some hackers barely know how to surf the Internet, whereas others write software that other hackers and ethical hackers alike depend on.

- **Script kiddies:** These are computer novices who take advantage of the hacker tools and documentation available for free on the Internet but don't have any knowledge of what's going on behind the scenes. They know just enough to cause you headaches but typically are very sloppy in their actions, leaving all sorts of digital fingerprints behind. Even though these guys are the stereotypical hackers that you hear about in the news media, they often need minimal skills to carry out their attacks.
- **Intermediate hackers:** These halfway hackers usually know just enough to cause serious problems. They know about computers and networks, and often use well-known exploits. Some want to be experts; given enough time and effort, they can be.
- **Elite hackers:** These are skilled hacking experts. These are the people who write many of the hacker tools, including the scripts and other programs that the script kiddies use. These folks write such malware as viruses and worms. They can break into systems and cover their tracks. They can even make it look like someone else hacked the systems.

  Elite hackers are often very secretive and share information with their "subordinates" only when they are deemed worthy. Typically, for lower-ranked hackers to be considered worthy, they must possess some unique information or prove themselves through a high-profile hack. These hackers are your worst enemies in information security. Okay, maybe they're not as bad as untrained end users, but that's another issue. Fortunately, elite hackers are not as plentiful as script kiddies.

Other hacktivists try to disseminate political or social messages through their work. A hacktivist wants to raise public awareness of an issue. Examples of hacktivism are the Web sites that were defaced with the *Free Kevin* messages in the name of freeing Kevin Mitnick from prison for his famous hacking escapades. Other cases of hacktivism include messages about legalizing marijuana, protests against the U.S. Navy spy plane that collided with the Chinese fighter jet in 2001, the common hacker attacks between India and Pakistan, and attacks against the U.S. White House Web site over the years.

Cyberterrorists attack government computers or public utility infrastructures, such as power grids and air-traffic-control towers. They crash critical systems or steal classified government information. Countries take these threats so seriously that many mandate information-security controls in such industries as the power industry to protect essential systems against these attacks.

Hackers for hire are part of organized crime on the Internet. In late 2003, the Korean National Police Agency busted the Internet's largest organized hacking ring, which had over 4,400 members. Prior to that, police in the Philippines busted a multimillion-dollar organized hacking ring that was selling cheap phone calls made through phone lines the ring had hacked into. Many of these hackers hire themselves out for money — and lots of it!

Why Hackers Hack

The main reason hackers hack is because they can! Okay, it goes a little deeper than that. Hacking is a casual hobby for some hackers — they just hack to see what they can and can't break into, usually testing only their own systems. These aren't the folks I'm writing about here. I'm focusing on those hackers who are obsessive and often have criminal intent.

Many hackers get a kick out of outsmarting corporate and government IT and security administrators. They thrive on making headlines and being notorious cyberoutlaws. Defeating an entity or possessing knowledge makes them feel better about themselves. Many of these hackers feed off instant gratification. They become obsessed with this feeling. Hackers can't resist the adrenaline rush they get when breaking into someone else's systems. Often, the more difficult the job is, the greater the thrill.

The knowledge that malicious hackers gain and the elevated ego that comes with that knowledge are like an addiction and a way of life. Some hackers want to make your life miserable, and others simply want to be seen or heard. Some common hacker motives are *revenge, basic bragging rights, curiosity, boredom, challenge, vandalism, theft for financial gain, sabotage, blackmail, extortion,* and *corporate espionage.*

Hackers often promote individualism — or at least the decentralization of information — because many believe that all information should be free. They think cyberattacks are different from attacks in the real world. They easily ignore or misunderstand their victims and the consequences of hacking.

Many hackers say they don't intend to harm or profit through their bad deeds, which helps them justify their work. They often don't look for tangible payoffs. Just proving a point is often a good enough reward for them.

Many business owners and managers — even some network and security administrators — believe that they don't have anything that a hacker wants or that hackers can't do much damage if they break in. This couldn't be further from the truth. This kind of thinking helps support hackers and their objectives. Hackers can compromise a seemingly unimportant system to access the network and use it as a launching pad for attacks on other systems.

It's worth repeating that hackers often hack because they can. Some hackers go for high-profile systems, but hacking into anyone's system helps them fit into hacker circles. Hackers use the false sense of security that many people have and go for almost any system they think they can compromise. They know that electronic information can be in more than one place at the same time. It's tough to prove that hackers took the information and possess it.

Similarly, hackers know that a simple defaced Web page — however easily attacked — is not good for business. The following Web sites show examples of Web pages that have been defaced in the past few years:

- `www.2600.com/hacked_pages`
- `www.onething.com/archive`

Hacked sites like these can persuade management and other nonbelievers that information threats and vulnerabilities should be addressed.

Hacking continues to get easier for several reasons:

- Increasing use of networks and Internet connectivity
- Anonymity provided by computer systems working over the Internet
- Increasing number and availability of hacking tools
- Computer-savvy children
- Unlikelihood that hackers are investigated or prosecuted if caught

Although most hacker attacks go unnoticed or unreported, hackers who are discovered are often not pursued or prosecuted. When they're caught, hackers often rationalize their services as being altruistic and a benefit to society: They're merely pointing out vulnerabilities before someone else does. Regardless, if justice is ever served, it helps eliminate the "fame and glory" reward system that hackers thrive on.

These criminal hackers are in the minority, so don't think that you're up against millions of these villains. Many other hackers just love to tinker and only seek knowledge of how computer systems work.

Hacking in the name of liberty

Many hackers exhibit behaviors that contradict what they're fighting for — that is, they fight for civil liberties and want to be left alone, and at the same time, they love prying into other people's business. Many hackers claim to be civil libertarians supporting the principles of personal privacy and freedom. However, they act in an entirely different way by intruding on the privacy and property of others. They often steal the property and rights of others, yet are willing to go to great lengths to get their own rights back from anyone who tries to take them away.

The case against copyrighted materials and the Recording Industry Association of America (RIAA) is a classic example. Hackers have gone to great lengths to prove a point, from defacing the Web sites of organizations that support copyrights to illegally sharing music by using otherwise legal mediums such as Kazaa, Gnutella, and Morpheus.

Planning and Performing Attacks

Hacking styles vary widely:

- **Some hackers prepare far in advance of a large attack.** They gather small bits of information and methodically carry out their hacks, as I outline in Chapter 4. These hackers are more difficult to track.
- **Other hackers — usually, the inexperienced script kiddies — act before they think things through.** For example, such hackers may try to telnet directly into an organization's router without hiding their identities. Other hackers may try to launch a DoS attack against a Microsoft Exchange e-mail server without first determining what version of Exchange is running or what patches are installed.

  These are the guys who usually get caught.

Although the hacker underground is a community, many of the hackers — especially the elite hackers — don't share information with the crowd. Most hackers do much of their work independently from other hackers. Hackers who network with one another use private bulletin board systems (BBSs), anonymous e-mail addresses, hacker Web sites, and Internet Relay Chat (IRC).

You can log on to many of these sites to see what hackers are doing.

Whatever approach they take, most malicious hackers prey on ignorance. They know the following aspects of real-world security:

- The majority of systems that hackers want to attack aren't managed properly. The computer systems aren't properly patched, hardened, and monitored as they should be. Hackers often can attack by flying below the average radar of the firewalls, IDSs, and authentication systems.

- Most network and security administrators simply can't keep up with the deluge of new vulnerabilities.
- Information systems grow more complex every year. This is yet another reason why overburdened administrators find it difficult to know what's happening across the wire and on the hard drives of their systems.

Time is a hacker's friend — and it always seems to be on the hacker's side. By attacking through computers rather than in person, hackers have more control over when they can carry out their attacks.

- Hack attacks can be carried out slowly, making them hard to detect.
- They're frequently carried out after typical business hours — often, in the middle of the night. Defenses are often weaker at night — with less physical security and less intrusion monitoring — when the typical network administrator (or security guard) is sleeping.

If you want detailed information on how some hackers work or want to keep up with the latest hacker methods, several magazines are worth checking out:

- *2600 — The Hacker Quarterly* magazine (`www.2600.com`). I've found gobs of great information in *2600*.
- *PHRACK* (`www.phrack.org`).
- *Computer Underground Digest* (`www.soci.niu.edu/~cudigest`).

Also, check out Lance Spitzner's Web site `www.tracking-hackers.com` for some great information on using honeypots to track hacker behavior.

Hackers learn from their hacking mistakes. Every mistake moves them one step closer to breaking into someone's system. They use this wisdom when carrying out future attacks.

Maintaining Anonymity

Smart hackers want to be as low-key as possible. Covering their tracks is a priority. In fact, success often depends on it. They don't want to raise suspicion so they can come back and access the systems in the future. Hackers often remain anonymous by using one of the following techniques:

- Borrowed or stolen dial-up accounts from friends or previous employers
- Public computers at libraries, schools, or kiosks at the local mall
- Internet proxy servers or anonymizer services
- Anonymous or disposable e-mail accounts from free e-mail services

- Open e-mail relays
- Unsecured computers — also called *zombies* — at other organizations
- Workstations or servers on the victim's own network

If hackers use enough steppingstones for their attacks, they are hard to trace.

Chapter 3

Developing Your Ethical Hacking Plan

In This Chapter

- Setting ethical hacking goals
- Selecting which systems to test
- Developing your ethical hacking testing standards
- Examining hacking tools

As an ethical hacker, you must plan your ethical hacking efforts before you start. A detailed plan doesn't mean that your testing must be elaborate. It just means that you're very clear and concise on what's done. Given the seriousness of ethical hacking, make this as structured a process as possible.

Even if you're just testing a single Web application or workgroup of computers, it's critical to establish your goals, define and document the scope of what you'll be testing, determine your testing standards, and gather and familiarize yourself with the proper tools for the task. This chapter covers these steps to help you create a positive ethical hacking environment so you can set yourself up for success.

Getting Your Plan Approved

Getting approval for ethical hacking is critical. First, obtain project sponsorship. This approval can come from your manager, an executive, a customer, or yourself (if you're the boss). Otherwise, your testing may be canceled suddenly, or someone can deny authorizing the tests. There can even be legal consequences for unauthorized hacking. Always make sure that what you're doing is known and visible — at least to the decision-makers. Chapter 20 outlines ten tips for getting upper management's buy-in on your security initiatives.

If you're an independent consultant or have a business with a team of ethical hackers, consider getting professional liability (also known as *errors and omissions*) insurance from an agent who specializes in business insurance coverage. This kind of insurance can be expensive, but it can be well worth it.

The authorization can be as simple as an internal memo from upper management if you're performing these tests on your own systems. If you're performing testing for a customer, you must have a signed contract in place, stating the customer's support and authorization. Get written approval as soon as possible to ensure that your time and efforts are not wasted. This documentation is your *security* if anyone questions what you're doing.

Establishing Your Goals

Your ethical hacking plan needs goals. The main goal of ethical hacking is to find vulnerabilities in your systems so you can make them more secure. You can then take this a step further:

- **Define more specific goals.** Align these goals with your business objectives.
- **Create a specific schedule with start and end dates.** These dates are critical components of your overall plan.

Before you begin any ethical hacking, you absolutely, positively need everything in writing and signed-off on.

Document everything, and involve upper management in this process. Your best ally in your ethical hacking efforts is a manager who supports what you're doing.

The following questions can start the ball rolling:

- Does ethical hacking support the mission of the business and its IT and security departments?
- What business goals are met by performing ethical hacking?

  These goals may include the following:

  - Prepping for the internationally accepted security framework of ISO 17799 or a security seal such as SysTrust or WebTrust
  - Meeting federal regulations
  - Improving the company's image
- How will ethical hacking improve security, IT, and the general business?
- What information are you protecting?

This could be intellectual property, confidential customer information, or private employee information.

- How much money, time, and effort are you and your organization willing to spend on ethical hacking?
- What specific deliverables will there be?

  Deliverables can include anything from high-level executive reports to detailed technical reports and write-ups on what you tested along with the outcomes of your tests. You can deliver specific information that is gleaned during your testing, such as passwords and other confidential information.
- What specific outcomes do you want?

  Desired outcomes include the justification for hiring or outsourcing security personnel, increasing your security budget, or enhancing security systems.

People within your organization may attempt to keep you from performing your ethical hacking plans. The best antidote is education. Show how ethical hacking helps support the business in everyone's favor.

After you know your goals, document the steps to get there. For example, if one goal is to develop a competitive advantage to keep existing customers and attract new ones, determine the answers to these questions:

- When will you start your ethical hacking?
- Will your ethical hacking be blind, in which you know nothing about the systems you're testing, or a knowledge-based attack, in which you're given specific information about the systems you're testing such as IP addresses, hostnames, and even usernames and passwords?
- Will this testing be technical in nature or involve physical security assessments or even social engineering?
- Will you be part of a larger ethical hacking team, often called a *tiger team* or *red team?*
- Will you notify your customers of what you're doing? If so, how?

  Customer notification is a critical issue. Many customers appreciate that you're taking steps to protect their information. Approach the testing in a positive way. Don't say, "We're breaking into our systems to see what information of yours is vulnerable to hackers." Instead, you can say that you're assessing the overall security of your systems so the information is as secure as possible from the bad guys.
- How will you notify customers that the organization is taking steps to enhance the security of their information?
- What measurements can ensure that these efforts are paying off?

Establishing your goals takes time, but you won't regret it. These goals are your road map. If you have any concerns, refer to these goals to make sure that you stay on track.

Determining What Systems to Hack

You probably don't want — or need — to assess the security of all your systems at the same time. This could be quite an undertaking and could lead to problems. I'm not saying you shouldn't eventually assess every computer and application you have. I'm just suggesting that whenever possible, you should break your ethical hacking projects into smaller chunks to make them more manageable. You may decide which systems to test based on a high-level risk analysis, answering questions such as:

- What are your most critical systems? Which systems, if hacked, would cause the most trouble or the greatest losses?
- Which systems appear to be most vulnerable to attack?
- Which systems are not documented, are rarely administered, or are the ones you know the least about?

After you've established your overall goals, decide which systems to test. This step helps you carefully define a scope for your ethical hacking so that you not only establish everyone's expectations up front, but also better estimate the time and resources for the job.

The following list includes systems and applications that you may consider performing your hacking tests on:

- Routers
- Firewalls
- Network infrastructure as a whole
- Wireless access points and bridges
- Web, application, and database servers
- E-mail and file/print servers
- Workstations, laptops, and tablet PCs
- Mobile devices (such as PDAs and cell phones) that store confidential information
- Client and server operating systems
- Client and server applications, such as e-mail or other in-house systems

What specific systems you should test depends on several factors. If you have a small network, you can test everything from the get-go. You may consider testing just public-facing hosts such as e-mail and Web servers and their associated applications. The ethical hacking process is flexible. Base these decisions on what makes the most business sense.

Start with the most vulnerable systems, and consider the following factors:

- Where the computer or application resides on the network
- Which operating system and application(s) it runs
- The amount or type of critical information stored on it

If you're hacking your own systems or a customer's systems, a previous security-risk assessment or vulnerability test may already have generated this information. If so, that documentation may help identify systems for more testing.

Ethical hacking goes a few steps beyond the higher-level information risk assessments and vulnerability testing. As an ethical hacker, you first glean information on all systems — including the organization as a whole — and then further assess the systems that appear most vulnerable. I discuss the ethical hacking methodology in more detail in Chapter 4.

Another factor to help you decide where to start is to assess the systems that have the greatest visibility. For example, focusing on a database or file server that stores customer or other critical information may make more sense — at least initially — than concentrating on a firewall or Web server that hosts marketing information about the company.

Creating Testing Standards

One miscommunication or slip-up can send your systems crashing during your ethical hacking tests. No one wants that to happen. To prevent mishaps, develop and document testing standards. These standards should include

- When the tests are performed, along with the overall timeline
- What tests are performed
- How the tests are performed, and from where
- How much knowledge of the systems you acquire in advance
- What you do when a major vulnerability is discovered

This is a list of general best practices. You can apply more standards for your situation.

Timing

You know they say that it's "all in the timing." This is especially true when performing ethical hacking tests. Make sure that the tests you're performing minimize disruption to business processes, information systems, and people. You want to avoid situations like miscommunicating the timing of tests and causing a DoS attack against a high-traffic e-commerce site in the middle of the day, or forcing yourself or others to perform password-cracking tests in the middle of the night. It's amazing what a 12-hour time difference can make! Everyone in the project should agree on a detailed timeline before you begin. This puts everyone on the same page and sets correct expectations.

Notify any Internet Service Providers (ISP) or Application Service Providers (ASPs) involved before performing any tests across the Internet. This way, ISPs and ASPs will be aware of the testing going on, which will minimize the chance that they will block your traffic if they suspect malicious behavior that shows up on their firewalls or Intrusion Detection Systems (IDSs).

The timeline should include specific short-term dates and times of each test, the start and end dates, and any specific milestones in between. You can develop and enter your timeline into a simple spreadsheet or Gantt chart, or you can include the timeline as part of your initial customer proposal and contract. For example, you could use a timeline similar to the following:

Test Performed	*Tester*	*Start Time*	*Projected End Time*
War dial	Tommy Tinker	July 1, 6:00 a.m.	July 1, 10:00 a.m.
Password cracking	Amy Trusty	July 2, 12:00 p.m.	July 2, 5:00 p.m.

This timeline will keep things simple and provide a reference during testing.

Specific tests

You may have been charged with performing a general *penetration test*, or you may want to perform specific tests, such as cracking passwords or war-dialing into a network. Or you might be performing a social-engineering test or assessing the Windows operating systems on the network. However you're testing, you may want to conceal the specifics of the testing to keep what you're doing covert or to protect your methodologies. In fact, your manager or customer may not want the details. Either way, document and make known at a high level what you're doing. This can help eliminate any potential miscommunication and keep you out of hot water.

A good way to provide evidence of what was tested, when it was tested, and more is to enable logging on the systems you're testing.

Sometimes, you may know the general tests that you're performing, but if you're using automated tools, it may be next to impossible to understand completely every test you're performing. This is especially true if the software you're using receives real-time vulnerability-testing updates from the vendor every time you run it. The potential for frequent updates underscores the importance of reading the documentation and readme files that come with the tools you're using.

I have experienced surprising vulnerability updates in the past. I was performing an automated assessment on a customer's Web site — the same test I had just performed the previous week. The customer and I had scheduled the test date and time in advance. What I didn't know is that the software vendor made some changes to its Web form submission tests, and I flooded the customer's Web application, creating a DoS condition.

Luckily, this DoS condition occurred after business hours and didn't affect the customer's operations. However, the customer's Web application was coded to generate an alert e-mail for every form submission. The application developer and company's president received 4,000 e-mails in their inboxes within about 10 minutes — ouch! I was lucky that the president was tech-savvy and understood the situation. It's important to have a contingency plan in case a situation like this occurs.

Blind versus knowledge assessments

It may be good to have some knowledge of the systems you're testing, but it's not required. However, a basic understanding of the systems you're hacking can protect you and others. Obtaining this knowledge shouldn't be difficult if you're hacking your own in-house systems. If you're hacking a customer's systems, you may have to dig a little deeper into how the systems work so you know what's what. That's how I've always done it. In fact, I've never had a customer ask for a fully blind assessment. Most people are scared of these assessments. This doesn't mean that blind assessments aren't valuable. The type of assessment you carry out depends on your specific needs.

The best approach is to plan on *unlimited* attacks, wherein any test is possible. The bad guys aren't hacking your systems within a limited scope, so why should you?

Consider whether the tests should be undetected. This isn't required but should be considered, especially for social-engineering and physical security tests. I outline specific tests for those subjects in Chapter 5 and Chapter 6.

A false sense of vigilance can be created if too many insiders know about your testing which can end up negating the hard work you're putting into this. This doesn't mean you shouldn't tell anyone. Always have a main point of contact within the organization — preferably someone with decision-making authority — that both you and all employees can contact if and when something goes wrong.

Location

The tests you're performing dictate where you must run them from. Your goal is to hack your systems from locations where malicious hackers can access the systems. You can't predict whether you'll be attacked by a hacker from outside or inside your network, so cover all your bases. Combine external (public Internet) tests and internal (private network) tests.

You can perform some tests, such as password cracking and network-infrastructure assessments, from the comfort of your office — inside the network. But it may be better to have a true outsider perform other tests on routers, firewalls, and public Web applications.

For your external hacks that require network connectivity, you may have to go off-site (a good excuse to work from home) or use an external proxy server. Better yet, if you can assign an available public IP address to your computer, plug into the network on the outside of the firewall for a hacker's-eye view of your systems. Internal tests are easy because you need only physical access to the building and the network.

Reacting to major exploits that you find

Determine ahead of time whether you'll stop or keep going when you find a critical security hole. Your manager or your customer may not ask you to, but I think it's best to keep going to see what else you can discover. I'm not saying to keep hacking until the end of time or until you crash all your systems. Simply pursue the path you're going down until you can't hack it any longer (pun intended).

Silly assumptions

You've heard what you make of yourself when you assume things. Even so, you must make assumptions when you hack your systems. Here are some examples of those assumptions:

- Computers, networks, and people are available when you're testing.
- You have all the proper hacking tools.
- The hacking tools you're using won't crash your systems.
- Your hacking tools actually work.
- You know all the risks of your tests.

You should document all assumptions and have management or your customer sign off on them as part of your overall approval process.

Selecting Tools

The required security-assessment tools *(hacking tools)* depend on the tests you're running. You can perform some ethical hacking tests with a pair of sneakers, a telephone, and a basic workstation on the network. However, comprehensive testing is easier with hacking tools.

Not only do you need an arsenal of tools, but you should also use the right tool for the task:

- If you're cracking passwords, a general port scanner such as SuperScan or Nmap may not do the trick. For this task, you need a tool such as LC4, John the Ripper, or pwdump.
- If you're attempting an in-depth analysis of a Web application, a Web-application assessment tool (such as Nikto or WebInspect) is more appropriate than a network analyzer such as Ethereal.

If you're not sure what tools to use, fear not. Throughout this book, I introduce a wide variety of tools — both free and commercial — that you can use to accomplish your tasks.

You can choose among hundreds, if not thousands, of tools for ethical hacking — everything from your own words and actions to software-based vulnerability-assessment programs to hardware-based network analyzers. Here's a rundown of some of my favorite commercial, freeware, and open-source security tools:

- Elcomsoft Proactive Windows Security Explorer
- Ethereal
- Foundstone SuperScan
- Qualys QualysGuard
- GFI LANguard Network Security Scanner
- John the Ripper
- Network Stumbler
- Nessus
- Nikto
- Nmap
- Pwdump2
- SPI Dynamics WebInspect
- THC-RUT
- ToneLoc

- Wellenreiter
- WildPackets EtherPeek and AiroPeek

I discuss these tools, including details on how to use many of them, in Parts II through V when I cover specific hack attacks. Appendix A contains a more comprehensive listing of these tools for your reference.

The capabilities of many security and hacking tools are often misunderstood. This misunderstanding has shed negative light on some excellent tools, such as SATAN (Security Administrator Tool for Analyzing Networks) and Nmap (Network Mapper). It's important to know what each tool can and can't do and how to use each one. I suggest reading the manual and other help files. Unfortunately, some tools have limited documentation, which can be pretty frustrating when you're trying to use those tools. You can search newsgroups and message boards and post a message if you're having trouble with a tool.

Hacking tools can be hazardous to your network's health. Be careful when using them. Always make sure that you understand what every option does before you use it. Try your tools on test systems if you're not sure how to use them. These precautions help prevent DoS conditions and loss of data integrity and availability on your production systems.

Look for these characteristics in the tools you select for ethical hacking:

- Adequate documentation.
- Detailed reports on the vulnerabilities, including how they may be exploited and fixed.
- Updates and support when needed.
- High-level reports that can be presented to managers or other nontechie types. These reports can save you time and effort when you're writing the report. I cover the reporting process in Chapter 17.

Know the limitations of your tools and of yourself. Many security-assessment tools generate false positives — alerting to a vulnerability when it doesn't really exist. Some even generate false negatives, which means they miss the vulnerabilities altogether. Likewise, if you're performing social-engineering tests or physical-security assessments, it's only human to miss specific vulnerabilities.

You may despise some "popular" freeware and open-source hacking tools. If these tools end up causing you more headaches than they're worth or don't do what you need them to do, consider purchasing commercial alternatives. They're often easier to use and typically generate better reports faster — especially high-level executive reports. Some commercial tools are quite expensive, but their ease of use and functionality may justify the cost.

Chapter 4

Hacking Methodology

In This Chapter

- Examining steps for successful ethical hacking
- Gleaning information about your organization from the Internet
- Scanning your network
- Looking for vulnerabilities

Before you start testing your systems, plan a basic methodology. Ethical hacking involves more than just penetrating and patching. Proven techniques can help guide you along the hacking highway and ensure that you end up at the right destination. Planning a methodology that supports your ethical hacking goals is what separates the professionals from the amateurs.

Setting the Stage

In the past, ethical hacking was mostly a manual process. Now, tools can automate various tasks. These tools allow you to focus on performing the tests instead of on your testing methods. However, it's important to follow a general methodology and understand what's going on behind the scenes.

Ethical hacking is similar to beta testing software. Think logically — like a programmer — dissecting and interacting with all the network components to see how they work. You gather information — often small pieces — and assemble the pieces of the puzzle. You start at point A with several goals in mind, hack (repeating many steps along the way), and move closer until you discover security vulnerabilities at point B.

The process that ethical hacking is built around is basically the same as what a malicious hacker would use. The goals and how you achieve them are different. In addition, as an ethical hacker, you will eventually attempt to assess *all* information-security vulnerabilities and properly address them, rather than run a single exploit. Today's attacks can come from any angle against any system, not just from the perimeter of your network and the Internet. Test *every* possible entry point, including partner, vendor, and customer networks, as well as home users, wireless LANs, and modems.

When you start rolling with your ethical hacking, keep detailed logs of every test you perform, every system you test, and your results. This information can help you do the following:

- Track what worked in previous tests and why.
- Help prove that you didn't maliciously hack the systems.
- Correlate your testing with intrusion-detection systems and other log files if questions arise.

In addition to taking general notes, it's also helpful to take screen captures of your results whenever possible. These will come in handy later if you need to show proof of what occurred, as well as when you're generating your final report. Chapter 1 lists the general steps of ethical hacking.

These steps don't include specific information on the low-tech hacking methods that you will use for social engineering and assessing physical security, but the techniques are basically the same. I cover these methods in more detail in Chapters 5 and 6.

Your main task is to simulate information-gathering and system compromises carried out by a hacker. This can be either a partial attack on one computer or a comprehensive attack against the entire organization. Generally, you're looking for what both inside and outside hackers see. You want to assess internal systems (processes and procedures that involve computers, networks, people, and physical infrastructures). Look for vulnerabilities; check how all your systems interconnect and how private systems and information are protected from untrusted elements.

If you're performing ethical hacking for a customer, you may go the blind-assessment route and start with just the company name and no other information that gives you a leg up, such as:

- IP addresses
- Host names
- Software versions
- Firewall rules
- Phone numbers
- Employee names

This blind-assessment approach allows you to start from ground zero and gives you a better sense of what information hackers can access publicly.

As an ethical hacker, you may not have to worry about covering your tracks or evading intrusion-detection systems, because everything you're doing is legitimate. But then again, one of your goals may be to test systems in a stealthy fashion. I discuss techniques that hackers use to conceal their actions in later chapters and outline some countermeasures for them as well. I don't discuss covering your tracks in the overall ethical hacking methodology.

Seeing What Others See

Your reconnaissance mission can turn up a ton of information about your organization and systems that the whole world can see. This process is often called *footprinting*. Here's how to gather the information:

- Start by using a Web browser to search the Web for information about your organization.

  With the resources available on the Internet, you can gather information until the end of time. Unless you're *really* bored or trying to take advantage of AOL's introductory offer to stay online for free for 23 hours a day, I don't recommend it!

- Discover more-specific information about your systems from a hacker's viewpoint. You can determine this information by running network scans, probing ports, and assessing vulnerability.

Whether you're searching generally or probing more technically, you ultimately should limit the amount of information you gather based on what's reasonable for you. You may spend an hour, a day, or a week gathering this information — it all just depends on how large your organization is and the complexity of your information systems.

Gathering public information

The amount of information you can passively gather usually is staggering. This information is all over the Internet. It's your job to find out what everyone knows about you. This information positions hackers to target specific areas, including departments and individuals.

Web search

Performing a Web search or simply browsing your Web site can turn up the following information:

- Employee names and contact info
- Important company dates
- Incorporation filings for private companies

- SEC filings for public companies
- Press releases on moves, organizational changes, and new products
- Mergers and acquisitions
- Patents and trademarks
- Presentations, articles, and Webcasts

My favorite tool — the favorite of many hackers — is Google (`www.google.com`). It ferrets out information — from word-processing documents to graphics files — on any publicly accessible computer. It's free, too! There are entire books on using Google. Appendix A lists my favorite resources. With Google, you can search the Internet several ways:

- **By typing keywords:** This often reveals dozens and sometimes hundreds of pages of information — such as files, phone numbers, and addresses — that you never guessed were available.
- **By performing more advanced Web searches:** Google's advanced search options can find sites that link back to your company's Web site. This type of search often reveals a lot of information about partners, vendors, clients, and other affiliations.
- **By using switches to dig deeper into a Web site:** For example, if you want to find a certain word or file on your Web site, simply enter a line like one of the following into Google:

```
site:www.your_domain.com keyword
site:www.your_domain.com filename
```

Web crawling

Web-crawling utilities such as BlackWidow can mirror your Web site by downloading every publicly accessible file from it. You can then inspect

- The Web site layout and configuration offline.
- The HTML source code of Web pages.
- Comment fields. These fields contain such information as names and e-mail addresses of the developers and internal IT personnel, server names, software versions, and internal addressing schemes.

Web sites

These Web sites may provide specific information about your organization:

- Government and business Web sites:
  - `www.hoovers.com` and `finance.yahoo.com` for detailed information about public companies

  - www.sec.gov/edgar.shtml for SEC filings on public companies
  - www.uspto.gov for patent and trademark registrations
  - The Web site for your state's Secretary of State or similar organization for incorporation and corporate officer information
- Background checks through companies such as ChoicePoint (www.choicepoint.com) and USSearch (www.ussearch.com)

Mapping the network

When you're mapping out your network, you can search public databases and resources to see what the hackers know about you.

Whois

The best starting point is to perform a Whois lookup by using any one of the Whois tools available on the Internet. *Whois* is the tool you've most likely used to check whether a particular Internet domain name is available.

For ethical hacking, Whois provides information that can give a hacker a leg up to start a social-engineering attack or to scan your network:

- Internet domain-name information, such as contact names and addresses
- DNS servers responsible for your domain

You can look up Whois information at one of the following places:

- A domain registrar's site, such as www.networksolutions.com or www.registerfly.com.
- An ISP's tech-support page.

My favorite Whois tool is Sam Spade (www.samspade.org). You can use its Web site or download its Windows-based tool, shown in Figure 4-1.

You can run DNS queries directly from the site or download the site's Windows-based tool and run it from your PC. Sam Spade can

- Display general domain-registration information
- Show which host handles e-mail (the Mail Exchanger or MX record) for a domain
- Determine whether the host is listed on some spam blacklists

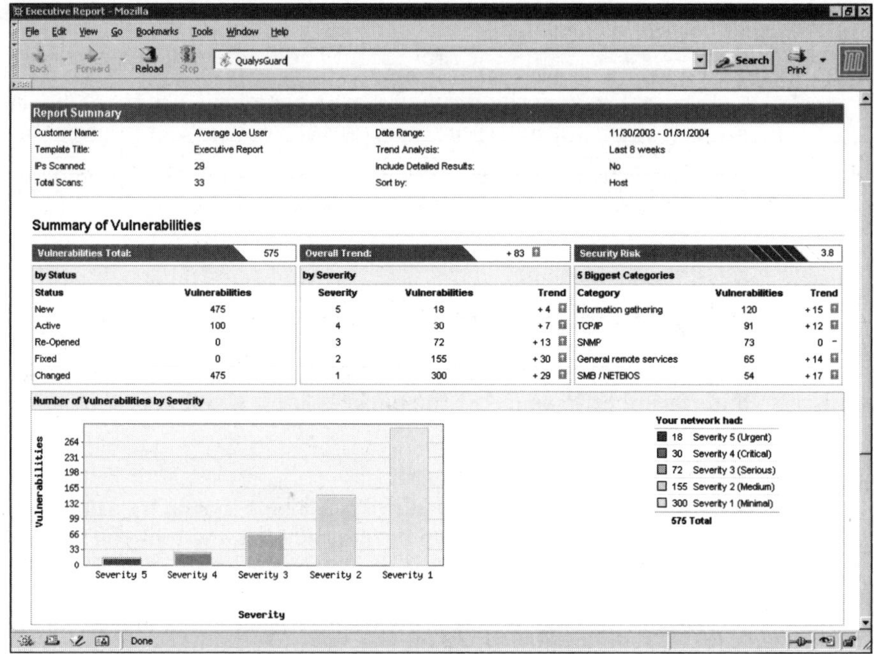

Figure 4-1: The Sam Spade graphical interface.

The following list runs down various lookup sites for other categories:

- **Government:** `whois.nic.gov`
- **Military:** `whois.nic.mil`
- **AfriNIC:** `www.afrinic.org` (emerging Regional Internet Registry for Africa)
- **APNIC:** `www.apnic.net/search/index.html` (Regional Internet Registry for the Asia Pacific Region)
- **ARIN:** `www.arin.net/whois/index.html` (Regional Internet Registry for North America, a portion of the Caribbean, and subequatorial Africa)
- **LACNIC:** Latin American and Caribbean Internet Addresses Registry `www.lacnic.net`
- **RIPE Network Coordination Centre:** `www.ripe.net/db/whois/whois.html` (Europe, Central Asia, African countries north of the equator, and the Middle East)

`Alldomains.com` offers a *reverse* Whois service called D-Tective. This paid service finds specific Internet domains for a domain name, a phone number, or an address.

Google groups

The Google Groups at `groups.google.com` can reveal surprising public network information. Search for such information as your hostnames, IP addresses, and usernames. You can search hundreds of millions of Usenet posts back to 1981 for public and often very private information.

You might find some information such as the following that you didn't realize was being made public:

- A tech-support or similar message that divulges too much information about your systems. Many people who post messages to Usenet don't realize that their messages are shared with the world.
- Disgruntled employees or customers who have posted confidential information about your company.

A few years ago, I was helping some folks at an Internet startup company select a telephone service vendor. I searched Google Groups for a vendor they were interested in and turned up some interesting information about the telephone service's network. Apparently, its network administrator had posted some messages to a tech-support site that revealed his full name and e-mail address, specific server names, IP addresses, and network configuration information of its internal systems. My customer used another vendor.

If you discover that confidential information is posted about your company, you may be able to get it removed. Check out the Google Groups help page at `groups.google.com/googlegroups/help.html` for details.

Privacy policies

Check your Web site's privacy policy. A good practice is to disclose basic information about how user information is protected.

Make sure that the people writing privacy policies don't divulge details about your information-security infrastructure. An Internet startup businessman once contacted me about business opportunities. During the conversation, he was bragging about his company's security systems to ensure the privacy of client information. I went to his Web site to check out his privacy policy. He had posted the brand and model of firewall he was using. Not a good idea!

Scanning Systems

Active information gathering produces more details about your network and helps you see your systems from a hacker's perspective. For instance, you can

- Use the information provided by your Whois lookups and start testing other closely related IP addresses and host names. When you map out — *enumerate* — your network, you see how your systems are laid out. This includes determining IP addresses, host names (both external and internal), running protocols, open ports, and running services and applications.
- Scan your internal hosts — if they are within the scope of your testing. These hosts may not be visible to outsiders, but you should test them. The hacker may be on the inside!

If you're not completely comfortable scanning your systems, consider first using a lab with test systems or a system running virtual-machine software such as VMware Workstation or Microsoft's Virtual PC. Some hacking tools may not work as designed when you run them on virtual-machine software. If you have trouble getting the software to load or hosts to respond, you may have to run your tests against physically separate computers.

Hosts

Scan and document specific hosts that are reachable from the Internet. Start by pinging either specific host names or IP addresses with one of these:

- The basic ping utility that's built into your operating system
- A third-party utility that allows you to ping multiple addresses at the same time, such as SuperScan (`www.foundstone.com`) and NetScanTools Pro (`www.netscantools.com`) for Windows and fping for UNIX (which allows you to ping more than one address)

The site `www.whatismyip.com` shows how your gateway IP address appears on the Internet. Just browse to that site. Your outermost public IP address (your firewall or router — preferably not your local computer) appears.

Modems and open ports

Scan for modems and open ports by using network-scanning tools:

- Check for unsecured modems with war-dialing software, such as ToneLoc, PhoneSweep, and THC-Scan. I cover war dialing in Chapter 8.
- Scan network ports with SuperScan or Nmap (`www.insecure.org/nmap`). You can use a happy-clicky-GUI version made for Windows called NMapWin, shown in Figure 4-2. See Chapter 9 for details.
- Listen to network traffic with a network analyzer such as Ethereal. I cover this topic in various chapters throughout the book.

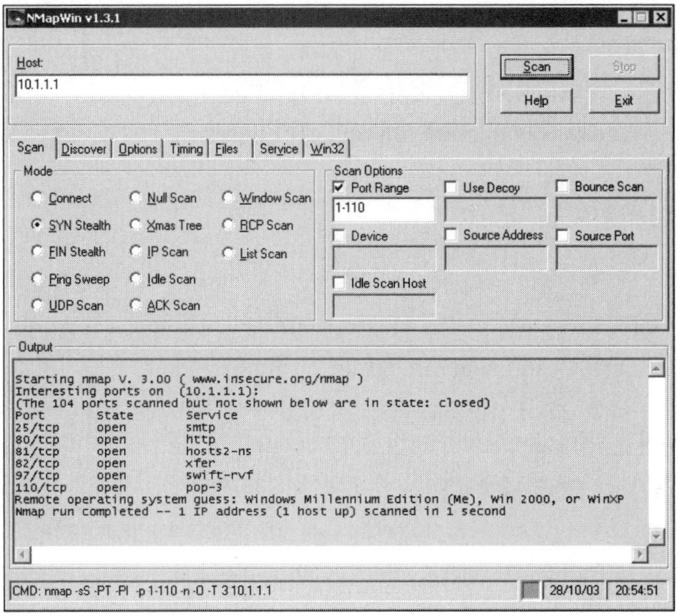
NMapWin v1.3.1
Host:
10.1.1.1
Scan
Stop
Help
Exit
Scan
Discover
Options
Timing
Files
Service
Win32
Mode
Connect
Null Scan
Window Scan
SYN Stealth
Xmas Tree
RCP Scan
FIN Stealth
IP Scan
List Scan
Ping Sweep
Idle Scan
UDP Scan
ACK Scan
Scan Options
Port Range
1-110
Use Decoy
Bounce Scan
Device
Source Address
Source Port
Idle Scan Host
Output
Starting nmap V. 3.00 (www.insecure.org/nmap)
Interesting ports on (10.1.1.1):
(The 104 ports scanned but not shown below are in state: closed)
Port State Service
25/tcp open smtp
80/tcp open http
81/tcp open hosts2-ns
82/tcp open xfer
97/tcp open swift-rvf
110/tcp open pop-3
Remote operating system guess: Windows Millennium Edition (Me), Win 2000, or WinXP
Nmap run completed -- 1 IP address (1 host up) scanned in 1 second
CMD: nmap -sS -PT -PI -p 1-110 -n -O -T 3 10.1.1.1
28/10/03
20:54:51

Figure 4-2: The NMapWin graphical interface.

Scanning *internally* is easy. Simply connect your PC to the network, load up the software, and fire away. Scanning from *outside* your network takes a few more steps, but it can be done:

- For war dialing, scanning shouldn't be an issue. You can just use one of your internal analog lines to dial out from.
- Pinging and scanning is more complicated. The easiest way to connect and get an "outside-in" perspective is to assign yourself a public IP address and plug your workstation into a switch or hub on the public side of your firewall or router. Physically, you're not on the Internet looking in, but this type of connection works just the same.

Determining What's Running on Open Ports

As an ethical hacker, you should glean as much information as possible after scanning your systems. You can often identify the following information:

- Protocols in use, such as IP, IPX, and NetBEUI
- Services running on the hosts, such as e-mail and database applications

- Available remote-access services, such as Windows Terminal Services and Secure Shell (SSH)
- VPN services, such as PPTP, SSL, and IPSec
- Required authentication for network shares

You can look for the following open ports (your network scanning program reports these as open):

- Ping (ICMP echo) replies; ICMP traffic is allowed to and from the host
- TCP port 20 and/or 21, showing that FTP is running
- TCP port 23, showing that telnet is running
- TCP ports 25 or 465 (SMTP), 110 or 995 (POP3), or 143 or 993 (IMAP), showing that an e-mail server is running
- TCP/UDP port 53, showing that a DNS server is running
- TCP ports 80 and 443, showing that a Web server is running
- TCP/UDP ports 137, 138, and 139, showing that an unprotected Windows host is running

Thousands of ports can be open — 65,535, to be exact. I cover many popular port numbers when describing hacks throughout this book. A listing of all well-known port numbers (ports 1–1023) and registered port numbers (ports 1024–49151), with their associated protocols and services, is located at `www.iana.org/assignments/port-numbers`. You can also perform a port-number lookup at `www.cotse.com/cgi-bin/port.cgi`.

If you detect a Web server running on the system you're testing, you can check the software version by using one of the following methods:

- Type the site's name, followed by a page that you know doesn't exist, such as `www.your_domain.com/1234.html`. Many Web servers return an error page showing detailed version information.
- Use Netcraft's Web server-search utility (`www.netcraft.com`), which connects to your server from the Internet and displays the Web-server version and operating system, as shown in Figure 4-3.

You can dig deeper for more specific information on your hosts. This reveals what software version is running on the systems and more:

- NMapWin can determine the system OS version; refer to Figure 4-2.
- An enumeration utility (such as DumpSec) can extract users, groups, and file and share permissions directly from Windows.
- Many systems return useful banner information when you connect to a service or application running on a port. For example, if you telnet to an

e-mail server on port 25 by entering `telnet mail.your_domain.com 25` at a command prompt, you may see something like this:

```
220 mail.your_domain.com ESMTP all_the_version_info_
        you'll_ever_need Ready
```

Most e-mail servers return detailed information, such as the version and the current service pack installed. After you have this information, you (and hackers) can determine what vulnerabilities are present on the system from some of the Web sites listed in the next section.

- An e-mail to an invalid address may return with detailed e-mail header information. A bounced message often discloses lots of information that can be used against you, including internal IP addresses and software versions. On certain Windows systems, you can map drives and establish other types of network connections. I cover these issues in Chapter 11.

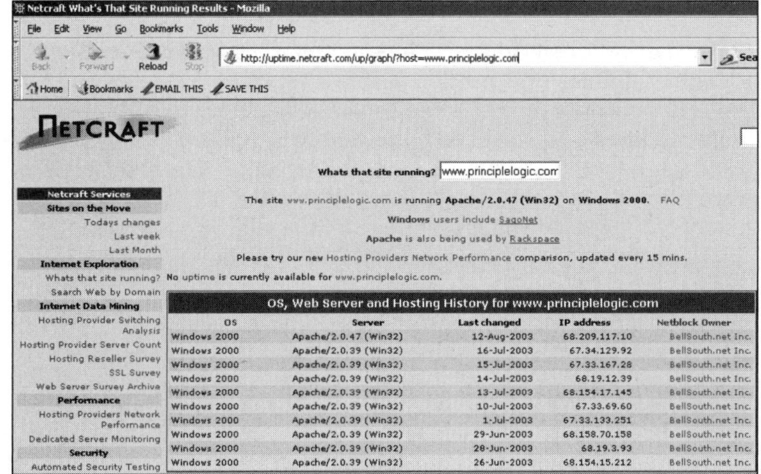

OS	Server	Last changed	IP address	Netblock Owner
Windows 2000	Apache/2.0.47 (Win32)	12-Aug-2003	68.209.117.10	BellSouth.net Inc.
Windows 2000	Apache/2.0.39 (Win32)	16-Jul-2003	67.34.129.92	BellSouth.net Inc.
Windows 2000	Apache/2.0.39 (Win32)	15-Jul-2003	67.33.167.28	BellSouth.net Inc.
Windows 2000	Apache/2.0.39 (Win32)	14-Jul-2003	68.19.12.39	BellSouth.net Inc.
Windows 2000	Apache/2.0.39 (Win32)	13-Jul-2003	68.154.17.145	BellSouth.net Inc.
Windows 2000	Apache/2.0.39 (Win32)	10-Jul-2003	67.33.69.60	BellSouth.net Inc.
Windows 2000	Apache/2.0.39 (Win32)	1-Jul-2003	67.33.133.251	BellSouth.net Inc.
Windows 2000	Apache/2.0.39 (Win32)	29-Jun-2003	68.158.70.158	BellSouth.net Inc.
Windows 2000	Apache/2.0.39 (Win32)	28-Jun-2003	68.19.3.93	BellSouth.net Inc.
Windows 2000	Apache/2.0.39 (Win32)	26-Jun-2003	68.154.15.212	BellSouth.net Inc.

Figure 4-3: Netcraft's Web-server version utility.

Assessing Vulnerabilities

After finding potential security holes, test whether they are vulnerabilities. Before you test, perform some manual searching. You can research hacker message boards, Web sites, and vulnerability databases, such as these:

- Common Vulnerabilities and Exposures (`cve.mitre.org/cve`)
- CERT/CC Vulnerability Notes Database (`www.kb.cert.org/vuls`)
- NIST ICAT Metabase (`icat.nist.gov/icat.cfm`)

These sites list practically every known vulnerability. If you can't find a vulnerability documented on one of these sites, search the vendor's site. You can find a list of commonly exploited vulnerabilities at www.sans.org/top20. This is the SANS Top 20 Internet Security Vulnerabilities consensus list, which is compiled and updated by information-security authorities.

If you're not keen on researching your potential vulnerabilities and can jump right into testing, you have a couple of options:

- **Manual assessment:** You can assess the potential vulnerabilities by connecting to the ports that are exposing the service or application and poking around. You should manually assess certain vulnerabilities (such as in Web applications). The vulnerability reports in the preceding databases often disclose how to do this — at least generally. If you have a lot of free time, performing these tests manually may be for you.
- **Automated assessment:** If you're like me, you'll assess vulnerabilities automatically when you can. Manual assessments are a great way to learn, but people usually don't have the time for most manual steps.

I love many of the available vulnerability-assessment tools. Some test for vulnerabilities on specific platforms (such as Windows and UNIX) and types of networks (either wired or wireless). They test for specific system vulnerabilities — some even focus on the SANS Top 20 list. Versions of these tools can map the business logic within an application; others can help software developers test for code flaws. The drawback to these tools is that they find only individual vulnerabilities, not correlating vulnerabilities. However, this is changing with the advent of event-correlation applications.

Many people love the Nessus tool (www.nessus.org). However, it's not best for beginners or without a Linux or UNIX server.

One of my favorite ethical hacking weapons is a vulnerability-assessment tool called QualysGuard by Qualys (www.qualys.com). It's both a port scanner and vulnerability-assessment tool. You don't even need a computer to run it.

QualysGuard — which has its roots in Nessus — is an application service provider-based commercial tool. Just browse to the Qualys Web site, log in, and enter the IP address of the systems you want to test. You schedule the assessment; it runs, then generates excellent reports, such as these:

- An executive report containing information like the partial screen capture of a QualysGuard report shown in Figure 4-4.
- A technical report of detailed explanations of the vulnerabilities and specific countermeasures.

Like most good security tools, you pay for QualysGuard — it's not the least expensive tool — but you get what you pay for. Some newer products offer similar technical capabilities while adding convenience.

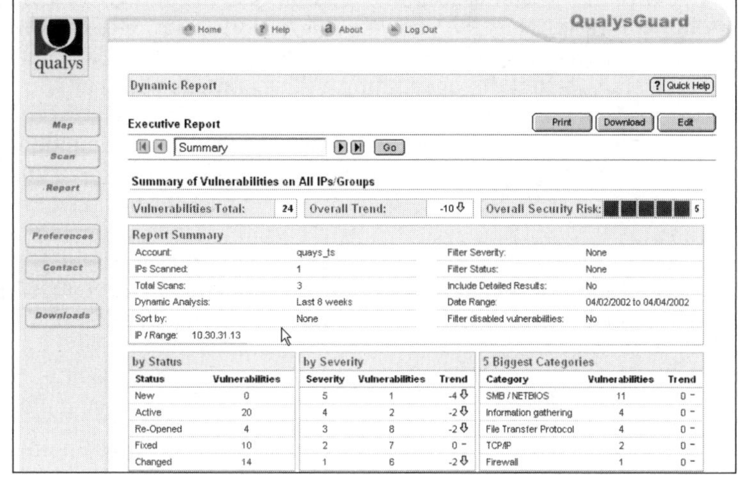

Figure 4-4: A sample QualysGuard vulnerability-assessment report.

Assessing vulnerabilities with a tool such as QualysGuard requires follow-up expertise. Study the reports to base your recommendations on the tested systems.

Penetrating the System

You can use identified critical security holes to do the following:

- Gain further information about the host and its data.
- Start or stop certain services or applications.
- Access other systems.
- Disable logging or other security controls.
- Capture screen shots.
- Install such hacker tools as *rootkits* (hacker programs that masquerade as legitimate OS programs) and network analyzers for later backdoor entry.
- Capture keystrokes.
- Send an e-mail as the administrator.
- Perform a buffer-overflow attack.
- Launch another type of DoS attack.
- Upload a file proving your victory.

You can exploit the vulnerabilities on your systems and go for complete system penetration. Ideally, you've already made your decision on this. You may want to leave well enough alone. There are also tasks you can't do — such as installing rootkits or planting a file — unless you try.

Leave the more-intrusive penetration to those with more time on their hands. Focus on correcting problems. Part VI of this book covers reporting, patching, and managing.

Don't take the steps I outline in this chapter too literally. General ethical hacking methodologies can be either too simplistic or too rigid. Ultimately, you are in control and can decide what to do and when to do it.

Part II
Putting Ethical Hacking in Motion

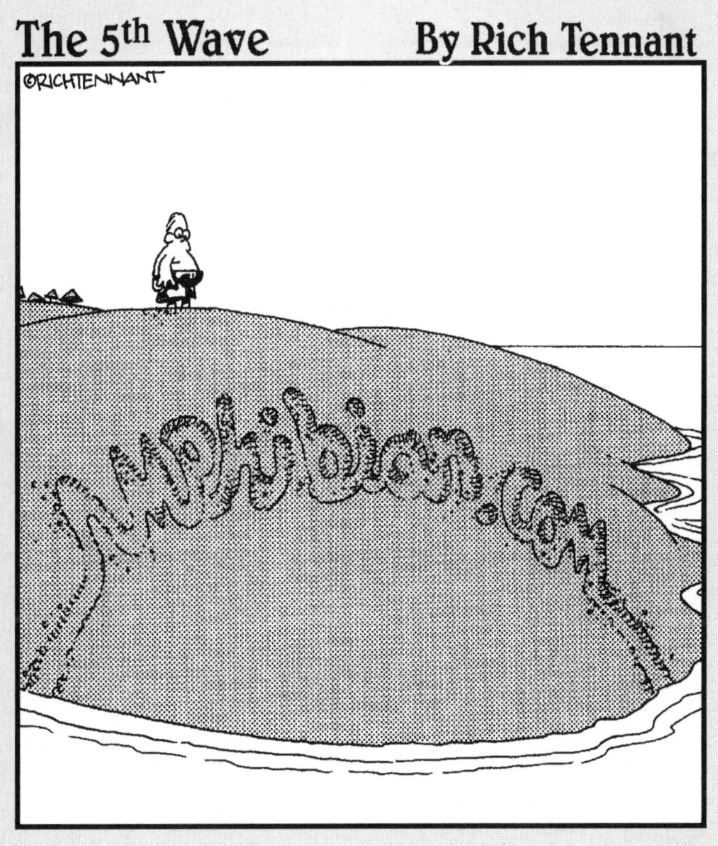

In this part . . .

Let the games begin! You've waited long enough — now's the time to start testing your systems. But where do you start? How about with your two *P*s — your people and your physical systems? These are, after all, two of the most easily and commonly attacked targets in your organization.

This part starts out with a discussion of hacking people. It then goes on to take a look at physical security vulnerabilities. Of course, I'd be remiss in a part about people if I skipped passwords, so I cover testing those as well. This is a great way to get the ball rolling to warm you up for the more specific hacks that come later in the book.

Chapter 5

Social Engineering

In This Chapter

- Introducing social engineering
- Examining the ramifications of social engineering
- Understanding social-engineering techniques
- Protecting your organization against social engineering

Social engineering takes advantage of the weakest link in any organization's information-security defenses: the employees. Social engineering is "people hacking" and involves maliciously exploiting the trusting nature of human beings for information that can be used for personal gain.

Social Engineering 101

Typically, hackers pose as someone else to gain information they otherwise can't access. Hackers then take the information obtained from their victims and wreak havoc on network resources, steal or delete files, and even commit industrial espionage or some other form of fraud against the organization they're attacking. Social engineering is different from *physical-security* issues, such as shoulder surfing and dumpster diving, but they are related.

Here are some examples of social engineering:

- **False support personnel** claim that they need to install a patch or new version of software on a user's computer, talk the user into downloading the software, and obtain remote control of the system.
- **False vendors** claim to need to make updates to the organization's accounting package or phone system, ask for the administrator password, and obtain full access.
- **False contest Web sites** run by hackers gather user IDs and passwords of unsuspecting contestants. The hackers then try those passwords on other Web sites, such as Yahoo! and Amazon.com, and steal personal or corporate information.

- **False employees** notify the security desk that they have lost their keys to the computer room, are given a set of keys, and obtain unauthorized access to physical and electronic information.

Sometimes, social engineers act as forceful and knowledgeable employees, such as managers or executives. Other times, they may play the roles of extremely uninformed or naïve employees. They often switch from one mode to the other, depending on whom they are speaking to.

Effective information security — especially for fighting social engineering — begins and ends with your users. Other chapters in this book provide great technical advice, but never forget that basic human communication and interaction also affect the level of security. The *candy-security* adage is "Hard crunchy outside, soft chewy inside." The *hard crunchy outside* is the layer of mechanisms — such as firewalls, intrusion-detection systems, and encryption — that organizations rely on to secure their information. The *soft chewy inside* is the people and the systems inside the organization. If hackers can get past the thick outer layer, they can compromise the (mostly) defenseless inner layer.

Social engineering is one of the toughest hacks, because it takes great skill to come across as trustworthy to a stranger. It's also by far the toughest hack to protect against because people are involved. In this chapter, I explore the ramifications of social engineering, techniques for your own ethical hacking efforts, and specific countermeasures to take against social engineering.

Before You Start

I approach the ethical hacking methodologies in this chapter differently than in subsequent hacking chapters. Social engineering is an art and a science. It takes great skill to perform social engineering as an ethical hacker and is dependent upon your personality and overall knowledge of the organization you're testing. If social engineering isn't natural for you, consider using the information in this chapter for educational purposes — at first — until you have more time to study the subject.

You can use the information in this chapter to perform specific tests or improve information-security awareness in your organization. Social engineering can harm people's jobs and reputations, and confidential information could be leaked. Proceed with caution and think before you act.

You can perform social-engineering attacks millions of ways. For this reason, and because it's next to impossible to train specific behaviors in one chapter, I don't provide how-to instructions on carrying out social-engineering attacks. Instead, I describe specific social-engineering scenarios that have worked for other hackers — both ethical and unethical. You can tailor these same tricks and techniques to specific situations.

A case study in social engineering with Ira Winkler

In this case study, Ira Winkler, a world-renowned social engineer, was gracious in sharing with me an interesting study in social engineering.

The Situation

Mr. Winkler's client wanted a general temperature of the organization's security awareness level. He and his accomplice went for the pot of gold and tested the organization's susceptibility to social engineering. Getting started, they scoped out the main entrance of the client's building and found that the reception/security desk was in the middle of a large lobby and was staffed by a receptionist. The next day, the two men walked into the building during the morning rush while pretending to talk on cell phones. They stayed at least 15 feet from the attendant and simply ignored her as they walked by.

After they were inside the facility, they found a conference room to set up shop. They sat down to plan the rest of the day and decided a facility badge would be a great start. Mr. Winkler called the main information number and asked for the office that makes the badges. He was forwarded to the reception/security desk. He then pretended to be the CIO and told the person on the other end of the line that he wanted badges for a couple of subcontractors. The person responded, "Send the subcontractors down to the main lobby."

When Mr. Winkler and his accomplice arrived, a uniformed guard asked what they were working on, and they mentioned computers. The guard then asked them if they needed access to the computer room! Of course they said, "That would help." Within minutes, they both had badges with access to all office areas and the computer operations center. They went to the basement and used their badges to open the main computer room door. They walked right in and were able to access a Windows server, load the user administration tool, add a new user to the domain, and make the user a member of the administrators' group. Then they quickly left.

The two men had access to the entire corporate network with administrative rights within two hours! They also used the badges to perform after-hours walkthroughs of the building. In doing this, they found the key to the CEO's office and planted a mock bug there.

The Outcome

Nobody outside the team knew what the two men did until they were told after the fact. After the employees were informed, the guard supervisor called Mr. Winkler and wanted to know who issued the badges. Mr. Winkler informed him that the fact that his area didn't know who issued the badges was a problem in and of itself, and that he does not disclose that information.

How This Could Have Been Prevented

According to Mr. Winkler, the security desk should have been located closer to the entrance, and the company should have had a formal process for issuing badges. In addition, access to special areas like the computer room should require approval from a known entity. After access is granted, a confirmation should be sent to the approver. Also, the server screen should have been locked, the account should not have been logged on unattended, and any addition of an administrator-level account should be audited and appropriate parties should be alerted.

Ira Winkler, CISSP, CISM, is considered one of the world's best social engineers. You can find more of his case studies in his book *Spies Among Us* (McGraw-Hill).

These social-engineering techniques may be best performed by an outsider to the organization. If you're performing these tests against your own organization, you may have difficulties acting as an outsider if everyone knows you. This may not be a problem in larger organizations, but if you have a small, close-knit company, people usually are on to your antics.

You can outsource social-engineering testing to a trusted consulting firm or even have a colleague perform the tests for you. The key word here is *trusted*. If you're involving someone else, you must get references, perform background checks, and have the testing approved by management in writing beforehand. I cover the topic of outsourcing ethical hacking in Chapter 19.

Why Hackers Use Social Engineering

Bad guys use social engineering to break into systems because they can. They want someone to open the door to the organization so that they don't have to break in and risk getting caught. Firewalls, access controls, and authentication devices can't stop a determined social engineer.

Most social engineers perform their attacks slowly, so they're not so obvious and don't raise suspicion. The bad guys gather bits of information over time and use the information to create a broader picture. Alternatively, some social-engineering attacks can be performed with a quick phone call or e-mail. The methods used depend on the hacker's style and abilities.

Social engineers know that many organizations don't have formal data classification, access-control systems, incident-response plans, and security-awareness programs.

Social engineers know a lot about a lot of things — both inside and outside their target organizations — because it helps them in their efforts. The more information social engineers gain about organizations, the easier it is for them to pose as employees or other trusted insiders. Social engineers' knowledge and determination give them the upper hand over average employees who are unaware of the value of the information social engineers are seeking.

Understanding the Implications

Most organizations have enemies that want to cause trouble through social engineering. These enemies could be current or former employees seeking revenge, competitors wanting a leg up, or basic hackers trying to prove their skills.

Regardless of who is causing the trouble, every organization is at risk. Larger companies spread across several locations are often more vulnerable, but small companies also are attacked. Everyone from receptionists to security guards to IT personnel are potential victims of social engineering. Help-desk and call-center employees are especially vulnerable because they are trained to be helpful and forthcoming with information. Even the average untrained end user is susceptible to attack.

Social engineering has serious consequences. Because the objective of social engineering is to coerce someone for ill-gotten gains, anything is possible. Effective social engineers can obtain the following information:

- User or administrator passwords
- Security badges or keys to the building and even the computer room
- Intellectual property such as design specifications, formulae, or other research and development documentation
- Confidential financial reports
- Private and confidential employee information
- Customer lists and sales prospects

If any of the preceding information is leaked out, it can cause financial losses, lower employee morale, jeopardize customer loyalty, and even create legal issues. The possibilities are endless.

One reason protecting against social-engineering attacks is difficult is that they aren't well documented. Because so many possible methods exist, recovery and protection are difficult after the attack. The *hard crunchy outside* created by firewalls and intrusion-detection systems often creates a false sense of security, making the problem even worse.

With social engineering, you never know the next method of attack. The best you can do is remain vigilant, understand the social engineer's methodology, and protect against the most common attacks. In the rest of this chapter, I discuss how you can do this.

Performing Social-Engineering Attacks

The process of social engineering is actually pretty basic. In general, social engineers find the details of organizational processes and information systems to perform their attacks. With this information, they know what to pursue. Hackers typically perform social-engineering attacks in four simple steps:

1. **Perform research.**
2. **Build trust.**
3. **Exploit relationship for information through words, actions, or technology.**
4. **Use the information gathered for malicious purposes.**

These steps can include myriad substeps and techniques, depending on the attack being performed.

Before social engineers perform their attacks, they need a goal in mind. This is the hacker's first step in this process, and this goal is most likely already implanted in the hacker's mind. What does the hacker want to accomplish? What is the hacker trying to hack? Does he want intellectual property, server passwords, or security badges; or does he simply want to prove that the company's defenses can be penetrated? In your efforts as an ethical hacker performing social engineering, determine this goal before you move forward.

Fishing for information

Social engineers typically start by gathering public information about their victim. Many social engineers acquire information slowly over time so they don't raise suspicion. Obviousness is a tip-off when defending against social engineering. I cover other warning signs throughout the rest of this chapter.

Regardless of the initial research method, all a hacker needs to start penetrating an organization is an employee list, a few key internal phone numbers, or a company calendar.

Using the Internet

Today's basic research medium is the Internet. A few minutes on Google or other search engines, using simple key words such as the company name or specific employees' names, often produces a lot of information. You can find even more information in SEC filings at `www.sec.gov` and at sites such as `www.hoovers.com` and `finance.yahoo.com`. In fact, many organizations — especially upper management — would be dismayed by what's available. By using this search-engine information and browsing the company's Web site, the hacker often has enough information to start.

Hackers can pay $100 or less for a comprehensive background check on individuals. These searches can turn up practically any public — and sometimes private — information about a person in minutes.

Dumpster diving

Dumpster diving is a more difficult method of obtaining information. This method is literally going through trash cans for information about a company.

Dumpster diving can turn up even the most confidential information, because many employees think that their information is safe after it goes into file 13. Most people don't think about the potential value of paper they throw away. These documents often contain a wealth of information that tips off the social engineer with information needed to penetrate the organization further. The astute social engineer looks for the following printed documents:

- Internal phone lists
- Organizational charts
- Employee handbooks, which often contain security policies
- Network diagrams
- Password lists
- Meeting notes
- Spreadsheets and reports
- E-mails containing confidential information

Shredding is effective if the paper is *cross-shredded* into tiny pieces of confetti. Inexpensive shredders that shred documents only in long strips are basically worthless against a determined social engineer. With a little time and tape, a social engineer can easily piece a document back together.

Hackers often gather confidential personal and business information from others by listening in on conversations held in restaurants, coffee shops, and airports. People who speak loudly when talking on a cell phone are a great source. Poetic justice, perhaps? While writing in public places, it's amazing what I've heard others divulge — and I wasn't trying to listen!

Hackers also look for floppy disks, CD-ROM and DVD discs, old computer cases (especially with hard drives) and backup tapes.

See Chapter 6 for more on trash and other physical-security issues, including countermeasures against these exploits.

Phone systems

Hackers can obtain information by using the dial-by-name feature built into most voice-mail systems. To access this feature, you usually just press 0 when calling into the company's main number or even someone's desk. This trick works best after hours to make sure that no one answers.

Hackers can protect their identifies if they can hide where they're calling from. Here are some ways that they can do that:

- **Residential phones** sometimes can hide their numbers from caller ID. The code to hide a residential phone number from a caller ID is *67. Just dial *67 before the number; it blocks the source number.

  This feature is usually disabled when you're calling toll-free (800, 888, 877) numbers.

- **Business phones** are more difficult to spoof from an office by using a phone switch. However, all the hacker usually needs is the user guide and administrator password for the phone-switch software. In many switches, the hacker can enter the source number — including a falsified number, such as the victim's home phone number.

Hackers find interesting bits of information, such as when their victims are out of town, just by listening to voice-mail messages. They even study victims' voices by listening to their voice-mail messages or Internet presentations and Webcasts to impersonate those people.

Building trust

Trust — so hard to gain, so easy to lose. Trust is the essence of social engineering. Most humans trust other humans until a situation occurs that forces them not to. We want to help one another, especially if trust can be built and the request for help is reasonable. Most people want to be team players in the workplace and don't know what can happen if they divulge too much information to a "trusted" source. This is why social engineers can accomplish their goals. Of course, building deep trust often takes time. Crafty social engineers gain it within minutes or hours. How do they build trust?

- **Likability:** Who can't relate to a nice person? Everyone loves courtesy. The friendlier the social engineer — without going overboard — the better his chances of getting what he wants. Social engineers often begin by establishing common interests. They often use information they gained in the research phase to determine what the victim likes and act as if they like those things as well. For instance, they can phone victims or meet them in person and, based on information they've learned about the person, start talking about local sports teams or how wonderful it is to be single again. A few low-key and well-articulated comments can be the start of a nice new relationship.

- **Believability:** Of course, believability is based in part on the knowledge that social engineers have and how likable they are. But social engineers also use impersonation — perhaps posing as a new employee or fellow employee that the victim hasn't met. They may even pose as a vendor that does business with the organization. They often modestly claim authority to influence people. The most common social-engineering trick is to do something nice so that the victim feels obligated to be nice in return or to be a team player for the organization.

Exploiting the relationship

After social engineers obtain the trust of their unsuspecting victims, they coax them into divulging more information than they should. Whammo — they can go in for the kill. They do this through face-to-face or electronic communications that victims feel comfortable with, or they use technology to get victims to divulge information.

Deceit through words and actions

Wily social engineers can get inside information from their victims many ways. They are often articulate and focus on keeping their conversations moving without giving their victims much time to think about what they're saying. However, if they're careless or overly anxious during their social-engineering attacks, the following tip-offs may give them away:

- Acting overly friendly or eager
- Mentioning names of prominent people within the organization
- Bragging about authority within the organization
- Threatening reprimands if requests aren't honored
- Acting nervous when questioned (pursing the lips and fidgeting — especially the hands and feet, because more conscious effort is required to control body parts that are farther from the face)
- Overemphasizing details
- Physiological changes, such as dilated pupils or changes in voice pitch
- Appearing rushed
- Refusing to give information
- Volunteering information and answering unasked questions
- Knowing information that an outsider should not have
- A known outsider using insider speech or slang

- Asking strange questions
- Misspelling words in written communications

A good social engineer isn't obvious with the preceding actions, but these are some of the signs that malicious behavior is in the works.

Hackers often do a favor for someone and then turn around and ask that person if he or she would mind helping them. This is a common social-engineering trick that works pretty well. Hackers also often use what's called reverse social engineering. This is where they offer help if a specific problem arises; some time passes, the problem occurs (often by their doing), and then they help fix the problem. They may come across as heroes, which can further their cause. Hackers also simply may ask an unsuspecting employee for a favor. Yes — they just outright ask for a favor. Many people fall for it.

Impersonating an employee is easy. Social engineers can wear a similar looking uniform, make a fake ID badge, or simply dress like the real employees. They often pose as employees. People think, "Hey — he looks and acts like me, so he must be one of us." Social engineers also pretend to be employees calling in from an outside phone line. This is an especially popular way of exploiting help-desk and call-center personnel. Hackers know that it's easy for these people to fall into a rut due to such repetitive tasks as saying, "Hello, can I get your customer number, please?"

Here's my story about how I was social-engineered because I didn't think before I spoke. One day, I was having trouble with my high-speed Internet connection. I figured I could just use dial-up access, because it's better than nothing for e-mail and other basic tasks. I contacted my ISP and told the tech-support guy I couldn't remember my dial-up password. This sounds like the beginning of a social-engineering stunt that I could've pulled off, but *I* got taken. The slick tech-support guy paused for a minute, as if he was pulling up my account info, and then asked, "What password did you try?"

Stupid me, I proceeded to mouth off all the passwords it could've been! The phone got quiet for a moment. He reset my password and told me what it was. After I hung up the phone, I thought, "What just happened? I just got social-engineered!" Man, was I mad at myself. I changed all the passwords that I divulged in case he used that information against me. I still bet to this day that he was just experimenting with me. Lesson learned: Never, ever, under any circumstances divulge your password to someone else.

Deceit through technology

Technology can make things easier — and more fun — for the social engineer. Often, the request comes from a computer or other electronic entity you think you can identify. But spoofing a computer name, an e-mail address, a fax number, or a network address is easy. Fortunately, you can take a few countermeasures against this, as described in the next section.

One way hackers deceive through technology is by sending e-mail for critical information. Such e-mail usually provides a link that directs victims to a professional- and legitimate-looking Web site that "updates" such account information as user IDs, passwords, and Social Security numbers

Many spam messages use this trick. Most users are inundated with so much spam and other unwanted e-mail that they often let their guard down and open e-mails and attachments that they shouldn't open. These e-mails usually look professional and believable. They often dupe people into disclosing information they should never give in exchange for a gift. These social-engineering tricks also occur when a hacker who has already broken into the network sends messages or creates fake Internet pop-up windows. The same tricks have occurred through instant messaging and cell-phone messaging.

In some well-publicized incidents, hackers e-mailed to their victims a patch purporting to come from Microsoft or another well-known vendor. Users think it looks like a duck and it quacks like a duck — but it's not Bill this time! The message is from a hacker wanting the user to install the "patch" so a Trojan-horse keylogger can be installed or a backdoor can be created into computers and networks. Hackers use these backdoors to hack into the organization's systems or use the victims' computers (known as *zombies*) as launching pads to attack another system. Even viruses or worms use social engineering. For instance, the LoveBug worm told users they had a secret admirer. When the victims opened the e-mail, it was too late. Their computers were infected; perhaps worse, they didn't have a secret admirer.

The *Nigerian 419* e-mail fraud scheme attempts to access unsuspecting people's bank accounts and money. These social engineers — scamsters — offer to transfer millions of dollars to the victim to repatriate a deceased client's funds to the United States. All the victim must provide is personal bank-account information and a little money up front to cover the transfer expenses. Victims have ended up having their bank accounts emptied.

Many computerized social-engineering tactics can be performed anonymously through Internet proxy servers, anonymizers, and remailers. When people fall for requests for confidential personal or corporate information, the sources of these social-engineering attacks are often impossible to track.

Social-Engineering Countermeasures

You have only a few good lines of defense against social engineering. Even with strong security systems, a naïve or untrained user can let the social engineer into the network. Never underestimate the power of social engineers.

Policies

Specific policies help ward off social engineering long-term in these areas:

- Classifying data
- Hiring employees and contractors and setting up user IDs
- Terminating employees and contractors, and removing user IDs
- Setting and resetting passwords
- Handling proprietary and confidential information
- Escorting guests

These policies must be enforceable and enforced — for everyone within the organization. Keep them up to date and tell your end users about them.

User awareness

The best line of defense against social engineering is an organization with employees who can identify and respond to social-engineering attacks. User awareness begins with initial training for everyone and follows with security-awareness initiatives to keep social-engineering defenses on everyone's mind. Align training and awareness with specific security policies.

Consider outsourcing security training to a seasoned security trainer. Employees often take training more seriously if it comes from an outsider. Outsourcing security training is worth the investment.

As you approach ongoing user training and awareness in your organization, the following tips help you combat social-engineering long term:

- Treat security awareness and training as a business investment.
- Train users on an ongoing basis to keep security fresh in their minds.
- Tailor your training content to your audience whenever possible.
- Create a social-engineering awareness program for your business functions and user roles.
- Keep your messages as nontechnical as possible.
- Develop incentive programs for preventing and reporting incidents.
- Lead by example.

Share these tips with your users to help prevent social-engineering attacks:

- Never divulge any information unless you can validate that the person requesting the information needs it and is who he says he is. If a request is made over the telephone, verify the caller's identity, and call back.
- Never click an e-mail link that supposedly loads a page with information that needs updating. This is especially true for unsolicited e-mails.
- Escort all guests within a building.
- Never send or open files from strangers.
- Never give out passwords.

A few other general suggestions can ward off social engineering:

- Never let a stranger connect to one of your network jacks — even for a few seconds. A hacker can place a network analyzer, Trojan-horse program, or other malware directly onto your network.
- Classify your information assets, both hard-copy and electronic. Train all employees to handle each asset type.
- Develop and enforce computer media and document destruction policies that help ensure data is handled carefully and stays where it should.
- Use cross-shredding paper shredders. Better, hire a document-shredding company that specializes in confidential document destruction.
- Never allow anonymous File Transfer Protocol (FTP) access into your FTP servers if you don't have to.

These techniques can reinforce the content of formal training:

- New-employee orientation, lunch 'n' learns, e-mails, and newsletters
- Social-engineering survival brochure with tips and FAQs
- Trinkets, such as screen savers, mouse pads, sticky notes, pens, and office posters

  Appendix A lists my favorite user-awareness trinket vendors to improve user awareness in your organization.

Chapter 6

Physical Security

In This Chapter

- Understanding the importance of physical security
- Q&A with a well-known physical-security expert
- Looking for physical-security vulnerabilities
- Implementing countermeasures for physical-security attacks

I'm a strong believer that information security is more dependent on nontechnical policies, processes, and procedures than on the technical hardware and software solutions that many people swear by. Physical security — *protection of physical property* — encompasses both technical and nontechnical components.

Physical security is an often overlooked aspect of an information-security program. Physical security is a critical component of information security. Your ability to secure your information depends on your ability to secure your site physically. In this chapter, I cover some common physical-security weaknesses, as they relate to computers and information security, to look for in your own systems. In addition, I outline free and low-cost countermeasures to minimize your vulnerabilities. I don't recommend breaking and entering, which is required for some physical-security tests. Instead, approach sensitive areas to see how far you *can* get. Take a fresh look — from an outsider's perspective — at the physical vulnerabilities I cover in this chapter. You may discover holes in your physical-security infrastructure.

Physical-Security Vulnerabilities

Whatever your computer and network-security technology, practically any hack is possible if a hacker is in your building or computer room. That's why it's important to look for physical-security vulnerabilities.

In small companies, some physical-security issues may not be a problem. Many physical security vulnerabilities depend on factors like the following:

- Size of the building
- Number of buildings or sites
- Number of employees
- Location and number of building entrance/exit points
- Placement of the computer room(s) and other confidential information

Literally thousands of possible physical-security vulnerabilities exist. The bad guys are always on the lookout for them — so you should find these vulnerabilities first. Here are some common physical-security vulnerabilities I've found when assessing security:

- No receptionist in a building
- No visitor sign-in or escort required for building access
- Employees trusting visitors just because they're wearing vendor uniforms or say they're there to work on the copier or computers
- No access controls on doors
- Doors propped open
- Publicly accessible computer rooms
- Backup media lying around
- Unsecured computer hardware and software media
- CDs and floppy disks with confidential information in trash cans

When these physical-security vulnerabilities are exploited, bad things can happen. Perhaps the biggest problem is that unauthorized people can enter your building. After intruders are in your building, they can wander the halls; log onto computers; rummage through the trash; and steal hard-copy documents, floppy disks and CDs, and even computers out of offices.

What to Look For

You should look for specific security vulnerabilities. Many potential physical-security exploits seem unlikely, but they happen to organizations that don't take physical security seriously.

Hackers can exploit many physical-security vulnerabilities, including weaknesses in a building's infrastructure, office layout, computer-room access, and design. In addition to these factors, consider the facility's proximity to local emergency assistance (police, fire, and ambulance) and the area's crime statistics (burglary, breaking and entering, and so on) so you can better understand what you're up against.

A Q&A on physical security with Jack Wiles

In this Q&A session, Jack Wiles, an information-security pioneer with over 30 years of experience, answered several questions on physical security and how a lack of it often leads to information insecurity.

How important do you think physical security is in relation to technical-security issues?

I've been asked that question many times in the past, and from decades of experience with both physical and technical security, I have a standard answer. Without question, many of the most expensive technical-security countermeasures and tools become worthless when physical security is weak. If I can get my team into your building(s) and walk up to someone's desk and log in as that person, I have bypassed all your technical-security systems. In past security assessments, after my team and I entered a building, we always found that people simply thought that we belonged there — that we were employees. We were always friendly and helpful when we came in contact with real employees. They would often return the kindness by helping us with whatever we asked for.

How were you able to get into most of the buildings when you conducted "red team" penetration tests for companies?

In many cases, we just boldly walked into the building and went up the elevator in multistory buildings. If we were challenged, we always had a story ready. Our typical story was that we thought that this was the HR department, and we were there to apply for a job. If we were stopped at the door and told which building to go to for HR, we simply left and then looked for other entrances to that same building. If we found an outside smoking area at a different door, we attempted *tailgating* and simply walked in behind other employees who were reentering the building after finishing their breaks. Tailgating also worked at most entrances that required card access. In my career as a red-team leader, we were never stopped and questioned. We simply said, "Thank you" as we walked in and compromised the entire building.

What kinds of things would you bring out of a building?

It was always easy to get enough important documentation to prove that we were there. In many cases, the documentation was sitting in a box next to someone's desk (especially if that person was someone important) marked RECYCLE. To us, that really said, "Steal me first"! We found it interesting that many companies just let their recycle boxes fill up before emptying them. We would also look for a room where strip-cut shredders were used. The documents that were shredded were usually stored in clear plastic bags. We loaded these bags into our cars and had many of the shredded documents put back together in a few hours. We found that if we pasted the strips from any page on cardboard with as much as an inch of space between the strips, the final document was still readable.

Jack Wiles is president of TheTrainingCo. and promotes the annual information-security conference Techno Security (`www.thetrainingco.com`).

The following sections list vulnerabilities to look for when assessing your organization's physical security. This won't take a lot of technical savvy or expensive equipment. Depending on the size of your facilities, these tests shouldn't take much time. The bottom line is to determine whether the physical-security systems are adequate for the risks involved. Above all, be practical and use common sense.

Building infrastructure

Doors, windows, and walls are critical components of a building — especially in a computer room or in an area where confidential information is stored.

Attack points

Hackers can exploit a handful of building-infrastructure vulnerabilities. Consider the following attack points, which are commonly overlooked:

- Are doors propped open? If so, why?
- Can gaps at the bottom of critical doors allow someone using a balloon or other device to trip a sensor on the inside of a "secure" room?
- Would it be easy to force doors open? Would a simple kick near the doorknob suffice?
- What is the building and/or computer room made of (steel, wood, concrete), and how sturdy are the walls and entryways? How resilient would the material be to earthquakes, tornadoes, strong winds, heavy rains, and vehicles driving into the building?
- Are any doors or windows made of glass? Is this glass clear? Is the glass shatterproof or bulletproof?
- Are doors, windows, and other entry points wired to an alarm system?
- Are there *drop ceilings* with tiles that can be pushed up? Are the walls slab-to-slab? If not, hackers can easily scale walls, bypassing any door or window access controls.

Countermeasures

Many physical-security countermeasures for building vulnerabilities may require other maintenance, construction, or operations experts. If building infrastructures is not your forte, you can hire outside experts during the design, assessment, and retrofitting stages to ensure that you have adequate controls. Here are some of the best ways to solidify building security:

- Strong doors and locks
- Windowless walls around computer rooms

- An alarm system that's connected to all access points and continuously monitored
- Lighting (especially around entry/exit points)
- Mantraps that allow only person at a time to pass through a door
- Fences (barbed wire and razor wire)

Utilities

You must consider building and computer-room utilities, such as power, water, and fire suppression, when accessing physical security. These utilities can help fight off such incidents as fire and keep other access controls running during a power loss. They can also be used against you if an intruder enters the building.

Attack points

Hackers often exploit utility-related vulnerabilities. Consider the following attack points, which are commonly overlooked:

- Is power-protection equipment (surge protectors, UPSs, and generators) in place? How easily accessible are the on/off switches on these devices? Can an intruder walk in and flip a switch?
- When the power fails, what happens to physical-security mechanisms? Do they fail *open,* allowing anyone through, or fail *closed,* keeping everyone in or out until the power is restored?
- Where are fire-detection and -suppression devices — including alarm sensors, extinguishers, and sprinkler systems — located? Determine how a malicious intruder can abuse them. Are these devices placed where they can harm electronic equipment during a false alarm?
- Where are water and gas shutoff valves located? Can you access them, or would you have to call maintenance personnel about an incident?
- Are local telecom wires (both copper and fiber) that run outside of the building located aboveground, where someone can tap into them with telecom tools? Can digging in the area cut them easily? Are they located on telephone poles that are vulnerable to traffic accidents?

Countermeasures

You may need to involve other experts during the design, assessment, or retrofitting stages. The key is *placement:*

- Where are the major utility controls placed?
- Can a hacker or other miscreant walking through the building access the controls to turn them on and off?

Covers for on/off switches and thermostat controls and locks for server power buttons and PCI expansion slots are effective defenses.

I once assessed the physical security of an Internet collocation facility for a very large computer company (whose name will remain anonymous). I made it past the front guard and tailgated through all the controlled doors to reach the data center. After I was inside, I walked by such equipment as servers, routers, firewalls, UPSs, and power cords that were owned by very large dot-com companies. All this equipment was completely exposed to anyone walking in that area. A quick flip of a switch or an accidental trip over a network cable dangling to the floor could bring an entire shelf — and a global e-commerce site — to the ground.

Office layout and usage

Office design and usage can either help or hinder physical security.

Hackers may exploit some office vulnerabilities. Consider these attack points:

- Does a receptionist or security guard monitor traffic in and out?
- Do employees have confidential information on their desks? What about mail and other packages — do they lie around outside someone's door or, even worse, outside the building, waiting for pickup?
- Where are trash cans and dumpsters located? Are they easily accessible by anyone? Are recycling bins or shredders used? Open recycling bins and other careless handling of trash are open invitations for *dumpster diving* — in which hackers search for confidential company information in phone lists and memos in the trash. Dumpster diving can lead to many security exposures.
- How secure are mail and copy rooms? If hackers can access these rooms, they can steal mail or company letterhead to use against you.
- Are closed-circuit television (CCTV) cameras used *and* monitored?
- What access controls are on doors and windows? Are regular keys, card keys, combination locks, or biometrics used? Who can access these keys, and where are they stored? Keys and programmable keypad combinations are often shared among users, making accountability difficult to determine. Find out how many people share these combinations and keys.

Countermeasures

Simple measures can reduce your exposure to office vulnerabilities:

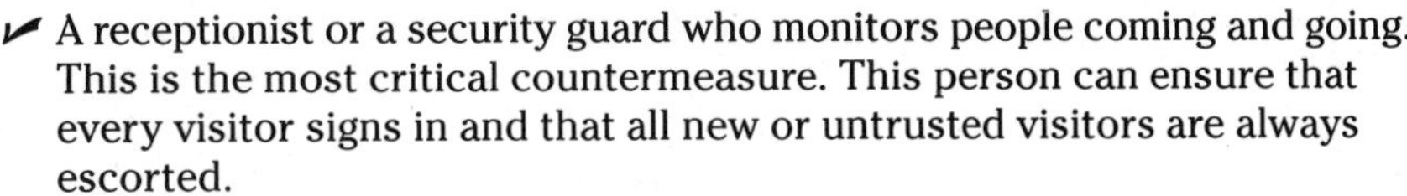

- A receptionist or a security guard who monitors people coming and going. This is the most critical countermeasure. This person can ensure that every visitor signs in and that all new or untrusted visitors are always escorted.

  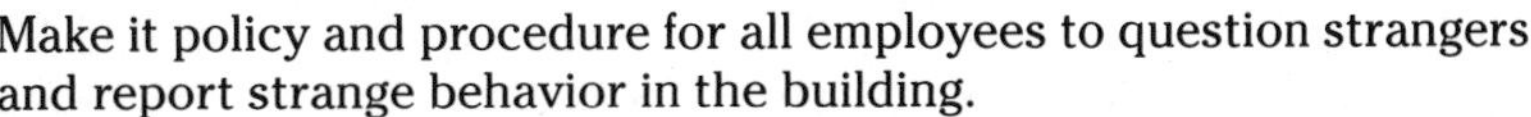

  Make it policy and procedure for all employees to question strangers and report strange behavior in the building.

  Employees Only or *Authorized Personnel Only* signs show the bad guys where they *should* go instead of deterring them from entering.

- CCTV cameras.
- Single entry/exit points to a building or computer room.
- Secure areas for dumpsters.
- Cross-cut shredders or secure recycling bins for hard-copy documents.
- Limited numbers of keys and pass-code combinations.

  Make keys and pass codes unique for each person, whenever possible.

- Biometrics identification systems can be very effective, but they can also be expensive and difficult to manage.

Network components and computers

After hackers obtain physical access to a building, they look for the computer room and other easily accessible computer and network devices.

Attack points

The keys to the kingdom are often as close as someone's desktop computer and not much farther than an unsecured computer room or wiring closet.

Malicious intruders can do the following:

- Obtain network access and send malicious e-mails as a logged-in user.
- Steal files from the computer by copying them onto a floppy disk or USB drive, or by e-mailing them to an external address.
- Enter unlocked computer rooms and mess around with servers, firewalls, and routers.
- Walk out with network diagrams, contact lists, and business-continuity and incident-response plans.
- Obtain phone numbers from analog lines and circuit IDs from T1, frame-relay, and other telecom equipment for future attacks.

Practically every bit of unencrypted information that traverses the network can be recorded for future analysis through one of the following methods:

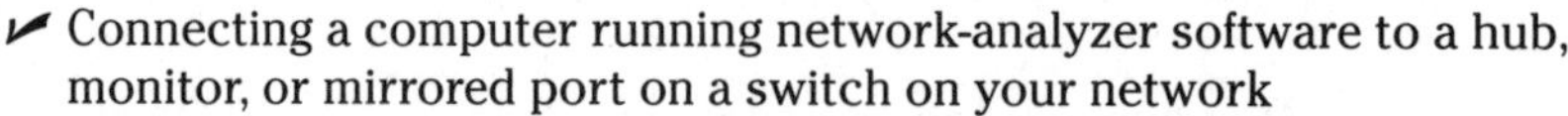

- Connecting a computer running network-analyzer software to a hub, monitor, or mirrored port on a switch on your network

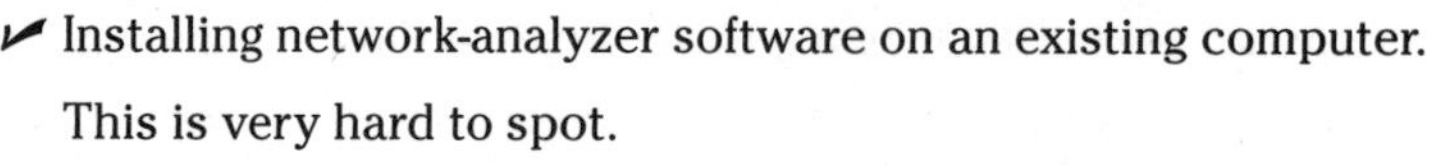

- Installing network-analyzer software on an existing computer.

  This is very hard to spot.

How would hackers access this information in the future?

- The easiest attack method is to either install remote-administration software on the computer or dial into a modem by using VNC or pcAnywhere.
- A crafty hacker with enough time can bind a public IP address to the computer if it's outside the firewall. Hackers with enough network knowledge can configure new firewall rules to do this.

Also consider these other vulnerabilities:

- How easily can someone's computer be accessed during regular hours? During lunchtime? After hours?
- Are servers, firewalls, routers, and switches mounted in locked racks?
- Are computers — especially laptops — secured to desks with locks?
- Are passwords stored on sticky notes on computer screens, keyboards, or desks?
- Are backup media lying around the computer room susceptible to theft?
- Are media safes used to protect backup media? Who can access the safe?
- How are laptops and hand-held computers handled in-house and when employees are working from home or traveling? Are personal digital assistants (PDAs) and cell phones sitting around unsecured? These devices are often at great risk because of their size and value. Also, they are typically unprotected by the organization's regular security controls. Are specific policies and technologies in place to help protect them? Is locking laptop bags and PDA cases required? What about power-on passwords? Also consider encryption in case these devices get into a hacker's hands.
- How easily can someone access a wireless *access point* (AP) signal or the AP itself to join the network?
- Are network firewalls, routers, switches, and hubs (basically, anything with an Ethernet connection) easily accessible, which would enable a hacker to plug into the network easily?

- Are all cables patched through on the patch panel in the wiring closet so all network drops are live?

  This is very common but a bad idea.

- Are cable traps/locks in place that prevent hackers from unplugging network cables from patch panels or computers to use those connections for their own computers?

Countermeasures

Network and computer security countermeasures are some of the simplest to implement, yet the most difficult to enforce because they involve everyday actions. Here is a rundown of these countermeasures:

- Require users to lock their screens — which usually takes a few clicks or keystrokes in Windows or UNIX — to keep intruders out of their systems.
- Ensure that strong passwords are used (as covered in Chapter 7).
- Require laptop users to lock their systems to their desks with a locking cable. This is especially important in larger companies or locations that receive a lot of foot traffic.
- Keep computer rooms and wiring closets locked, and monitor those areas for malicious wrongdoings.
- Keep a current inventory of hardware and software within the organization — especially in computer rooms — so it's easy to determine when extra equipment appears or other equipment is missing.
- Properly secure computer media — such as floppy disks, CD-ROMs, tapes, and hard drives — when stored and during transport.
- Use a bulk eraser on magnetic media before it's discarded.

Chapter 7
Passwords

In This Chapter

- Identifying password vulnerabilities
- Examining password-hacking tools and techniques
- Hacking operating-system passwords
- Hacking password-protected files
- Protecting your systems from password hacking

Password hacking is one of the easiest and most common ways hackers obtain unauthorized computer or network access. Although strong passwords that are difficult to *crack* (or guess) are easy to create and maintain, users often neglect this. Therefore, passwords are one of the weakest links in the information-security chain. Passwords rely on secrecy. After a password is compromised, its original owner isn't the only person who can access the system with it. That's when bad things start happening.

Hackers have many ways to obtain passwords. They can glean passwords simply by asking for them or by looking over the shoulders of users as they type them in. Hackers can also obtain passwords from local computers by using password-cracking software. To obtain passwords from across a network, hackers can use remote cracking utilities or network analyzers.

This chapter demonstrates just how easily hackers can gather password information from your network. I outline common password vulnerabilities that exist in computer networks and describe countermeasures to help prevent these vulnerabilities from being exploited on your systems.

If you perform the tests and implement the countermeasures outlined in this chapter, you're well on your way to securing your systems' passwords.

Password Vulnerabilities

When you balance the cost of security and the value of the protected information, the combination of *user ID* and *secret password* is usually adequate.

However, passwords give a false sense of security. The bad guys know this and attempt to crack passwords as a step toward breaking into computer systems.

One big problem with relying solely on passwords for information security is that more than one person can know them. Sometimes, this is intentional; often, it's not. You can't know who has a password other than the owner.

Knowing a password doesn't make someone an authorized user.

Here are the two general classifications of password vulnerabilities:

- **Organizational or end-user vulnerabilities:** This includes lack of password awareness on the part of end users and the lack of password policies that are enforced within the organization.
- **Technical vulnerabilities:** This includes weak encryption methods and insecure storage of passwords on computer systems.

Before computer networks and the Internet, the user's physical environment was an additional layer of password security. Now that most computers have network connectivity, that protection is gone.

Organizational password vulnerabilities

It's human nature to want convenience. This makes passwords one of the easiest barriers for an attacker to overcome. Almost 3 trillion (yes, trillion with a *t* and 12 zeros) eight-character password combinations are possible by using the 26 letters of the alphabet and the numerals 0 through 9. However, most people prefer to create passwords that are easy to remember. Users like to use such passwords as "password," their login name, or a pet's name.

Unless users are educated and reminded about using strong passwords, their passwords usually are

- Weak and easy to guess.
- Seldom changed.
- Reused for many security points. When bad guys crack a password, they try to access other systems with the same password and user name.
- Written down in nonsecure places. The more complex a password is, the more difficult it is to crack. However, when users create more complex passwords, they're more likely to write them down. Hackers can find these passwords and use them against you.

A case study in Windows password vulnerabilities with Philippe Oechslin

In this case study, Dr. Philippe Oechslin, a researcher and independent information security consultant, shared with me his recent research findings on Windows password vulnerabilities.

The Situation

In 2003, Dr. Oechslin discovered a new method for cracking Windows passwords. While testing a brute-force password-cracking tool, he thought it was a waste of time for everyone using the same tool to have to generate the same hashes over and over again. He believed that generating a huge dictionary of all possible hashes would make it easier to crack Windows passwords, but then he quickly realized that a dictionary of the LAN Manager (LM) hashes of all possible alphanumerical passwords would require over a terabyte of storage.

During his research, Dr. Oechslin discovered a technique called time-memory trade-offs, where hashes are computed in advance but only a small fraction are stored (approximately one in a thousand). He discovered that how the LM hashes are organized allows you to find any password if you spend some time recalculating some of the hashes. This technique saves memory but takes a lot of time. Studying this method, he found a way to make it more efficient, making it possible to find any of the 80 billion unique hashes by using a table of 250 million entries (1GB worth of data) and performing only 4 million hash calculations. This process is much faster than a brute-force attack, which must generate 50 percent of the hashes (40 billion) on average.

This research is based on the absence of a random element when Windows passwords are hashed. This is true for both the LM hash and the NT hash built into Windows. As a result, the same password produces the same hash on any Windows machine. Although it is known that Windows hashes have no random element, no one has used a technique like the one that Dr. Oechslin discovered to crack Windows passwords.

For a short time, Dr. Oechslin and his team had an interactive tool on their Web site (`lasecwww.epfl.ch`) that enabled visitors to submit hashes and have them cracked. Over a six-day period, the tool cracked 1,845 passwords in an average of 7.7 seconds! They deactivated the demo after a week (and a million hits) and did not release the tool because they didn't want to help hackers. Dr. Oechslin did say that he has heard about other tools (such as RainbowCrack) that use the same method but are being developed independently.

The Outcome

So what's the big deal, you say? This password-cracking method can crack any alphanumerical password in a few seconds, whereas current brute-force tools can take several hours. Dr. Oechslin and his research team have generated a table with which they can crack any password made of letters, numbers, and 16 other characters in less than a minute, demonstrating that passwords made up of letters and numbers aren't good enough. He also stated that this method is useful for ethical hackers who have only limited time to perform their testing. Unfortunately, hackers have the same benefit and can perform their attacks before anyone detects them!

Philippe Oechslin, PhD, CISSP, is a lecturer and senior research assistant at the Swiss Federal Institute of Technology in Lausanne and spends his spare time as an independent information-security consultant.

Technical password vulnerabilities

You can often find these serious technical vulnerabilities after exploiting organizational password vulnerabilities:

- Weak password-encryption schemes. Hackers can break weak password storage mechanisms by using cracking methods that I outline in this chapter. Many vendors and developers believe that passwords are safe from hackers if they don't publish the source code for their encryption algorithms. *Wrong!* A persistent, patient hacker can usually crack this *security by obscurity* fairly quickly. After the code is cracked, it is soon distributed across the Internet and becomes public knowledge.

  Password-cracking utilities take advantage of weak password encryption. These utilities do the grunt work and can crack any password, given enough time and computing power.
- Software that stores passwords in memory and easily accessed databases.
- End-user applications that display passwords on the screen while typing.

The ICAT Metabase (an index of computer vulnerabilities) currently identifies over 460 technical password vulnerabilities, 230 of which are labeled as high-severity. You can search for some of these issues at `icat.nist.gov/icat.cfm` to find out how vulnerable some of your systems are from a technical perspective.

Cracking Passwords

Password cracking is one of the most enjoyable hacks for the bad guys. It fuels their sense of exploration and desire to figure things out. You may not have a burning desire to explore everyone's passwords, but it helps to approach password cracking with this thinking. So where should you start hacking the passwords on your systems? Generally speaking, any user's password works. After you obtain one password, you can obtain others — including administrator or root passwords.

Administrator passwords are the pot of gold. With unauthorized administrative access, you can do virtually anything on the system. When looking for your organization's password vulnerabilities, I recommend first trying to obtain the highest level of access possible (such as administrator) through the most discreet method possible. That's what the hackers do.

You can use low-tech ways and high-tech ways to exploit the vulnerabilities and obtain passwords. For example, you can deceive users into divulging passwords over the telephone or simply observe what a user has written down on a piece of paper. Or you can capture passwords directly from a computer or over a network or the Internet with tools covered in the following sections.

Cracking passwords the old-fashioned way

A hacker can use low-tech methods to crack passwords. These methods include using social-engineering techniques, shoulder surfing, and simply guessing passwords from information that you know about the user.

Social engineering

The most popular low-tech method is *social engineering,* which is covered in detail in Chapter 5. Social engineering takes advantage of the trusting nature of human beings to gain information that can later be used maliciously.

Techniques

To obtain a password through social engineering, you just ask for it. For example, you can simply call a user and tell him that he has some important-looking e-mails stuck in the mail queue and you need his password to log in and free them up. This is how hackers try to get the information!

If your colleague gives you his password, make sure that he changes it.

Countermeasures

User awareness is the best defense against social engineering. Train users to spot attacks (such as suspicious phone calls or deceitful e-mails) and respond effectively. Their best response is to not give out any information and to alert the appropriate information-security officer in the organization to see whether the inquiry is legitimate and whether a response is necessary. For this defense to be successful, the organization must enforce a security policy and provide ongoing security-awareness training to users.

Shoulder surfing

Shoulder surfing is an effective, low-tech password hack.

Techniques

To mount this attack, you must be near the user and not look obvious. Simply watch either the user's keyboard or screen when logging in.

A hacker with a good eye may watch whether the user is glancing around his desk for either a reminder of the password or the password itself.

Many folks have experienced shoulder surfing at the grocery-store checkout line. You swipe your debit card to pay for your chips and dip; you enter your PIN to authorize the transaction; and before you know it, the guy in line behind you has your PIN! He simply watched you enter it into the keypad.

You can try shoulder surfing yourself — though preferably not in the grocery-store checkout line. Just walk around the office and perform random spot checks. Go to users' desks, and ask them to log in to their computers, the network, or even their e-mail applications. Just don't tell them what you're doing beforehand, or they'll be on to you and attempt to hide what they're typing or where they're looking for their password — two things that they should've been doing all along!

Countermeasures

Encourage users to be aware of their surroundings and not enter their passwords when they suspect that someone is looking over their shoulder. Instruct users that if they suspect someone is looking over their shoulder while they're logging in, they should politely ask the person to look away.

Inference

Inference is simply guessing passwords from information you know about users — such as their date of birth, favorite television show, and phone numbers. It sounds silly, but you can determine passwords by guessing!

The best defense against an inference hack attack is to educate users about creating secure passwords that do not include information that can be associated with them. You can't easily enforce this practice with technical controls, so you need a sound security policy and ongoing awareness training to remind users of the importance of secure password creation.

Weak authentication

Hackers can obtain — or simply avoid having to use — passwords by taking advantage of older operating systems, such as Windows 9*x* and Me. These operating systems don't require passwords to log in.

Bypassing authentication

On a Windows 9*x* or similar workstation that's prompting for a password, you can press Esc on the keyboard to get right in. After you're in, you can find other passwords stored in such places as dial-up networking connections and screen savers. These weak systems can serve as *trusted* machines — meaning that it's assumed that they're secure — and provide good launching pads for network-based password attacks as well.

Countermeasures

The only true defense against this hack is to not use operating systems that employ weak authentication. To eliminate this vulnerability, upgrade to Windows XP, or use Linux or the flavors of UNIX, including Mac OS X.

More modern authentication systems (such as Kerberos, which is used in newer versions of Windows), directory services (such as Novell's eDirectory), and network-based e-mail systems (such as Exchange) encrypt user passwords or don't communicate the passwords across the network. These measures create an extra layer of security, but these authentication systems still have some vulnerabilities, which I discuss shortly.

High-tech password cracking

High-tech password cracking involves using a program that tries to guess a password by determining all possible password combinations. These high-tech methods are mostly automated after you access the computer and password database files.

Password cracking software

You can try to crack your organization's operating-system and Internet-application passwords with various password cracking tools:

- LC4 (previously called L0phtcrack) can sniff out password hashes from the wire. Go to `www.atstake.com/research/lc`
- Proactive Windows Security Explorer, a password security test tool. Go to `www.elcomsoft.com/pwsex.html`
- NetBIOS Auditing Tool (NAT) specializes in network-based password attacks. Go to `www.securityfocus.com/tools/543`
- Chknull (`www.phreak.org/archives/exploits/novell`) for Novell NetWare password testing
- These tools require physical access on the tested computer:
  - John the Ripper (`www.openwall.com/john`)
  - pwdump2 (`razor.bindview.com/tools/desc/pwdump2_readme.html`)
  - Crack (`coast.cs.purdue.edu/pub/tools/unix/pwdutils/crack`)
  - Brutus (`www.hoobie.net/brutus`)
  - Pandora (`www.nmrc.org/project/pandora`)
  - NTFSDOS Professional (`www.winternals.com`)
- Various other handy password tools exist, such as
  - GetPass for decrypting login passwords for Cisco routers (`www.boson.com/promo/utilities/getpass/getpass_utility.htm`)
  - Win Sniffer for capturing FTP, e-mail, and other types of passwords off the network
  - Cain and Abel for capturing, cracking, and even calculating various types of passwords on a plethora of systems (`www.oxid.it/cain.html`)

You may be wondering what value a password-cracking tool offers if you need physical access to your systems to test them. Some would say that if a hacker can obtain physical access to your systems and password files, you have more than just basic information-security problems to worry about. But this kind of access is entirely possible! What about a summer intern, a disgruntled employee, or an outside consultant with malicious intent?

Password-cracking utilities take a set of known passwords and run them through a password-hashing algorithm. The resulting hashes — or an encrypted form of a data set — are then compared at lightning speed to the password hashes extracted from the original password database. When a match is found between the newly generated hash and the hash in the original database, the password has been cracked. It's that simple.

Other password-cracking programs simply attempt to logon using a predefined set of user IDs and passwords. In fact, NAT can do just that. NAT takes advantage of some known weaknesses in Microsoft's Server Message Block (SMB) protocol, which is used for file and print sharing.

Try running NAT in a real-world scenario. Simply download NAT from the preceding address, and extract it to a temporary directory on your hard drive. NAT comes with some predefined usernames and passwords in the `userlist.txt` and `passlist.txt` files, but you can modify them or add your own. For a quick test of a Windows NT or 2000 machine across the network, enter this basic NAT command at a command prompt:

```
nat -u userlist.txt -p passlist.txt IP_address_of_the_computer_you're_testing
```

Figure 7-1 shows the output of my test server when I ran NAT against it. NAT used the default password list to crack the administrator password in just a few seconds. If you don't have any luck, consider using one of the dictionary files listed in the next section. Just give the test some time. If you use one of the larger lists, the process may take quite a while.

```
DOS Prompt
C:\passwords>nat -u userlist.txt -p passlist.txt 10.11.12.200

[*]--- Reading usernames from userlist.txt
[*]--- Reading passwords from passlist.txt

[*]--- Checking host: 10.11.12.200
[*]--- Obtaining list of remote NetBIOS names
[*]--- Remote systems name tables:

    WINNT
    DOMAIN1
    ☺☻__MSBROWSE__☻
    ADMINISTRATOR

[*]--- Attempting to connect with name: *
[*]--- Unable to connect

[*]--- Attempting to connect with name: WINNT
[*]--- CONNECTED with name: WINNT
[*]--- Attempting to connect with protocol: MICROSOFT NETWORKS 1.03
[*]--- Server time is Sun Aug 3 12:33:00 2003
[*]--- Timezone is UTC-4.0
[*]--- Remote server wants us to encrypt, telling it not to

[*]--- Attempting to connect with name: WINNT
[*]--- CONNECTED with name: WINNT
[*]--- Attempting to establish session
[*]--- Was not able to establish session with no password
[*]--- Attempting to connect with Username: `ADMINISTRATOR' Password: `administr
ator'
[*]--- Attempting to connect with Username: `ADMINISTRATOR' Password: `password'

[*]--- Attempting to connect with Username: `ADMINISTRATOR' Password: `share'
[*]--- CONNECTED: Username: `ADMINISTRATOR' Password: `share'
C:\passwords>
```

Figure 7-1: Output from the NetBIOS Auditing Tool.

Passwords that are subjected to cracking tools eventually lose. You have access to the same tools as the bad guys. These tools can be used for both legitimate auditing and malicious attacks. You want to audit your passwords before the bad guys do, and in this section, I show you some of my favorite methods for auditing Windows and Linux/UNIX passwords.

When trying to crack passwords, the associated user accounts may be locked out, which could interrupt your users. Be careful if you have intruder lockout enabled — you may have to go back in and reenable locked accounts.

Passwords are typically stored on a computer in an encrypted fashion, using an encryption or one-way hash algorithm such as DES or MD5. Hashed passwords are then represented as fixed-length encrypted strings that always represent the same passwords with exactly the same strings. These hashes are irreversible for all practical purposes, so passwords can never be decrypted.

Password storage locations vary by operating system:

- Windows usually stores passwords in these locations:
  - Security Accounts Manager (SAM) database (`c:\winnt\system32\config`)
  - Active Directory database file that's stored locally or spread across domain controllers (`ntds.dit`)

  Windows sometimes stores passwords in either a backup of the SAM file in the `c:\winnt\repair` directory or on an emergency repair disk.

  Some Windows applications store passwords in the Registry or as plaintext files on the hard drive!

- Linux and other UNIX variants typically store passwords in these files:
  - `/etc/passwd` (readable by everyone)
  - `/etc/shadow` (accessible by root only)
  - `/etc/security/passwd` (accessible by root only)
  - `/.secure/etc/passwd` (accessible by root only)

Two high-tech password-cracking methods are dictionary attacks and brute-force attacks.

Dictionary attacks

Dictionary attacks against passwords quickly compare a set of words — including many common passwords — against a password database. This database is a text file with thousands of words typically listed in alphabetical order. For instance, suppose that you have a dictionary file that you downloaded from one of the sites in the following list. The English dictionary file at the Purdue site contains one word per line starting with *10th, 1st* . . . all the way to *zucchini* and *zygote.*

Many password-cracking utilities can use a separate dictionary that you create or download from the Internet. Here are some popular sites that house dictionary files and other miscellaneous word lists:

- ftp://ftp.cerias.purdue.edu/pub/dict
- ftp://ftp.ox.ac.uk/pub/wordlists
- packetstormsecurity.nl/Crackers/wordlists
- www.outpost9.com/files/WordLists.html

Most dictionary attacks are good for *weak* (easily guessed) passwords. However, some special dictionaries have common misspellings of words such as pa$$w0rd (password) and 5ecur1ty (security), non-English words, and thematic words from religions, politics, or *Star Trek*.

Brute-force attacks

Brute-force attacks can crack any password, given sufficient time. Brute-force attacks try every combination of numbers, letters, and special characters until the password is discovered. Many password-cracking utilities let you specify such testing criteria as the characters and password length to try.

A brute-force test can take quite a while, depending on the number of accounts, their associated password complexities, and the speed of the computer that's running the cracking software.

Smart hackers attempt logins slowly or at random times so the failed login attempts aren't as predictable or obvious in the system log files. Some malicious users may even call the IT help desk to attempt a reset of the account they've just locked out. This social-engineering technique could be a major issue, especially if the organization has no or minimal mechanisms in place to verify that locked-out users are who they say they are.

Can an expiring password deter a hacker's attack and render password-cracking software useless? Yes. After the password is changed, the cracking must start again if the hacker wants to test all the possible combinations. This is one reason why passwords must be changed periodically. Shortening the change interval can reduce the risk of a password's being cracked.

Exhaustive password-cracking attempts usually aren't necessary. Most passwords are fairly weak. Even minimum password requirements, such as a password length, can help you in your testing; you may be able to give your cracking programs more defined cracking parameters, which eliminates combinations for faster results.

Cracking passwords with pwdump2 and John the Ripper

The following steps use two of my favorite utilities to test the security of current passwords on Windows systems:

- pwdump2 (to extract password hashes from the Windows SAM database)
- John the Ripper (to crack the hashes of Windows and UNIX passwords)

This test requires administrative access to either your Windows NT/2000 stand-alone workstation or server:

1. **Create a new directory called** `passwords` **from the root of your Windows C: drive.**
2. **Download and install a decompression tool, if you don't have one.**

   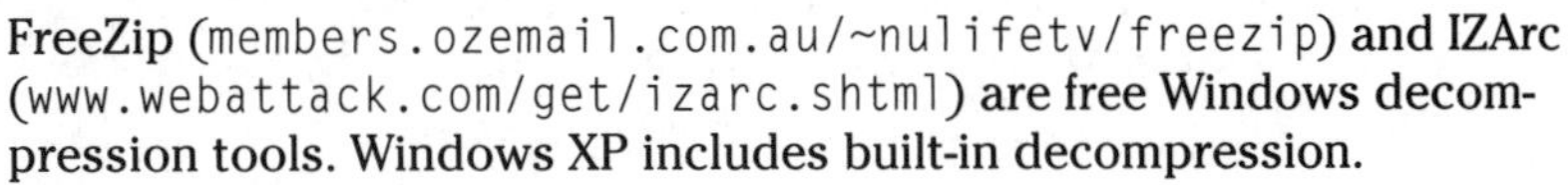

   TIP

   FreeZip (`members.ozemail.com.au/~nulifetv/freezip`) and IZArc (`www.webattack.com/get/izarc.shtml`) are free Windows decompression tools. Windows XP includes built-in decompression.
3. **Download, extract, and install the following software, if you don't already have it on your system:**
   - pwdump2 — download the file from `razor.bindview.com/tools/desc/pwdump2_readme.html`
   - John the Ripper — download the file from `www.openwall.com/john`
4. **Enter the following command to run pwdump2 and redirect its output to a file called** `cracked.txt`**:**

   ```
   pwdump2 > cracked.txt
   ```

   This file will be used to store the Windows SAM password hashes that will later be cracked with John the Ripper. Figure 7-2 shows the contents of the `cracked.txt` file that contains the local Windows SAM-database password hashes.

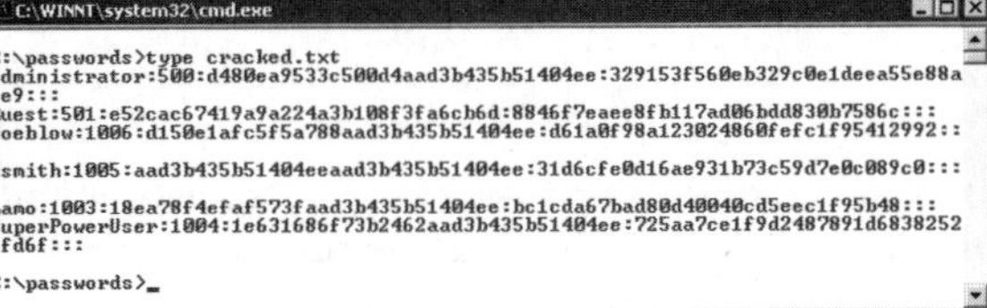

Figure 7-2: Output from pwdump2.

5. **Enter the following command to review the contents from the resulting hashes:**

   ```
   type cracked.txt
   ```

   All the users on your system are listed (similar to Figure 7-3), whether you run this on a stand-alone Windows NT/2000 system or Windows Primary Domain Controller (PDC).

```
C:\WINNT\system32\cmd.exe

C:\passwords>john cracked.txt
Loaded 5 passwords with no different salts (NT LM DES [24/32 4K])
PASS             (Guest:1)
GUESS            (Lamo:1)
GUM              (joeblow:1)
ROOT             (Administrator:1)
TUFF             (SuperPowerUser:1)
guesses: 5  time: 0:00:00:05 (3)  c/s: 319789  trying: SHRK - RM45

C:\passwords>_
```

Figure 7-3: Cracked password file hashes from pwdump2.

6. **Enter the following command to run John the Ripper against the Windows SAM password hashes to display the cracked passwords:**

   ```
   john cracked.txt
   ```

   You should see something similar to the following:

   ```
   Loaded 3 passwords with no different salts (NT LM DES [24/32 4K])
   123         (Weak:1)
   PASS        (Newuser:1)
   GUESS       (Lame:1)
   guesses: 3 time: 0:00:00:00 (3) c/s: 165146 trying: SAMELL - SANDIT
   ```

   This process can take seconds or days, depending on the number of users and the complexity of their associated passwords. My Windows example took only five seconds to crack five weak passwords.

John the Ripper can crack UNIX passwords. You need root access to your system and to the password (`/etc/passwd`) and shadow password (`/etc/shadow`) files. Perform the following steps for cracking UNIX passwords:

1. **Download the UNIX source files from** `www.openwall.com/john`**.**
2. **Extract the program by entering the following command:**

   ```
   tar -zxf john-1.6.tar.gz
   ```

3. **Change into the** `/src` **directory that was created when you extracted the program, and enter the following command:**

   ```
   make generic.
   ```

4. **Change into the** `/run` **directory, and enter the following command to use the unshadow program to combine the passwd and shadow files and copy them to the file** `cracked.txt`**:**

   ```
   ./unshadow /etc/passwd /etc/shadow > cracked.txt
   ```

5. **Enter the following command to start the cracking process:**

   ```
   ./john cracked.txt
   ```

   When John the Ripper is complete (and this could take some time), you get an output similar to the results of the preceding Windows process.

After completing the preceding Windows or UNIX steps, you can either

- Force users to change passwords that don't meet specific password policy requirements.
- Create a password policy from scratch.

Be careful handling the results of your password cracking. Password information for others is confidential and should be treated with care.

Checking for null passwords in NetWare

Using the chknull program, you can test for NetWare users that have empty passwords, passwords that match their username, or passwords that match a specific password that you supply on the command line. Figure 7-4 shows the output of a chknull session against a NetWare server without being logged in: Four users have blank passwords, three users have the password "123," and one user's password is the same as his username (avadminuser).

```
Select DOS Prompt

C:\netware>chknull -p 123
37800000  0001  JOHNNYD HAS a NULL password
3b800000  0001  DOCTORX HAS a NULL password
3c800000  0001  NIKKI HAS a NULL password
3d800000  0001  MARY HAS a NULL password
FOUND 3e800000  0001  BILLY : 123
FOUND 3f800000  0001  SANDMAN : 123
FOUND 40800000  0001  KBEAVER : 123
FOUND 43800000  0001  AVADMINUSER : AVADMINUSER

C:\netware>
```

Figure 7-4: NetWare password weaknesses found with chknull.

General password-hacking countermeasures

A password for one system usually equals passwords for many other systems, because many people use the same passwords on every system they use. For this reason, instruct users to create different passwords for different systems, especially on the systems that protect more sensitive information.

Strong passwords are important, but balance security and convenience:

- You can't expect users to memorize passwords that are insanely complex and changed every week.
- You can't afford weak passwords or no passwords at all.

Passwords by the numbers

One hundred twenty-eight different ASCII characters are used in typical computer passwords. (Technically, only 126 characters are used, because you can't use the NULL and the carriage return characters.) A truly random eight-character password that uses 126 different characters can have 63,527,879,748,485,376 different combinations. Taking that a step further, if it were possible (and it is, in Linux and UNIX) to use all 256 ASCII characters (254, without NULL and carriage return) in a password, 17,324,859,965,700,833,536 different combinations are possible. This is approximately 2.7 billion times more combinations than there are people on earth!

A text file containing all these possible passwords would require millions of terabytes of storage space. Even if you included just the more realistic combination of 95 or so ASCII letters, numbers, and standard punctuation characters, such a file would still fill thousands of terabytes of storage space. These storage requirements require password-cracking programs to form the password combinations on the fly, instead of reading all possible combinations from a text file. That's why brute-force attacks are more effective at cracking passwords than dictionary attacks.

Given the effectiveness of brute-force password attacks, it's not unrealistic to think that in the future, anyone will be able to crack all possible password combinations, given the current technology and average lifespan. It probably won't happen, but many of us also thought in the mid-1980s that 640KB of RAM and 10MB hard drives in our PCs were all we needed.

Storing passwords

If you have to choose between weak passwords that your users can memorize and strong passwords that your users must write down, I recommend having readers write down passwords and store the information securely. Train users to store their written passwords in a secure place — not on keyboards or in easily cracked password-protected computer files (such as spreadsheets). Users should store a written password in either of these locations:

- A locked file cabinet or office safe
- An encrypted file or database, using such tools as
  - PGP (`www.pgpi.org` for the free open-source version or `www.pgp.com` for the commercial version)
  - Open-source Password Safe, originally developed by Counterpane (`passwordsafe.sourceforge.net`)

No sticky notes!

Policy considerations

As an ethical hacker, you should show users the importance of securing their passwords. Here are some tips on how to do that:

- Demonstrate how to create secure passwords. You may want to refer to them as pass codes or pass phrases, because people tend to take the word *passwords* literally and use only words, which can be less secure.
- Show what can happen when weak passwords are used or passwords are shared.
- Diligently build user awareness of social-engineering attacks.

Enforce (or encourage the use of) a strong password-creation policy that includes the following criteria:

- Use upper- and lowercase letters, special characters, and numbers. (Never use only numbers. These passwords can be cracked quickly.)
- Misspell words or create acronyms from a quote or a sentence. (An *acronym* is a word created from the initials of a phrase. For example, *ASCII* is an acronym for *American Standard Code for Information Interchange.)*
- Use punctuation characters to separate words or acronyms.
- Change passwords every 6 to 12 months.
- Use different passwords for each system. This is especially important for network-infrastructure hosts, such as servers, firewalls, and routers.
- Use variable-length passwords. This can throw off the hackers, because they won't know the required minimum or maximum length of passwords and must try all password length combinations.
- Don't use common slang words or words that are in a dictionary.
- Don't use similar-looking characters, such as *3* instead of *E, 5* instead of *S,* or *!* instead of *1.* Password-cracking programs can check for this.
- Don't reuse the same password within 12 months.
- Use password-protected screen savers.
- Don't share passwords.
- Avoid storing user passwords in a central place, such as an unsecured spreadsheet on a hard drive. This is an invitation for disaster. Use PGP, Password Safe, or a similar program to store user passwords.

Other considerations

Here are some other password-hacking countermeasures that I recommend:

- Enable security auditing to help monitor and track password attacks.
- Test your applications to make sure they aren't storing passwords in memory or writing them to disk.

Some password-cracking Trojan-horse applications are transmitted through worms or simple e-mail attachments, such as `VBS.Network.B` and `PWSteal.SoapSpy`. These applications can be lethal to your password-protection mechanisms if they're installed on your systems. The best defense is malware protection software, such as antivirus protection (from a vendor like Norton or McAfee), spyware protection (such as PestPatrol or Spybot), or malicious-code behavioral protection (such as Finjan's offerings).

- Keep your systems patched. Passwords are reset or compromised during buffer overflows or other DoS conditions.
- Know your user IDs. If an account has never been used, delete or disable the account until it's needed. You can determine unused accounts by manual inspection or by using a tool such as DumpSec (`www.somarsoft.com`), which can enumerate the Windows operating system and gather user ID and other information.

As the security administrator in your organization, you can enable *account lockout* to prevent password-cracking attempts. Most operating systems and some applications have this capability. Don't set it too low (less than five failed logins), and don't set it too high to give a malicious user a greater chance of breaking in. Somewhere between 5 and 50 may work for you. I usually recommend a setting of around 10 or 15.

- To use account lockout and prevent any possibilities of a user DoS condition, require two different passwords, and don't set a lockout time for the first one.
- If you permit auto reset of the account after a certain time period — often referred to as *intruder lockout* — don't set a short time period. Thirty minutes often works well.

A failed login counter can increase password security and minimize the overall effects if the account is being compromised by an automated attack. It can force a password change after a number of failed attempts. If the number of failed login attempts is high, and they all occurred in a short period of time, the account has likely experienced an automated password attack.

Some more password-protection countermeasures include the following:

- Use stronger authentication methods, such as challenge/response, smart cards, tokes, biometrics, or digital certificates.
- Automate password reset. This functionality lets users to manage most of their password problems without getting others involved. Otherwise, this support issue becomes expensive, especially for larger organizations.
- Password-protect the system BIOS (basic input/output system). This is especially important on servers and laptops that are susceptible to physical-security threats and vulnerabilities.

Password-protected files

Do you wonder how vulnerable word-processing, spreadsheet, and zip files are as users send them into the wild blue yonder? Wonder no more. Some great utilities can show how easily passwords are cracked.

Cracking files

Most password-protected files can be cracked in seconds or minutes. You can demonstrate this "wow-factor" security vulnerability to users and management. Here's a real-world scenario:

- Your CFO wants to send some confidential financial information in an Excel spreadsheet to the company's outside financial advisor.
- She protects the spreadsheet by assigning a password to it during the file-save process in Excel 2002.
- For good measure, she uses WinZip to compress the file, and adds another password to make it *really* secure.
- The CFO sends the spreadsheet as an e-mail attachment, assuming that it will reach its destination securely.

  The financial advisor's network has content filtering, which monitors incoming e-mails for keywords and file attachments. Unfortunately, the financial advisory firm's network administrator is looking in the content-filtering system to see what's coming in.
- This rogue network administrator finds the e-mail with the confidential attachment, saves the attachment, and realizes that it's password-protected.
- The network administrator remembers some great password-cracking utilities from ElcomSoft (`www.elcomsoft.com`) that can help him out. He may see something like Figures 7-5 and 7-6.

Cracking password-protected files is as simple as that! Now all that the rogue network administrator must do is forward the confidential spreadsheet to his buddies or the company's competitors.

If you carefully select the right options in Advanced ZIP Password Recovery and Office XP Password Recovery, you can drastically shorten your testing time. For example, if you know that a password is not over 5 characters or is lowercase letters only, you can cut the cracking time in half.

I recommend performing these file password-cracking tests on files that you capture with a content-filtering or network-analysis tool.

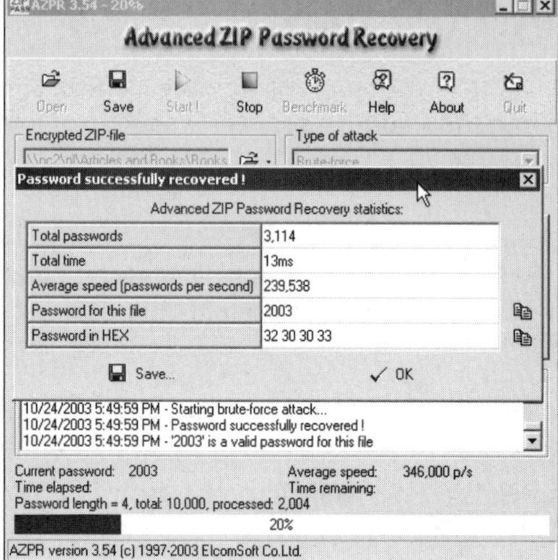

Figure 7-5: ElcomSoft's Advanced ZIP Password Recovery cracking a zip file.

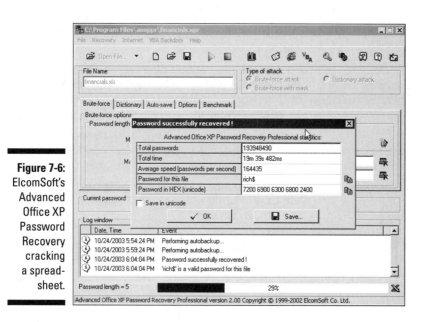

Figure 7-6: ElcomSoft's Advanced Office XP Password Recovery cracking a spreadsheet.

Countermeasures

The best defense against weak file password protection is to require your users to use a stronger form of file protection, such as PGP, when necessary. Ideally, you don't want to rely on users to make decisions about what they should use this method to secure, but it's better than nothing. Stress that a file-encryption mechanism such as PGP is secure only if users keep their passwords confidential and never transmit or store them in clear text.

If you're concerned about nonsecure transmissions through e-mail, consider one of these options:

- Block all outbound e-mail attachments that aren't protected on your e-mail server.
- Use an encryption program, such as PGP, to create self-extracting encrypted files.
- Use content-filtering applications.

Other ways to crack passwords

Over the years, I've found other ways to crack passwords, both technically and through social engineering.

Keystroke logging

One of the best techniques for cracking passwords is remote *keystroke logging* — the use of software or hardware to record keystrokes as they're being typed into the computer.

Be careful with keystroke logging. Even with good intentions, monitoring employees can raise some legal issues. Discuss what you'll be doing with your legal counsel, and get approval from upper management.

Logging tools

With keystroke-logging tools, you can later assess the log files of your application to see what passwords people are using:

- Keystroke-logging applications can be installed on the monitored computer. I recommend that you check out eBlaster and Spector Pro by SpectorSoft (`www.spectorsoft.com`). Another popular tool that you can use is Invisible KeyLogger Stealth, at `www.amecisco.com/iks.htm`, as well as the hardware-based KeyGhost (`www.keyghost.com`). Dozens of other such tools are available on the Internet.
- Hardware-based tools fit between the keyboard and the computer or replace the keyboard altogether.

A shared computer can capture the passwords of every user who logs in.

Countermeasures

The best defense against the installation of keystroke-logging software on your systems is a spyware-detection program or popular antivirus products.

The potential for hackers to install keystroke-logging software is another reason to ensure that your users aren't downloading and installing random shareware or opening attachments in unsolicited e-mails. Consider locking down your desktops by setting the appropriate user rights through local or group security policy in Windows. Alternatively, you could use a commercial lock-down program, such as Fortres 101 (`www.fortres.com`) for Windows or Deep Freeze (`www.deepfreezeusa.com`) for Windows and Mac OS X.

Weak password storage

Many legacy and stand-alone applications such as e-mail, dial-up network connections, and accounting software store passwords locally, making them vulnerable to password hacking. By performing a basic text search, I've found passwords stored in clear text on the local hard drives of machines.

Searching

You can try using your favorite text-searching utility — such as the Windows search function, `findstr`, or `grep` — to search for *password* or *passwd* on your drives. You may be shocked to find what's on your systems. Some programs even write passwords to disk or leave them stored in memory.

This is a hacker's dream. Head it off if you can.

Countermeasures

The only reliable way to eliminate weak password storage is to use only applications that store passwords securely. This may not be practical, but it's your only guarantee that your passwords are secure.

Before upgrading applications, contact your software vendor or search for a third-party solution.

Network analyzer

A network analyzer sniffs the packets traversing the network. This is what the bad guys do if they can gain control over a computer or gain physical network access to set up their network analyzer. If they gain physical access, they can look for a network jack on the wall and plug right in!

Testing

Figure 7-7 shows how crystal-clear passwords can be through the eyes of a network analyzer. This figure shows the password packet from an EtherPeek capture of a POP3 session using Microsoft Outlook to download messages from an e-mail server. Look in the POP — Post Office Protocol section for the password of "MyPassword". These same clear-text password vulnerabilities can apply to instant messaging, Web-site logins, telnet sessions, and more. Basically, if traffic is not being tunneled through a VPN, SSH, SSL, or some other form of encrypted link, it's vulnerable to attack.

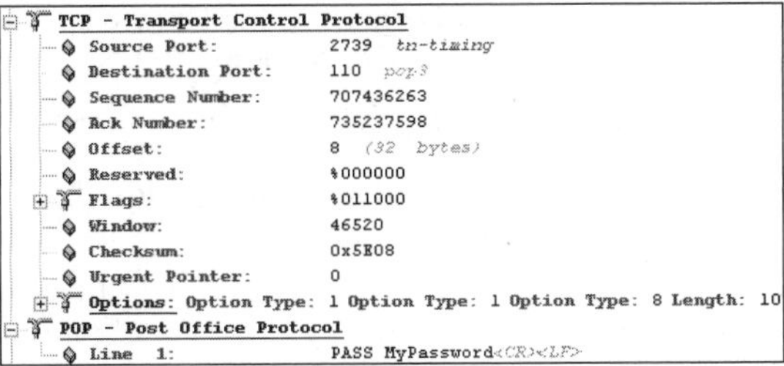

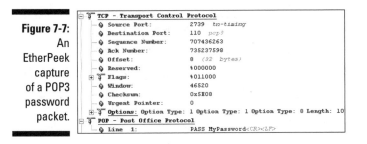

Figure 7-7: An EtherPeek capture of a POP3 password packet.

Although you can benefit from using a commercial network analyzer such as EtherPeek, you don't need to buy one for your testing. An open-source program, Ethereal, runs on Windows and UNIX platforms. You can search for password traffic on the network a million ways. For example, to capture POP3 password traffic, set up a trigger to search for the PASS command. When the network analyzer sees the PASS command in the packet, it starts capturing data until your specified time or number of packets.

Capture this data on a hub segment of your network, or plug your network-analyzer system into a monitor port on a switch. Otherwise, you can't see anyone else's data traversing the network — just yours. Check your switch's user's guide for whether it has a monitor or mirror port and instructions on how to configure it. You can connect your network analyzer to a hub on the public side of your firewall. You'll capture only those packets that are entering or leaving your network — not internal traffic.

Countermeasures

Here are some good defenses against network-analyzer attacks:

- Use switches on your network, not hubs.

  TIP

  If you must use hubs on network segments, a program such as sniffdet, cpm, and sentinel can detect network cards in *promiscuous mode* (accepting all packets, whether destined for it or not). Network cards in this mode are signs of a network analyzer running on the network.

  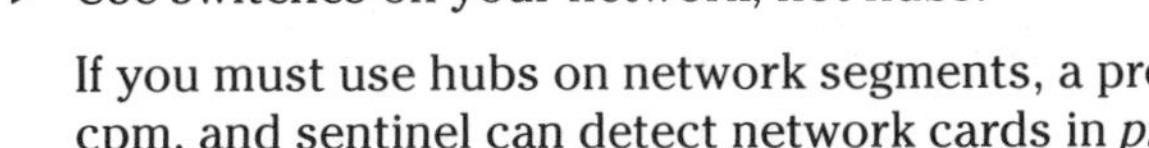

- Don't let a hacker gain physical access to your switches or the network connection on the public side of your firewall. With physical access, a hacker can connect to a switch monitor port, or tap into the unswitched network segment outside the firewall and capture packets.

Switches do not provide complete security because they are vulnerable to ARP poisoning attacks, which I cover in Chapter 9.

Most computer BIOSs allow power-on passwords and/or setup passwords to protect the computer's hardware settings that are stored in the CMOS chip. Here are some ways around these passwords:

- You can usually reset these passwords by either unplugging the CMOS battery or changing a jumper on the motherboard.
- Password-cracking utilities for BIOS passwords are available.

Some systems (especially laptops) can't be reset easily. You can lose all the hardware settings and lock yourself out of your own computer. If you plan to hack your own BIOS passwords, check for information in your user manual or on `labmice.techtarget.com/articles/BIOS_hack.htm` on doing this safely.

Weak passwords in limbo

Bad guys often exploit user accounts that have just been reset by a network administrator or help desk. Accounts may need to be reset if users forget their passwords, or if the accounts have been locked out because of failed attempts.

Weaknesses

Here are some reasons why user accounts can be vulnerable:

- When user accounts are reset, they often are assigned an easily cracked password (such as the user's name or the word *password*). The time between resetting the user account and changing the password is a prime opportunity for a break-in.
- Many systems have either default accounts or unused accounts with weak passwords or no passwords at all. These are prime targets.

Countermeasures

The best defenses against attacks on passwords in limbo are solid help-desk policies and procedures that prevent weak passwords from being available at *any* given time during the password-reset process. Perhaps the best ways to overcome this vulnerability are as follows:

- Require users to be on the phone with the help desk, or have a help-desk member perform the reset at the user's desk.
- Require that the user immediately log in and change his password.
- If you need the ultimate in security, implement stronger authentication methods, such as challenge/response, smart cards, or digital certificates.
- Automate password-reset functionality on your network so users can manage most of their password problems without help from others.

For a good list of default system passwords for vendor equipment, check `www.cirt.net/cgi-bin/passwd.pl`.

Password-reset programs

Network administrators occasionally use administrator password-resetting programs, which can be used against a network.

Tools

One of my favorites for Windows is NTAccess (www.mirider.com/ntaccess.html). This program isn't fancy, but it does the job.

Countermeasures

The best safeguard against a hacker using a password-reset program against your systems is to ensure the hacker can't gain physical access. When a hacker has physical access, all bets are off.

Securing Operating Systems

You can implement various operating-system security measures to ensure that passwords are protected.

Regularly perform these low-tech and high-tech password-cracking tests to make sure that your systems are as secure as possible — perhaps as part of a monthly, quarterly, or biannual audit.

Windows

The following countermeasures can help prevent password hacks on Windows systems:

- Some Windows passwords can be gleaned by simply reading the clear text or crackable cipher text from the Windows Registry. Secure your registries by doing the following:
  - Allowing only administrator access.
  - Hardening the operating system by using well-known hardening best practices, such as such as those from SANS (www.sans.org), NIST (csrc.nist.gov), the National Security Agency Security Recommendation Guides (www.nsa.gov/snac/index.html), and the ones outlined in *Network Security For Dummies,* by Chey Cobb (Wiley Publishing, Inc.).
- Use SYSKEY for enhanced Windows password protection.
  - By default, Windows 2000 encrypts the SAM database that stores hashes of the Windows account passwords. It's not the default in Windows NT.
  - You can use the SYSKEY utility to encrypt the database for Windows NT machines and to move the database-encryption key from Windows 2000 and later machines.

  Don't rely only on the SYSKEY utility. Tools such as ElcomSoft's Advanced EFS Data Recovery program can crack SYSKEY encryption.

- Keep all SAM-database backup copies secure.
- Disable the storage of LM hashes in Windows for passwords that are shorter than 15 characters.

  For example, in Windows 2000 SP2 and later, you can create and set the NoLMHash registry key to a value of 1 under `HKEY_LOCAL_MACHINE\SYSTEM\CurrentControlSet\Control\Lsa`.
- Use passfilt.dll or local or group security policies to help eliminate weak passwords on Windows systems before they're created.
- Disable null sessions in your Windows version:
  - In Windows XP, enable the Do Not Allow Anonymous Enumeration of SAM Accounts and Shares option in the local security policy.
  - In Windows 2000, enable the No Access without Explicit Anonymous Permissions option in the local security policy.
  - In Windows NT, enable the following Registry key:

```
HKLM/System/CurrentControlSet/Control/LSA/RestrictAnonymous=1
```

Linux and UNIX

The following countermeasures can help prevent password cracks on Linux and UNIX systems:

- Use shadowed MD5 passwords.
- Help prevent weak passwords from being created. You can use either built-in operating-system password filtering (such as cracklib in Linux) or a password auditing program (such as npasswd or passwd+).
- Check your `/etc/passwd` file for duplicate root UID entries. Hackers can exploit such entries as root backdoors.

Part III
Network Hacking

"Daddy and I are going to give you all the love.com, care.com, and opportunities.com that we possibly can."

In this part . . .

Now that you're off and running with your ethical hacking tests, it's time to take things to a new level. The previous tests — at least the social engineering and physical security tests — have started at a high level and were not that technical. Times are a-changin'! You now need to look at network security. This is where things start getting more technical.

This part starts out by looking into one of the most overlooked information security vulnerabilities. By that, I mean rogue modems installed on computers randomly throughout your network. This part then moves on to look at the network as a whole from the inside and the outside for everything from perimeter security to network scanning to DoS vulnerabilities and more. Finally, this part takes a look at how to assess the security of the wireless LAN technology that's introducing some serious security vulnerabilities into networks these days.

Chapter 8

War Dialing

In This Chapter

- Controlling dial-up access
- Testing for war dialing weaknesses
- Preventing war dialing

War dialing — the act of using a computer to scan other computers automatically for accessible modems — was made popular in the movie *War Games*. War dialing seems old-fashioned and less sexy than other hacking techniques these days; however, it's a very critical test to run against your network. This chapter shows how to test for war dialing vulnerabilities and outlines countermeasures to help keep your network from being victimized.

War Dialing

It's amazing how often end users and careless network administrators connect modems to computers inside the network. Some companies spend an astonishing amount of money and effort to roll out intrusion-prevention software, application firewalls, and forensics protection tools while ignoring that an unsecured modem on the network can render that protection worthless.

Modem safety

Modems are still on today's networks because of leftover remote access servers (RAS) that provide remote connectivity into the corporate network. Many network administrators — hesitant to deploy a VPN — still have modems on their servers and other hosts for other reasons, such as for administering the network, troubleshooting problems remotely, and even providing connectivity to remote offices. Some network administrators have legitimate modems installed for third-party monitoring purposes and business continuity; modems are a low-cost alternative network access method if the Internet connection is down. Many of these modems — and their software — run in default mode with weak passwords or none at all.

Practically every computer sold today has a modem. End users create dial-up networking connections so they can bypass the firewall-blocking and employee-monitoring systems in place on the corporate network. Many users want to dial into their work computers from home. Some users even set up their modems to send and receive faxes so that they eliminate every possible reason to leave their desks during the work day.

It's not as big a deal if the modem is configured for *outbound* access only, but there's always a chance that someone can use it to obtain *inbound* access. A software misconfiguration or a weak password can give a hacker access.

So what's the bottom line? Unsecured modems inside the network — and even ones with basic passwords — can put your entire network at risk. Many of these modems have remote-connectivity software such as pcAnywhere, Procomm Plus, and even Apple Remote Access and Timbuktu Pro for Apple computers. This software can provide backdoor access to the entire network. In many cases, a hacker can take over the computer with the modem attached and communications software running, gaining full access to everything the currently logged-in user can access. Ouch!

General telephone-system vulnerabilities

A war-dialing attack can uncover other telephone-system vulnerabilities:

- **Dial tone:** Many phone switches support a *repeat,* or *second dial tone,* for troubleshooting or other outbound call purposes. This allows a phone technician, a user, or even a hacker to enter a password at the first dial tone and make outbound calls to anywhere in the world — all on your organization's dime. Many hackers use war dialing to detect repeat dial tones so they can carry out these phone attacks in the future.
- **Voice mail:** Voice-mail systems — especially PC-based types — and entire private branch exchange (PBX) phone switches can be probed by war-dialing software and later compromised by a hacker.

Attacking

War dialing is not that complicated. Depending on your tools and the amount of phone numbers you're testing, this can be an easy test. War dialing involves these basic hacking methodologies:

- Gathering public information and mapping your network
- Scanning your systems
- Determining what's running on the systems discovered
- Attempting to penetrate the systems discovered

A case study in war dialing with David Rhoades

In this case study, David Rhoades, a well-known war dialing and Web-application security expert, shared an experience performing an ISDN war dial. Here's an account of what happened.

The situation

A few years ago, Mr. Rhoades had an Integrated Services Digital Network (ISDN) circuit in his home office for two voice lines. ISDN also allowed him 128Kbps Internet access. His *ISDN terminal adapter* (sometimes incorrectly called an *ISDN modem*) allowed him to call other ISDN numbers extremely fast. He decided to write an ISDN war dialer that would take advantage of the amazing speed of ISDN. In about one second, he could dial the number and determine whether the other side was ISDN, ISDN with a busy signal, or a regular analog line. Analog war dialing is much slower. An analog modem would require at least 30 seconds to dial the number and recognize the other end as a modem — and that assumes the other end answers on the first ring. So an ISDN war dialer is very fast at locating other ISDN lines. The only downsides are that not all ISDN equipment can detect analog modems, and you may have to dial in a second time to detect them properly. Why bother locating ISDN numbers with a war dial? If the other end is ISDN, a terminal adapter or some other piece of equipment might be remotely accessible just by calling it.

Shortly after Mr. Rhoades wrote the ISDN war dialer, his company got a request for a war dial for a large German bank. The only catch was that the project called for an ISDN war dial, because ISDN was popular in Europe and his customer knew that the bank had lots of ISDN circuits. Mr. Rhoades soon found himself on a flight to Frankfurt with his software and ISDN terminal adapter.

The outcome

Mr. Rhoades found several ISDN and analog lines within the bank's system. His biggest challenge was becoming familiar with the dial-in software packages, which were popular in Europe but unknown in the United States. Fortunately for Mr. Rhoades, most vendors offered free demos of their software, which he could use to access the remote systems.

The bottom line is that if you want to be certain that no dial-up connections to your network exist, consider other methods of communication, such as ISDN. Also, never assume that well-known communications software is being used on the dial-up connection. If you don't recognize what's answering, explore it further. The bad guys most certainly will.

David Rhoades is a principal consultant with Maven Security Consulting Inc. (`www.mavensecurity.com`) and teaches at security conferences around the globe for USENIX, the MIS Training Institute, and ISACA.

The process of war dialing is as simple as entering phone numbers into your freeware or commercial war-dialing software and letting the program work its magic — preferably overnight, so you can get some sleep!

Before you get started, keep in mind that it might be illegal to war-dial in your jurisdiction, so be careful! Also, make sure you war-dial only the numbers you're authorized to dial. Even though you will most likely perform your war dialing after hours — at night or over a weekend — make sure that upper management and possibly even the people who are working know what you're doing. You don't want anyone being surprised by this!

War dialing is slow, because it can take anywhere from 30 to 60 seconds or longer to dial and test one number. A war-dialing test can take all night or even a weekend to dial all the numbers in one exchange. To counter this, if you use ToneLoc for your war dialing, there's a neat utility called Prescan, part of the ToneLoc Utilities Phun-Pak (`www.hackcanada.com/ice3/phreak`) that will let you fill in ToneLoc data files with known exchanges before you ever get started. This can save a ton of time!

You may have several thousand phone numbers to test if you need to test an entire exchange, so this process can take some time. If you use several modems at once for your tests, you can speed the testing time dramatically. However, before you can do this, several things have to be in place:

- You need multiple analog lines to dial out from. Today, these analog lines can be hard to get.
- Given the complexities involved, you may have to do one of the following:
  - Be present during the tests so you can manage all the war-dialing sessions you have to load.
  - Automate the tests with batch files.
  - Use a commercial war-dialing utility that supports simultaneous testing with multiple modems.

Gathering information

To get started, you need phone numbers to test for modems. You can program these numbers into your war-dialing software and automate the process.

You need to find two kinds of phone numbers for testing:

- *Dialing ranges* assigned to your organization, such as the following:
  - 555-0000 through 555-9999 (10,000 possible numbers)
  - 555-0100 through 555-0499 (400 possible numbers)
  - 555-1550 through 555-1599 (50 possible numbers)
- *Nonstandard analog numbers* that have a different exchange from your main digital lines. These numbers may not be publicly advertised.

To find or verify your organization's phone numbers, check these resources:

- *Local telephone white and yellow pages.* Either refer to hard copies or check out Internet sites such as `www.switchboard.com`.
- *Internet searches* for your company name and main phone number. (Check your organization's Web site, too.)

Google may find published numbers in surprising places, such as chamber of commerce and industry association listings.

- *Internet domain name Whois entries* at a lookup site such as `www.samspade.org`. The Whois database often contains direct phone numbers and other contact information that can give a hacker a leg up on the phone-number scheme within your organization.
- *Phone-service documentation,* such as monthly phone bills and phone-system installation paperwork

Selecting war-dialing tools

War dialing requires outbound phone access, software tools, and a compatible modem.

Software

Most war-dialing tools are freeware or shareware, but a few commercial war-dialing tools are also available, such as PhoneSweep by Sandstorm Enterprises (`www.sandstorm.net/products/phonesweep`).

These two freeware tools are very effective:

- ToneLoc (`www.securityfocus.com/data/tools/auditing/pstn/tl110.zip`), written by Minor Threat and Mucho Maas
- THC-Scan, written by The Hacker's Choice (`www.thc.org/releases.php`)

There's a list of war-dialing programs at `www.pestpatrol.com/pestinfo/phreaking_tool.asp`. If the freeware tools don't have features you need, consider a commercial product, such as PhoneSweep.

Modems

A plain Hayes-compatible modem usually is fine for outbound war dialing.

I've had trouble running both ToneLoc and THC-Scan on various modems, so you may have to tinker with COM port settings, modem initialization strings, and even modem types until you find a combinations that works.

The best way to determine what type of modem to use is to consult your war-dialing software's documentation:

- If in doubt, go with a name-brand model, such as U.S. Robotics, 3Com, or an older Hayes unit.
- As a last resort, check the modem documentation for features that the modem supports.

You can use this information to ensure you have the best software and hardware combination to minimize any potential headaches.

Some modems can increase war-dialing efficiency by detecting

- *Voices,* which can speed up the war-dialing process
- *Second dial tones,* which allows more dialing from the system

Dialing in from the outside

War dialing is pretty basic — you enter the phone numbers you want to dial into your war-dialing software, kick off the program, and let it do its magic. When the war-dialing software finds a carrier (which is basically a valid modem connection), the software logs the number, hangs up, and tries another number you programmed it to test.

Keep the following in mind to maximize your war-dialing efforts:

- Configure your war-dialing software to dial the list of numbers *randomly* instead of sequentially, if possible.

  Some phone switches, war-dialing detection programs (such as Sandstorm Enterprises' Sandtrap), and even the phone company itself may detect and stop war dialing — especially when an entire exchange of phone numbers is dialed sequentially or quickly.
- If you're dialing from a line that can block Caller ID, dial *67 immediately before dialing the number so your phone number isn't displayed. This may not work if you're calling toll-free numbers.
- If you're dialing long-distance numbers during your testing, make sure that you know about the potential charges. Costs can add up fast!

Using tools

ToneLoc and THC-Scan are similar in usage and functionality:

- Run a configuration utility to configure your modem and other dial settings.
- Run the executable file to war-dial.

There are a few differences between the two, such as timeout settings and other enhanced menu functionality that was introduced in THC-Scan. You can get an outline of all the differences at `web.textfiles.com/software/toneloc.txt`.

Configuration

In this example, I use my all-time favorite tool — ToneLoc — for war dialing. To begin the configuration process for ToneLoc, run the `tlcfg.exe` utility. You can tweak modem, dialing, and logging settings.

Two settings on the ModemOptions menu are likely to need adjustments, as shown in Figure 8-1:

- Serial port
  - Enter 1, 2, 3, or 4 for the specific COM port where your modem is installed.
  - Leave the Port Address and Port IRQ settings at 0 for the default settings unless you've made configuration changes to your modem.

If you're not sure what port your modem is installed on, run `msinfo32.exe` from the Windows Start/Run prompt, and browse to the Components/Modem folder. The modem's COM port value is listed in the Attached To item, as shown in Figure 8-2.

- Baud rate. Enter at least 19,200 if your modem supports it — preferably 115,000 if you have a 56K modem.

You may not be able to war-dial some older — and much slower — modems if the rates don't match.

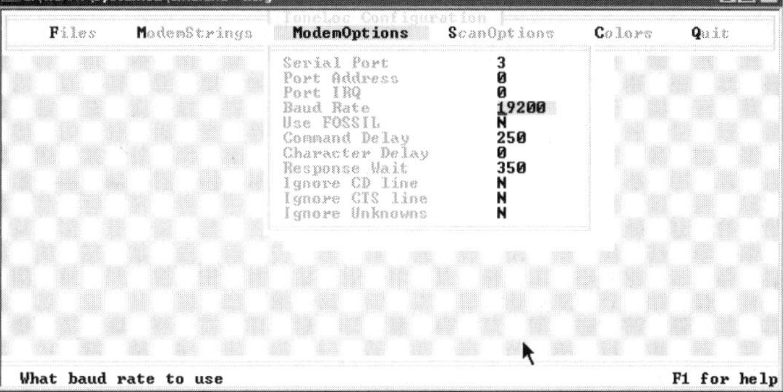

Figure 8-1: Configuring the modem in ToneLoc's TLCFG utility.

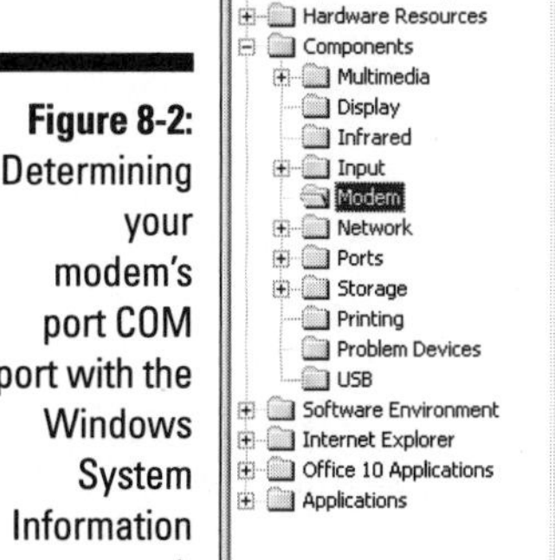

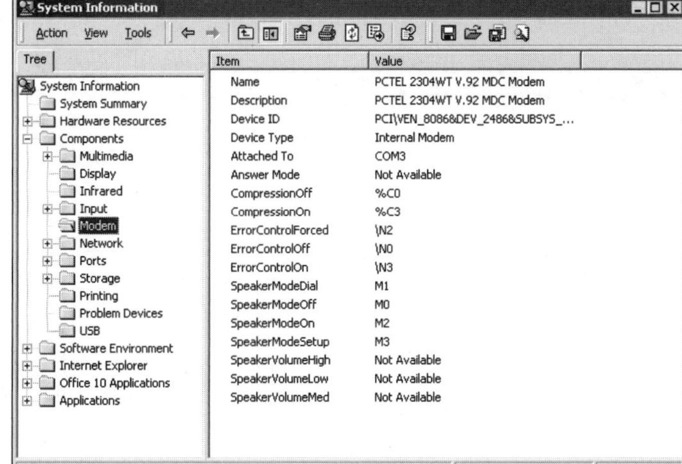

Figure 8-2: Determining your modem's port COM port with the Windows System Information tool.

Testing

After you've configured ToneLoc, you're ready to start war dialing with one of the following options:

- *Number range.* For a range of numbers from 770-555-1200 through 770-555-1209, enter the following command at a command prompt:

  ```
  toneloc 770-555-12XX /R:00-09
  ```

  This command tells ToneLoc to dial all numbers beginning with 404-555-15 numbers and then use the range of 00 through 99 in place of `XX`.

- *Single number.* To test one number (770-555-1234), enter it at a command prompt like this:

  ```
  toneloc 770-555-123X /R:4-4
  ```

To see all the command-line options, enter `toneloc` by itself at a command prompt.

After you enter the appropriate command (if you've configured the program correctly and your modem is working), ToneLoc produces test results in two forms:

- *Activity and counter display.* As shown in Figure 8-3, ToneLoc displays its activity and increments its counters, such as the number of carriers and busy signals.
- `tone.log` *file.* The following information is stored in this log file:
  - Records of all activities during testing. You can peruse this file for failed attempts (such as busy signals) to retest later.
  - Lists the carriers that ToneLoc discovered and such as the information displayed as a login prompt. You can use this information to penetrate your systems further.

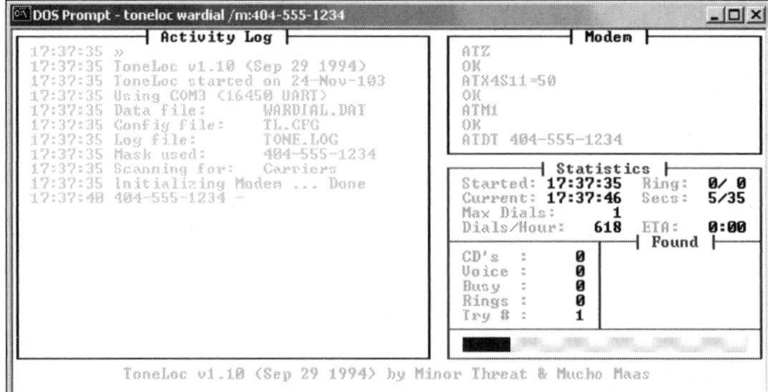
DOS Prompt - toneloc wardial /m:404-555-1234
Activity Log
17:37:35 »
17:37:35 ToneLoc v1.10 (Sep 29 1994)
17:37:35 ToneLoc started on 24-Nov-103
17:37:35 Using COM3 (16450 UART)
17:37:35 Data file: WARDIAL.DAT
17:37:35 Config file: TL.CFG
17:37:35 Log file: TONE.LOG
17:37:35 Mask used: 404-555-1234
17:37:35 Scanning for: Carriers
17:37:35 Initializing Modem ... Done
17:37:40 404-555-1234 -
Modem
ATZ
OK
ATX4S11=50
OK
ATM1
OK
ATDT 404-555-1234
Statistics
Started: 17:37:35 Ring: 0/ 0
Current: 17:37:46 Secs: 5/35
Max Dials: 1
Dials/Hour: 618 ETA: 0:00
Found
CD's : 0
Voice : 0
Busy : 0
Rings : 0
Try # : 1
ToneLoc v1.10 (Sep 29 1994) by Minor Threat & Mucho Maas

Figure 8-3: ToneLoc in the middle of a war dial.

An abbreviated `tone.log` file is as follows:

```
01:18:20 -
01:18:20 ToneLoc v1.10 (Sep 29 1994)
01:18:20 ToneLoc started on 31-Jan-104
01:18:20 Using COM1 (16450 UART)
01:18:20 Data file:   770-555-.DAT
01:18:20 Config file:  TL.CFG
01:18:20 Log file:    TONE.LOG
01:18:20 Mask used:   770-555-12XX
01:18:20 Range used:   00-09
01:18:20 Scanning for:  Carriers
01:18:20 Initializing Modem ... Done
01:18:24 770-555-1208 - Timeout (0)
01:19:02 770-555-1201 - Busy
01:19:40 770-555-1205 - No Carrier
. . .
01:22:52 770-555-1207 - * CARRIER *
01:23:30 770-555-1204 - Timeout (0)
01:24:08 Autosaving
01:24:48 770-555-1206 - Timeout (0)
01:25:20 All 10 numbers dialed
01:25:20 Sending exit string ... Done
01:25:21 Dials = 10, Dials/hour = 94
01:25:21 0:07 spent current scan
01:25:21 Exit with errorlevel 0
```

In the sixth line of the preceding example, ToneLoc is configured to read the `TL.CFG` file for its configuration options. With the seventh line, the findings are written to the `TONE.LOG` file.

The range of numbers dialed is 770-555-1200 through 770-555-1209. You can determine this by substituting the Range values (00-09) for the `XX` in the mask. ToneLoc dials numbers randomly, as you can see since it started with 770-555-1208, and so forth. The 1208, 1204, and 1206 numbers just timed out (meaning that no modem was detected). The 1201 number was apparently busy at the time, and the 1205 number didn't answer at all. ToneLoc found a carrier (modem) on the 1207 number. Ah ha! Time to dig deeper to see what's on the other end — such as what you're prompted with and details about the remote system that are given.

Rooting through the systems

When you identify phone numbers with modems attached, take one of these actions to penetrate the system further and test for related vulnerabilities:

- Stop your testing, determine whether the modems are legitimate, and disable or remove any rogue modems.

- Attempt to penetrate the systems further by
  - Determining what application is listening on the other end by using a communications program, such as Carbon Copy, Procomm Plus, or the free HyperTerminal that's built into Windows.
  - Attempting to crack passwords, if necessary.

Commercial tools such as PhoneSweep automate this process for you — making purchasing such a tool a lot more attractive.

A few questions can help you determine what's listening on the other end and decide whether to investigate this device and possibly remove it:

- How many rings does it take for the carrier to pick up?
- Is the carrier available only during certain time periods?
- What type of authentication prompt is presented (password only, user ID and password, or another combination)?
- Does login screen or banner tell you about the software that's running?

Countermeasures

A few countermeasures can help protect your network against war dialing.

Phone numbers

You can protect your phone numbers — especially those that are assigned to modems on critical computer systems — by:

- Limiting the phone numbers that are made public.

  Work with human resources, marketing, and management to ensure that only necessary phone numbers are unveiled.
- Obtaining analog-line phone numbers that aren't within the standard exchange of your main digital lines. This prevents hackers from finding modems within your main phone-number block.

Modem operation

You can help prevent unauthorized modem usage and operation by:

- Documenting, publishing, and educating *all* end users on modem usage. If users need modem access, require them to present the business reason.
- Requiring strong passwords on all communications software.

- Purchasing dial-only modems or disabling inbound access in your communications software.
- *Legacy applications* may require occasional modem access. Make it policy — and train your users — to keep the modem powered off or unplugged from the phone line when it's not being used.

When installing modems into computers within the organization, require all dial-up networking through either a VPN or a modem pool connected to a RAS server that IT/security manages centrally. Review all telephone bills each month to ensure that you don't have unauthorized lines installed.

Installation

Secure modem placement maximizes security, prevents war-dialing attacks, and makes modem management and future ethical hacking tests much easier:

- *External modems* are usually easy to see, but they can be hidden under desks and forgotten.
- *Internal modems* may require you to inspect every networked computer physically for a phone cable plugged into the back.

Digital phone-line converters can allow a user to connect an analog modem to a digital line — which normally fries the modem.

Chapter 9

Network Infrastructure

In This Chapter

- Selecting tools
- Scanning network hosts
- Assessing security with a network analyzer
- Preventing denial-of-service and infrastructure vulnerabilities

Your computer systems and applications require one of the most fundamental communications systems in your organization — your network. Your network consists of such devices as routers, firewalls, and even generic hosts (including servers and workstations) that you must assess as part of the ethical hacking process.

Many people refer to ethical hacking in terms of performing security tests from a network-only perspective. This is only part of the overall issue. You can't discount the basics of old-fashioned network security tests. I outline them in this chapter, with some solid countermeasures to foil attacks against your network.

There are thousands of possible network vulnerabilities, equally as many tools, and even more testing techniques. You don't need to test your network for *every* possible vulnerability, using every tool available and technique imaginable. The tests in this chapter produce a good overall assessment of your network.

You can eliminate many well-known network vulnerabilities by simply patching your network hosts with the latest vendor software and firmware patches. Odds are that your network *will not* be attacked to exploit most of these vulnerabilities. Even if it is, the results are not likely to be detrimental. You can eliminate many other vulnerabilities by following some security best practices on your network. The tests, tools, and techniques in this chapter offer the most bang for your ethical hacking buck.

A case study in hacking network infrastructures with Laura Chappell

Laura Chappell — one of the world's foremost authorities on network protocols and analysis — shared with me an interesting experience she had when assessing a customer's network. Here's her account of what happened.

The Situation

Ms. Chappell had a customer call with a routine "the network is slow" problem. Upon her arrival onsite, the customer mentioned sporadic outages and poor performance when connecting to the Internet as well. First, she examined individual flows between various clients and servers. Localized communications appeared normal, but any communication that flowed through the firewall to the Internet or other branch offices was severely delayed. It was time to sniff the traffic going through the firewall to see whether she could isolate the cause of the delay.

The Outcome

A quick review of the traffic crossing the firewall indicated that the outside links were saturated, so it was time to review and classify the traffic. Using the Sniffer Network Analyzer, Ms. Chappell plugged in to examine the protocol distribution. She saw that almost 45 percent of the traffic was listed as "others" and was unrecognizable. She captured some data and found several references to pornographic images. Further examination of the packets led her to two specific port numbers that appeared consistently in the trace files — port 1214 (Kazaa) and 6346 (Gnutella), two peer-to-peer (P2P) file sharing applications. She did a complete port scan of the network to see what was running and found over 30 systems running either Kazaa or Gnutella. Their file transfer processes were eating up the bandwidth and dragging down all communications. It would have been simple to shut down these systems and remove the applications, but she wanted to investigate them further without the users' knowledge.

Ms. Chappell decided to use her own Kazaa and Gnutella clients to look through the shared folders of the systems. By becoming a peer member with the other hosts on the network, she could perform searches through other shared folders, which indicated some of the users had shared their network directories! Through these shared folders, she was able to obtain the corporate personnel roster, including home phone numbers and addresses, accounting records, and several confidential memos that provided timelines for projects under way at the company!

Many users said they shared these folders to regain access to the P2P network, because they had previously been labeled *free loaders* because their shares contained only a few files. They were under the delusion that because no one knew the filenames contained in the network directories, no one would search for matching values. Although this on-site visit started with a standard performance and communication review, it ended with the detection of some huge security breaches in the company. Anyone can use these P2P tools to get onto the network and grab the files in the shared folders — with no authorization or authentication required!

Laura Chappell is Senior Protocol Analyst at the Protocol Analysis Institute, LLC (`www.packet-level.com`). A best-selling author and lecturer, Ms. Chappell has trained thousands of network administrators, security technicians, and law enforcement personnel on packet-level security, troubleshooting, and optimization techniques. I highly recommend that you check out her Web site for some excellent technical content to help you become a better ethical hacker.

Network Infrastructure Vulnerabilities

Network infrastructure vulnerabilities are the foundation for all technical security issues in your information systems. These lower-level vulnerabilities affect everything running on your network. That's why you need to test for them and eliminate them whenever possible.

Your focus for ethical hacking tests on your network infrastructure should be to find weaknesses that others can see in your network so you can quantify your level of exposure.

Many issues are related to the security of your network infrastructure. Some issues are more technical and require you to use various tools to assess them properly. You can assess others with a good pair of eyes and some logical thinking. Some issues are easy to see from outside the network, and others are easier to detect from inside your network.

Network infrastructure security involves assessing such areas as

- Where such devices as a firewall or IDS (intrusion detection system) are placed on the network and how they are configured
- What hackers see when they perform port scans and how they can exploit vulnerabilities in your network hosts
- Network design, such as Internet connections, remote-access capabilities, layered defenses, and placement of hosts on the network
- Interaction of installed security devices
- Protocols in use
- Commonly attacked ports that are unprotected
- Network host configuration
- Network monitoring and maintenance

If any of these network security issues is exploited, bad things can happen:

- A DoS attack can take down your Internet connection — or even your entire network.
- A hacker using a network analyzer can steal confidential information in e-mails and files being transferred.
- Backdoors into your network can be set up.
- Specific hosts can be attacked by exploiting local vulnerabilities across the network.

Before moving forward with assessing your network infrastructure security, remember to do the following:

- Test your systems from both the outside in and the inside out.
- Obtain permission from partner networks that are connected to your network to check for vulnerabilities on their ends that can affect *your* network's security, such as open ports and lack of a firewall or a misconfigured router.

Choosing Tools

Your tests require the right tools. Great commercial, shareware, and freeware tools are available.

If you're looking for easy-to-use security tools with all-in-one packaging, *you get what you pay for* — most of the time — especially for the Windows platform. Tons of security professionals swear by many free security tools, especially those that run on UNIX-based operating systems. Many of these tools offer a lot of value — if you have the time, patience, and willingness to learn their ins and outs.

You can equip your toolbox with scanners and vulnerability-assessment tools.

You need more than one tool. No tool does everything you need.

Scanners

These scanners provide practically all the port-scanning and network-testing tools you'll need:

- **Sam Spade for Windows** (`samspade.org/ssw`) for network queries from DNS lookups to traceroutes
- **SuperScan** (`www.foundstone.com`) for ping sweeps and port scanning
- **NetScanTools Pro** (`www.netscantools.com`) for dozens of network security-assessment functions, including ping sweeps, port scanning, and SMTP relay testing
- **Nmap** (`www.insecure.org/nmap`) or **NMapWin** (`sourceforge.net/projects/nmapwin`) as a happy-clicky-GUI front end for host-port probing and operating-system fingerprinting
- **Netcat** (`www.atstake.com/research/tools/network_utilities`) the most versatile security tool for such security checks as port scanning and firewall testing
- **WildPackets EtherPeek** (`www.wildpackets.com`) for network analysis

Vulnerability assessment

These vulnerability-assessment tools will allow you to test your network hosts for various known vulnerabilities as well as potential configuration issues that could lead to security exploits:

- **GFI LANguard Network Security Scanner** (`www.gfi.com`) for port scanning and other vulnerability testing
- **Nessus** (`www.nessus.org`) as a free all-in-one tool for such tests as ping sweeps, port scanning, and vulnerability testing
- **Qualys QualysGuard** (`www.qualys.com`) as a great all-in-one tool for in-depth vulnerability testing, if you can justify the cost

Scanning, Poking, and Prodding

Performing these ethical hacks on your network infrastructure involves following basic hacking steps:

1. Gather information and map your network.
2. Scan your systems to see which are available.
3. Determine what's running on the systems discovered.
4. Attempt to penetrate the systems discovered, if you choose to.

Every network card driver and implementation of TCP/IP in most operating systems, including Windows and Linux, and even in your firewalls and routers, has quirks that result in different behaviors when scanning, poking, and prodding your systems. This can result in different responses from your varying systems. Refer to your administrator guides or vendor Web sites for details on any known issues and possible patches that are available to fix them. If you have all your systems patched, this shouldn't be an issue.

Port scanners

A port scanner shows you what's what on your network. It's a software tool that basically scans the network to see who's there.

Port scanners provide basic views of how the network is laid out. They can help identify unauthorized hosts or applications and network host configuration errors that can cause serious security vulnerabilities.

The big-picture view from port scanners often uncovers security issues that may otherwise go unnoticed. Port scanners are easy to use and can test systems regardless of what operating systems and applications they're running. The tests can be performed very quickly without having to touch individual network hosts, which would be a real pain otherwise.

The real trick to assessing your overall network security is interpreting the results you get back. You can get false positives on open ports, and you may have to dig deeper. For example, UDP scans — like the protocol itself — are less reliable than TCP scans and often produce false positives, because many applications don't know how to respond to random incoming UDP scans.

A feature-rich scanner — usually, a commercial product — often can identify ports and see what's running in one step.

Port-scan tests take time. The length of time depends on the number of hosts you have, the number of ports you scan, the tools you use, and the speed of your network links.

Scan more than just the important hosts. These *other* systems often bite you if you ignore them. Also, perform the same tests with different utilities to see whether you get different results. Not all tools find the same open ports and vulnerabilities. This is unfortunate, but it's a reality of ethical hacking tests.

If your results don't match after you run the tests using different tools, you may want to explore the issue further. If something doesn't look right — such as a strange set of open ports — it probably isn't. Test it again; if you're in doubt, use another tool for a different perspective.

As an ethical hacker, you should scan all 65,535 UDP and 65,535 TCP ports on each network host that's found by your scanner. If you find questionable ports, look for documentation that the application is known and authorized.

For speed and simplicity, you can scan commonly hacked ports (listed in Table 9-1).

Table 9-1 Commonly Hacked Ports

Port Numbers	*Service*	*Protocols*
7	Echo	TCP, UDP
19	Chargen	TCP, UDP
20	FTP data (File Transfer Protocol)	TCP
21	FTP control	TCP
22	SSH	TCP
23	Telnet	TCP

Port Numbers	Service	Protocols
25	SMTP (Simple Mail Transfer Protocol)	TCP
37	Daytime	TCP, UDP
53	DNS (Domain Name System)	UDP
69	TFTP (Trivial File Transfer Protocol)	UDP
79	Finger	TCP, UDP
80	HTTP (Hypertext Transfer Protocol)	TCP
110	POP3 (Post Office Protocol version 3)	TCP
111	SUN RPC (remote procedure calls)	TCP, UDP
135	RPC/DCE end point mapper for Microsoft networks	TCP, UDP
137, 138, 139	NetBIOS over TCP/IP	TCP, UDP
161	SNMP (Simple Network Management Protocol)	TCP, UDP
220	IMAP (Internet Message Access Protocol)	TCP
443	HTTPS (HTTP over SSL)	TCP
512, 513, 514	Berkeley *r* commands (such as rsh, rexec, and rlogin)	TCP
1214	Kazaa and Morpheus	TCP, UDP
1433	Microsoft SQL Server	TCP, UDP
1434	Microsoft SQL Monitor	TCP, UDP
3389	Windows Terminal Server	TCP
5631, 5632	pcAnywhere	TCP
6346, 6347	Gnutella	TCP, UDP
12345, 12346, 12631, 12632, 20034, 20035	NetBus	TCP
27444	Trinoo	UDP
27665	Trinoo	TCP
31335	Trinoo	UDP
31337	Back Orifice	UDP
34555	Trinoo	UDP

Ping sweep

A ping sweep of all your network subnets and hosts is a good way to find out which hosts are alive and kicking on the network. A ping sweep is when you ping a range of addresses using Internet Control Message Protocol (ICMP) packets. Figure 9-1 shows the command and the results of using Nmap to perform a ping sweep of a class C subnet range.

Dozens of Nmap command-line options exist, which can be overwhelming when you just want to do a basic scan. You can just enter `nmap` on the command line to see all the options available.

These command-line options can be used for an Nmap ping sweep:

- `-sP` tells Nmap to perform a ping scan.
- `-n` tells Nmap to not perform name resolution.

  TIP: You may want to omit this if you want to resolve hostnames to see which systems are responding. Name resolution may take slightly longer, though.

  - `-T 4 option` tells Nmap to perform an aggressive (faster) scan.
  - `192.168.1.1-254` tells Nmap to scan the entire 192.168.1.x subnet.

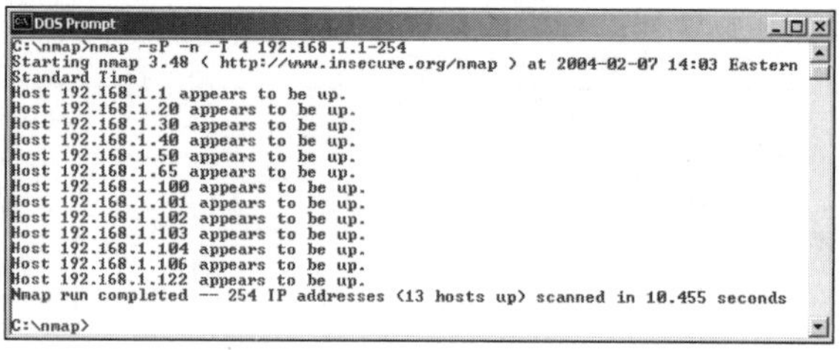

```
DOS Prompt
C:\nmap>nmap -sP -n -T 4 192.168.1.1-254
Starting nmap 3.48 ( http://www.insecure.org/nmap ) at 2004-02-07 14:03 Eastern
Standard Time
Host 192.168.1.1 appears to be up.
Host 192.168.1.20 appears to be up.
Host 192.168.1.30 appears to be up.
Host 192.168.1.40 appears to be up.
Host 192.168.1.50 appears to be up.
Host 192.168.1.65 appears to be up.
Host 192.168.1.100 appears to be up.
Host 192.168.1.101 appears to be up.
Host 192.168.1.102 appears to be up.
Host 192.168.1.103 appears to be up.
Host 192.168.1.104 appears to be up.
Host 192.168.1.106 appears to be up.
Host 192.168.1.122 appears to be up.
Nmap run completed -- 254 IP addresses (13 hosts up) scanned in 10.455 seconds

C:\nmap>
```

Figure 9-1: Performing a ping sweep of an entire class C network with Nmap.

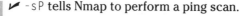

Port scanning

Most port scanners operate in three steps:

1. The port scanner sends TCP SYN requests to the host or range of hosts you set it to scan.

   Some port scanners, such as SuperScan, perform ping sweeps to determine which hosts are available before starting the TCP port scans.

   WARNING! Most port scanners scan only TCP ports by default. Don't forget about UDP ports. You can scan UDP ports with a UDP port scanner such as Nmap LANguard Network Security Scanner.

2. The port scanner waits for replies from the available hosts.
3. The port scanner probes these available hosts for up to 65,535 possible TCP and UDP ports — based on which ports you tell it to scan — to see which ones have available services on them.

The port scans provide the following information about the live hosts on your network:

- Hosts that are active and reachable through the network
- Network addresses of the hosts found
- Services or applications that the hosts *may be* running

After performing a generic sweep of the network, you can dig deeper into specific hosts you've found.

SuperScan

My favorite tool to perform generic TCP port scans is SuperScan. Figure 9-2 shows the results of my scan and a few interesting ports open on several hosts, including Windows Terminal Server and SSH.

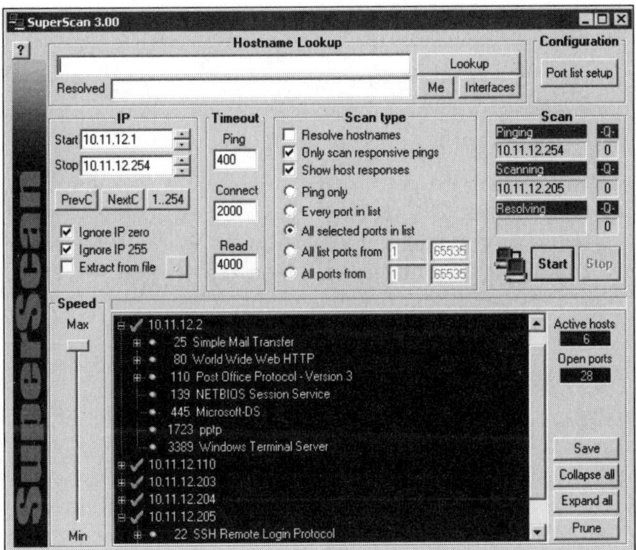

Figure 9-2: A TCP port scan using SuperScan.

In Figure 9-2, I selected the Only Scan Responsive Pings and All Selected Ports in List options. However, you may want to select some other options:

- If you don't want to ping each host first — which helps make the test run more efficiently — deselect the Only Scan Responsive Pings option. (ICMP can be blocked, which can cause the scanner to not find certain hosts.)
- If you want to scan a certain range of well-known ports or ports specific to your systems, you can configure SuperScan to do so. I recommend these settings:
    - If you want to perform a scan on well-known ports, at least select the All Selected Ports in List option.
    - If this is your initial scan, scan all ports from 1 to 65,535.

Nmap

After you have a general idea of what hosts are available and what ports are open, you can perform fancier scans to verify that the ports are actually open and not being reported as a false positive. If you wish to do this, Nmap is the perfect tool to use. Nmap allows you to run the following additional scans:

- **Connect:** This basic TCP scan looks for any open TCP ports on the host. You can use this scan to see what's running and determine whether IDSs, firewalls, or other logging devices log the connections.
- **UDP Scan:** This basic UDP scan looks for any open UDP ports on the host. You can use this scan to see what's running and determine whether IDSs, firewalls, or other logging devices log the connections.
- **SYN Stealth:** This scan creates a half-open TCP connection with the host possibly evading IDS systems and logging. This is a good scan for testing IDSs, firewalls, and other logging devices.
- **FIN Stealth, Xmas Tree, and Null:** These scans let you mix things up a bit — no pun intended — by sending strangely formed packets to your network hosts so you can see how they respond. These scans basically change around the flags in the TCP headers of each packet, which allows you to test how each host handles them to point out weak TCP/IP implementations and patches that may need to be applied.

Be careful when performing these scans. You can create your own DoS attack and potentially crash applications or entire systems. Unfortunately, if you have a host with a weak TCP/IP stack (the software that controls TCP/IP communications on your hosts), there is no good way to prevent this. The best way to reduce the chance of this occurring is to use the slow Nmap timing options — Paranoid, Sneaky, or Polite — when running your scans.

Figure 9-3 shows the NMapWin Scan tab, where you can select all these options. If you're a command-line fan, you see the command-line parameters displayed in the lower-left corner of the NMapWin screen. This helps when you know what you want to do and the command-line help isn't enough.

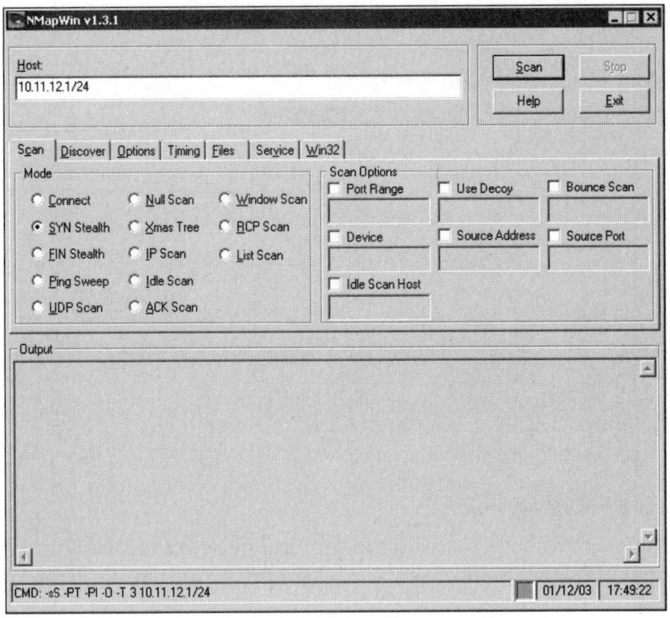

Figure 9-3: In-depth port-scanning options in NMapWin.

If you connect to a single port carefully enough (as opposed to several all at once) without making too much noise, you may be able evade your IDS/IDP system. This is a good test of your IDS and firewall systems, so assess your logs to see what they saw during this process.

Countermeasures

You can implement various countermeasures to typical port scanning.

Traffic restriction

Enable only the traffic you need to access internal hosts — preferably as far as possible from the hosts you're trying to protect. You apply these rules in two places:

- External router for inbound traffic
- Firewall for outbound traffic

  Configure firewalls to look for potentially malicious behavior over time (such as the number of packets received in a certain period of time), and have rules in place to cut off attacks if a certain threshold is reached, such as 100 port scans in one minute.

  Most firewalls, IDSs, and IDPs detect port scanning and cut it off in real time. Figure 9-4 shows an example: A basic Nmap OS fingerprint scan was detected and cut off (hence the black slash) by ISS's BlackICE personal firewall and IDP product in real time.

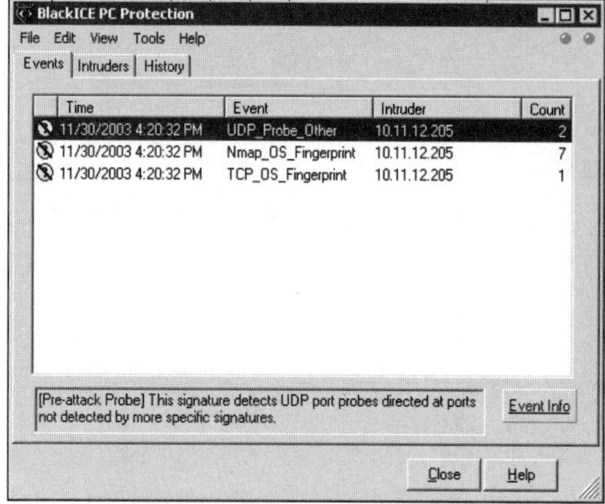

Figure 9-4: BlackICE logs showing how an Nmap scan was cut off.

Gathering network information

NetScanTools Pro is a great tool for general network information, such as the number of unique IP addresses, NetBIOS names, and MAC addresses found.

The following report is an example of the NetScanner (network scanner) output of NetScanTools Pro 2000:

```
Statistics for NetScanner
Scan completion time = Sat, 7 Feb 2004 14:11:08
Start IP address: 192.168.1.1
End IP address: 192.168.1.254
Number of target IP addresses: 254
Number of IP addresses responding to pings: 13
Number of IP addresses sent pings: 254
Number of intermediate routers responding to pings: 0
Number of successful NetBIOS queries: 13
Number of IP addresses sent NetBIOS queries: 254
Number of MAC addresses obtained by NetBIOS queries: 13
Number of successful Subnet Mask queries: 0
Number of IP addresses sent Subnet Mask queries: 254
Number of successful Whois queries: 254
```

Traffic denial

Deny ICMP traffic to specific hosts you're trying to protect. Most hosts don't need to have ICMP enabled — especially inbound ICMP requests — unless it's needed for a network management system that monitors hosts using this protocol.

You *can* break applications on your network, so make sure that you analyze what's going on, and understand how applications and protocols are working, before you disable such network traffic as ICMP.

SNMP scanning

Simple Network Management Protocol (SNMP) is a protocol built into virtually every network device. Network management programs (such as HP OpenView and LANDesk) use SNMP for remote network host management. Unfortunately, SNMP also presents security vulnerabilities.

Vulnerabilities

The problem is that most network hosts run SNMP that isn't hardened or patched to prevent known security vulnerabilities. The majority of network devices have SNMP enabled and don't even need it!

If SNMP is compromised, a hacker can gather such network information as ARP tables and TCP connections to attack your systems. If SNMP shows up in port scans, you can bet that a hacker will try to compromise the system. Figure 9-5 shows how GFI LANguard determined the NetWare version running (Version 6, Service Pack 3) by simply querying a host running unprotected SNMP. Here are some other utilities for SNMP enumeration:

- The commercial tool SolarWinds (`www.solarwinds.net`)
- Free Windows GUI-based Getif (`www.wtcs.org/snmp4tpc/getif.htm`)
- Text-based SNMPUTIL for Windows (`www.wtcs.org/snmp4tpc/FILES/Tools/SNMPUTIL/SNMPUTIL.zip`)

```
SNMP info (system)
  sysDescr - Novell NetWare 5.60.03 March 27, 2003__null
  sysUpTime - 24 days, 2 hours, 56 seconds
  sysContact - null
  sysName - FSMAIN
  sysLocation - null
  Object ID - 1.2.3.4.5.6.78.9.0 (Novell Netware Box)
  Vendor - Novell
```

Figure 9-5: Information gathered by querying a vulnerable SNMP host.

Countermeasures

Preventing SNMP attacks can be as simple as A-B-C:

- Always disable SNMP on hosts if you're not using it — period.
- Block the SNMP port (UDP port 161) at the network perimeter.
- Change the default SNMP community string from *public* to another value that's more difficult to guess. This makes SNMP harder to hack.

Banner grabbing

Banners are the welcome screens that divulge software version numbers and other host information to a network host. This banner information may identify the operating system, the version number, and the specific service packs, so hackers know possible vulnerabilities. You can grab banners by using either plain old telnet or Netcat.

telnet

You can telnet to hosts on the default telnet port (TCP port 23) to see whether you're presented with a login prompt or any other information. Just enter the following line at the command prompt in Windows or UNIX:

```
telnet ip_address
```

You can telnet to other commonly used ports with these commands:

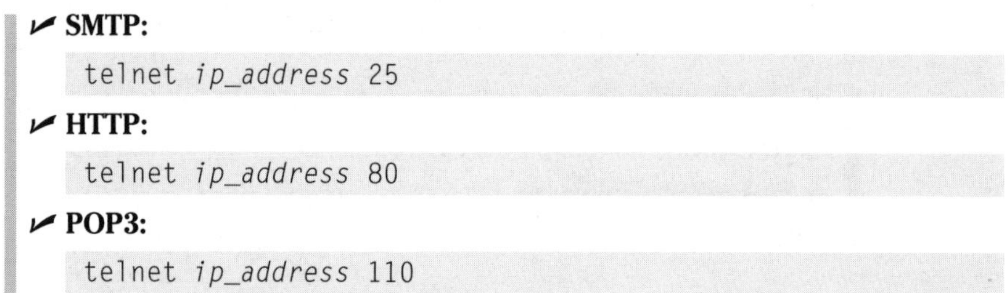

- **SMTP:**

  ```
  telnet ip_address 25
  ```

- **HTTP:**

  ```
  telnet ip_address 80
  ```

- **POP3:**

  ```
  telnet ip_address 110
  ```

Figure 9-6 shows specific version information about an Exchange 2003 server when telnetting to it on port 25.

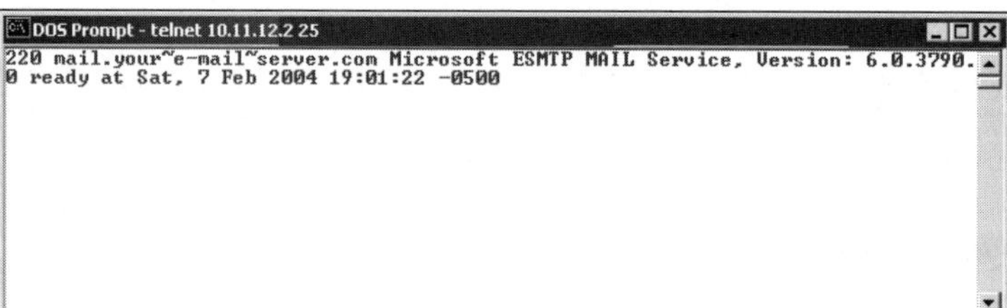

Figure 9-6: Information gathered about Exchange 2003 via telnet.

Netcat

Netcat can grab banner information from routers and other network hosts, such as a wireless access point or managed Ethernet switch.

The following steps bring back information about a host that runs a Web server for remote management purposes:

1. **Enter the following line to initiate a connection on port 80:**

   ```
   nc -v ip_address 80
   ```

2. **Wait for the initial connection.**

   Netcat returns the message `hostname [ip_address] 80 (http) open`.

3. **Enter the following line to grab the home page of the Web server:**

   ```
   GET / HTTP/1.0
   ```

4. **Press Enter a couple of times to load the page.**

   Figure 9-7 shows some typical results with Netcat.

```
Select DOS Prompt
C:\netcat>nc -v 10.11.12.2 80
server1 [10.11.12.2] 80 (http) open
GET / HTTP/1.0

HTTP/1.1 200 OK
Date: Mon, 01 Dec 2003 19:12:24 GMT
Server: Apache/2.0.47 (Win32)
Last-Modified: Thu, 11 Sep 2003 05:21:07 GMT
ETag: "2e8c-2a50-f792253b"
Accept-Ranges: bytes
Content-Length: 10832
Connection: close
Content-Type: text/html; charset=ISO-8859-1
```

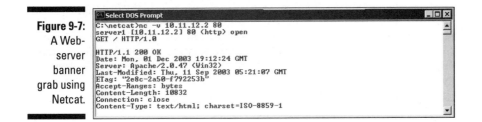

Figure 9-7: A Web-server banner grab using Netcat.

Countermeasures

The following steps can reduce the chance of banner-grabbing attacks:

- If there is no business need for services that offer banner information, disable those unused services on the network host.
- If there is no business need for the default banners, or if you can customize the banners displayed, configure the network host's application or operating system to either disable the banners or remove information from the banners that could give an attacker a leg up.

If you can customize your banners, check with your lawyer about adding a warning message similar to this:

> *Warning!!! This is a private system. All use is monitored and recorded. Any unauthorized use of this system may result in civil and/or criminal prosecution to the fullest extent of the law.*

Firewall rules

As part of your ethical hacking, you can test your firewall rules to make sure they're working like they're supposed to.

Testing

A few tests can verify that your firewall actually does what it says it's doing. You can connect through it on the ports you believe are open, but what about all the other ports that can be open and shouldn't be?

Some security-assessment tools can not only test for open ports, but also determine whether traffic is actually allowed to pass through the firewall.

All-in-one tools

All-in-one tools aren't perfect, but their broad testing capabilities make the network scanning process a lot less painful and can save you tons of time! Their reporting is really nice, too, especially if you will show your test results to upper management.

Nessus, QualysGuard, and GFI LANguard Network Security Scanner provide similar results. Figure 9-8 is partial output from LANguard. It identifies open ports on the test network and presents information on SNMP, operating-system information, and special alerts to look for.

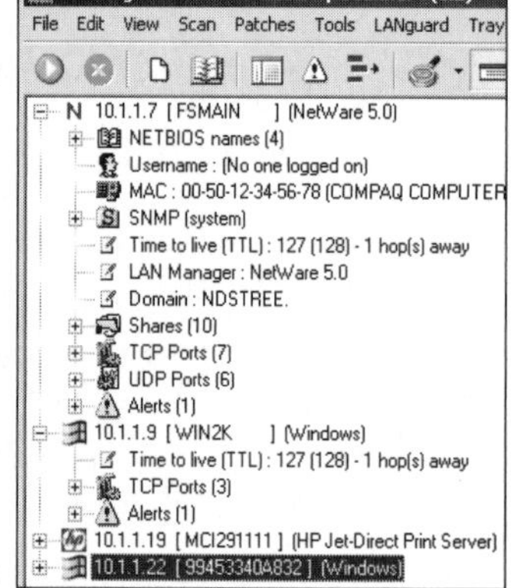

Figure 9-8: Information gathered from a network scan using LANguard Network Security Scanner.

You can use LANguard Network Security Scanner and QualysGuard to find operating-system vulnerabilities and patches that need to be applied. Pretty slick! I show you more on this in Chapter 11, which covers Windows.

Netcat

Netcat can test certain firewall rules without having to test a production system directly. For example, you can check whether the firewall allows port 23 (telnet) through. Follow these steps to see whether a connection can be made through port 23:

1. **Load Netcat on a client machine *inside* the network.**

   This allows you to test from the inside out.

2. **Load Netcat on a testing computer *outside* the firewall.**

   This allows you to test from the outside in.

3. **Enter the Netcat listener command on the client (internal) machine with the port number you're testing.**

   For example, if you're testing port 23, enter this command:

   ```
   nc -l -p 23 cmd.exe
   ```

4. **Enter the Netcat command to initiate an inbound session on the testing (external) machine. You must include the following information:**

   - The IP address of the internal machine you're testing
   - The port number you're testing

   For example, if the IP address of the internal (client) machine is 10.11.12.2 and the port is 23, enter this command:

   ```
   nc -v 10.11.12.2 23
   ```

If Netcat presents you with a new command prompt (that's what the `cmd.exe` is for in Step 3) on the external machine, it means that you connected and are now executing commands on the internal machine! This can serve several purposes, including testing firewall rules and — well, uhhhmmm — executing commands on a remote system!

Alternative testing tools

These utilities test firewall rules more robustly than Netcat:

- **Firewalk:** A UNIX-based tool (`www.packetfactory.net/firewalk`)
- **Firewall Informer:** A commercial tool by BLADE Software (`www.blade-software.com`)

Countermeasures

The following countermeasures can prevent a hacker from testing your firewall:

- Limit traffic to what's needed.

  Set rules on your firewall (and router, if needed) to pass only traffic that you absolutely must pass. For example, have rules in place that allow HTTP inbound to an internal Web server and outbound for external Web access.

  This is the best defense against someone poking at your firewall.
- Block ICMP to help prevent abuse from some automated tools, such as Firewalk.
- Enable stateful packet inspection on the firewall, if you can. It can block unsolicited requests.

Looking through a network analyzer

A network analyzer is a tool that allows you to look into a network and analyze data going across the wire for network optimization, security, and/or troubleshooting purposes. Like a microscope for a lab scientist, a network analyzer is a must-have tool for any security professional.

Network analyzers are often generically referred to as *sniffers,* though that's actually the name and trademark of a specific product from Network Associates, *Sniffer* (the original network-analysis tool).

A network analyzer is handy for *sniffing* packets. Watch for the following network traffic behavior:

- What do packet replies look like? Are they coming from the host you're testing or from an intermediary device?
- Do packets appear to traverse a network host or security device, such as a router, a firewall, IDS, or a proxy server?

When assessing security and responding to security incidents, a network analyzer can help you

- View anomalous network traffic and even track down an intruder.
- Develop a baseline of network activity and performance before a security incident occurs, such as protocols in use, usage trends, and MAC addresses.

When your network behaves erratically, a network analyzer can help you

- Track and isolate malicious network usage
- Detect malicious Trojan-horse applications
- Monitor and track down DoS attacks

You can use one of the following programs for network analysis:

- EtherPeek by WildPackets (`www.wildpackets.com`) is my favorite network analyzer. It delivers a ton of features that the higher-end network analyzers of yesterday have for a fraction of their cost. EtherPeek is available for the Windows operating systems.
- I download the open-source Ethereal network analyzer from `www.ethereal.org` if I need a quick fix and don't have my laptop nearby. It's not as user-friendly as EtherPeek, but it is very powerful if you're willing to learn its ins and outs. Ethereal is available for both Windows and UNIX-based operating systems.

- Two other powerful and free utilities can perform such functions as network analysis:
  - ettercap (`ettercap.sourceforge.net`) for Windows and UNIX-based operating systems. I cover ettercap in more detail in "ARP spoofing," later in the chapter.
  - dsniff (`www.monkey.org/~dugsong/dsniff`) for UNIX-based operating systems.

A network analyzer is just software running on a computer with a network card. It works by placing the network card in *promiscuous mode,* which enables the card to see all the traffic on the network, even traffic not destined to the network-analyzer host. The network analyzer performs the following functions:

- Captures all network traffic
- Interprets or decodes what is found into a human-readable format
- Displays it all in chronological order

Here are a few caveats for using a network analyzer:

- To capture all traffic, you must connect the analyzer to either
  - A hub on the network
  - A monitor/span/mirror port on a switch
- You should connect the network analyzer to a hub on the outside of the firewall, as shown in Figure 9-9, as part of your testing so you can see traffic similar to what a network-based IDS sees:
  - What's entering your network *before* the firewall filters eliminates the junk traffic
  - What's leaving your network *after* the traffic goes past the firewall

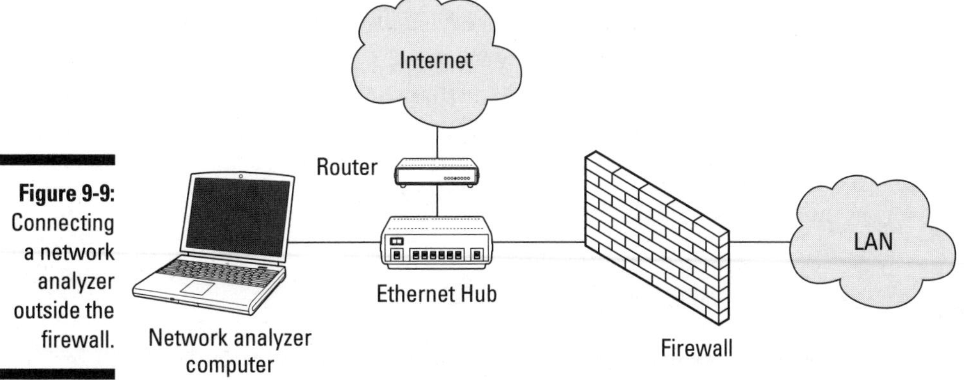

Figure 9-9: Connecting a network analyzer outside the firewall.

Whether you connect your network analyzer inside or outside your firewall, you see immediate results. It can be an overwhelming amount of information, but you can look for these issues first:

- Odd traffic, such as
  - Unusual amount of ICMP packets
  - Excessive amounts of multicast or broadcast traffic
  - Packet types that don't belong, such as NetBIOS in a NetWare environment
- Internet usage habits, which can help point out malicious behavior of a rogue insider or system that has been compromised, such as
  - Web surfing
  - E-mail
  - IM
- Questionable usage, such as
  - Many lost or oversized packets
  - High bandwidth consumption that may point to a Web or FTP server that doesn't belong
- Reconnaissance probes and system profiling from port scanners and vulnerability-assessment tools, such as a significant amount of inbound traffic from unknown hosts — especially over ports that are not used very much, such as FTP or telnet.
- Hacking in progress, such as tons of inbound UDP or ICMP echo requests, SYN floods, or excessive broadcasts.
- Nonstandard host names on your network. For example, if your systems are named Computer1, Computer2, and so on, a computer named GEEKz4evUR should raise a red flag.
- Hidden servers (especially Web, SMTP, FTP, and DHCP) that may be eating network bandwidth or serving illegal software or even access into your network hosts.
- Attacks on specific applications that show such commands as `/bin/rm`, `/bin/ls`, `echo`, and `cmd.exe`.

You may need to let your network analyzer run for quite a while — several hours to several days, depending on what you're looking for.

Before getting started, configure your network analyzer to capture and store the most relevant data:

- If your network analyzer permits it, configure your network analyzer software to use a first-in, first-out buffer.

This overwrites the oldest data when the buffer fills up, but it may be your only option if memory and hard drive space are limited on your network-analysis computer.

- If your network analyzer permits it, record all the traffic into a capture file, and save it to the hard drive. This is the ideal scenario — especially if you have a large hard drive, such as 50GB or more.

You can easily fill a several-gigabyte hard drive in a short period of time.

- When network traffic doesn't look right in a network analyzer, it probably isn't. It's better to be safe than sorry.

  Run a baseline when your network is working normally. You can see any obvious abnormalities when an attack occurs.

Clear-as-day decoding makes a network analyzer worth every penny you may pay.

Figure 9-10 shows what a Smurf DoS attack can do to a network in just 30 seconds. (I created this attack with BLADE Software's IDS Informer, but you can use other tools.) On a small network with very little traffic, the utilization number is 823 kilobits/second — not too large a number for a 100-megabit/second Ethernet network. However, on a busy network with a lot more traffic, the number would be staggering.

Figure 9-10: What a Smurf DoS attack looks like through a network analyzer.

Figure 9-11 shows the Smurf DoS attack on EtherPeek's conversation monitor. Three million bytes were transmitted in this short period of time — from one host.

Figure 9-12 shows what a WANRemote backdoor remote administration tool (RAT) looks like across the network using EtherPeek. It shows the commands sent to get files from the local C: drive, kill UNIX processes, and unload X-Window.

Net Node 1 (Client)	Net Node 2	Packets	Bytes	Duration
10.11.12.203	IP Broadcast	2,812	3,006,028	
ICMP		2,812	3,006,028	00:00:29.422

Figure 9-11: A Smurf DoS conversation via EtherPeek.

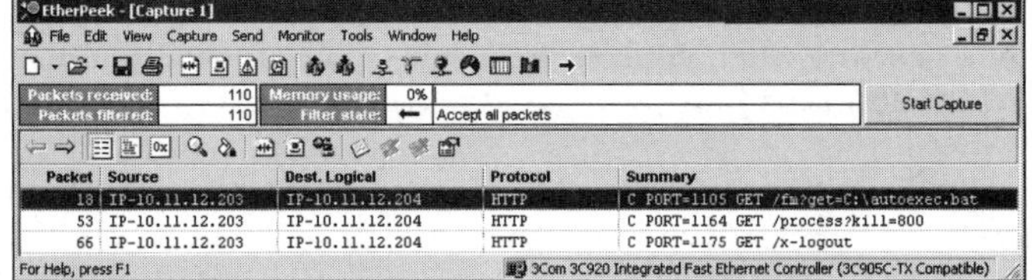

Figure 9-12: WANRemote RAT-attack traffic.

If one workstation consumes considerably more bandwidth than the others — such as the 10.11.12.203 host in Figure 9-13 — dig deeper to see what's going on. (Such network hosts as servers often send and receive more traffic than other hosts.)

Figure 9-14 shows an indication that a port scan is being run on the network. It shows all the different protocols and the small number of packets this analysis found, including Gnutella, telnet, and rlogin.

Net Node 1 (Client)	Net Node 2	Packets	Bytes
0.0.0.0	255.255.255.255	1	594
10.11.12.0	10.11.12.203	3,614	326,888
10.11.12.1	255.255.255.255	1	347
10.11.12.2	10.11.12.255	98	14,799
10.11.12.2	10.11.12.1	2	128
10.11.12.156	10.11.12.255	52	6,664
10.11.12.201	224.1.0.1	2	128
10.11.12.201	224.0.1.40	2	128
10.11.12.203	10.11.12.110	574,028	236,306,248
10.11.12.203	255.255.255.255	29,478	31,508,354
10.11.12.203	10.11.12.205	6,754	443,245
10.11.12.203	10.11.12.255	86	11,420
10.11.12.203	10.11.12.1	18	1,887
10.11.12.203	10.11.12.204	34,616	32,728,743
10.11.12.203	10.11.12.2	2,760	470,924
10.11.12.204	10.11.12.255	45	9,732
10.11.12.205	10.11.12.255	2	128
10.11.12.205	10.11.12.0	2	128

Figure 9-13: Higher-than-normal network usage (as shown by the 10.11.12.203 host).

Protocol	Percentage	Bytes	Packets
FTP	0.040%	384	6
RPC	0.027%	256	4
X-Windows	0.020%	192	3
WINS	0.020%	192	3
WhoIs	0.020%	192	3
TNS	0.020%	192	3
TELNET	0.020%	192	3
TDS	0.020%	192	3
SQL	0.020%	192	3
SMTP	0.020%	192	3
SLP	0.020%	192	3
SCCP	0.020%	192	3
RTSP	0.020%	192	3
rtelnet	0.020%	192	3
rsh	0.020%	192	3
RPC/NFS	0.020%	192	3
rlogin	0.020%	192	3

Figure 9-14: Many nonstandard protocols can indicate that a port scan is taking place.

Check your network for a high number of ARP requests and ICMP echo requests proportionate to your overall traffic, as shown in Figure 9-15.

Countermeasures

A network analyzer can be used for good or evil. All these tests can be used against you, too. A few countermeasures can help prevent someone from using an unauthorized network analyzer, but there's no way to completely prevent it.

If hackers can connect to your network (physical or wireless), they can capture packets on the network, even if you're using a switch.

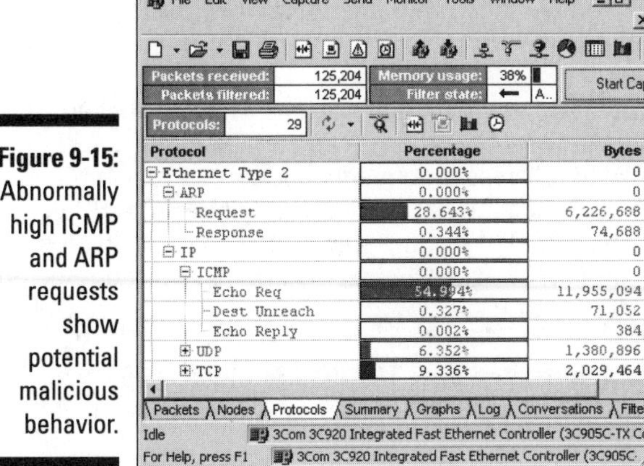

Figure 9-15: Abnormally high ICMP and ARP requests show potential malicious behavior.

Physical security

Ensure that adequate physical security is in place to prevent a hacker from plugging into your network:

- Keep the bad guys out of your server room and wiring closet.

  A special monitor port on a switch where a hacker can plug in a network analyzer is especially sensitive. Make sure it's extra secure.
- Make sure that such unsupervised areas as unoccupied desks don't have live network connections.

Network-analyzer detection

You can use a network- or host-based utility to determine if someone is running an unauthorized network analyzer on your network:

- sniffdet (`sniffdet.sourceforge.net`) for UNIX-based systems
- PromiscDetect (`ntsecurity.nu/toolbox/promiscdetect`) for Windows

These tools enable you to monitor the network for Ethernet cards that are running in promiscuous mode. You simply load the programs on your computer, and the programs alert you if they see promiscuous behaviors on the network (sniffdet) or local system (PromiscDetect).

The MAC-daddy attack

Attackers can use ARP (Address Resolution Protocol) running on your network to make their systems appear to be either your system or another authorized host on your network.

ARP spoofing

An excessive amount of ARP requests can be a sign of an *ARP poisoning* attack (or *ARP spoofing*) on your network.

What happens is that a client running a program such as the UNIX-based dsniff or the UNIX- and DOS/Windows-based ettercap can change the ARP tables — the tables that store IP addresses to *media access control (MAC)* mappings — on network hosts. This causes the victim computers to think they need to send traffic to the attacker's computer, rather than the true destination computer, when communicating on the network. This is often referred to as a Man-in-the-Middle (MITM) attack.

This security vulnerability is inherent in how TCP/IP communications are handled.

Here's a typical ARP spoofing attack with a hacker's computer (Hacky) and two legitimate network users' computers (Joe and Bob):

1. Hacky poisons the ARP caches of victims Joe and Bob by using dsniff, ettercap, or a utility he wrote.
2. Joe associates Hacky's MAC address with Bob's IP address.
3. Bob associates Hacky's MAC address with Joe's IP address.
4. Joe's traffic and Bob's traffic are sent to Hacky's IP address first.
5. Hacky's network analyzer captures Joe's traffic and Bob's traffic.

   If Hacky is configured to act like a router and forward packets, it forwards the traffic to its original destination. The original sender and receiver never know the difference!

Figure 9-16 shows the juicy e-mail stuff I found with ettercap. I loaded ettercap on my Windows computer, selected 10.11.12.204 as the source and 10.11.12.2 as the destination, and used ARP poisoning. Voilà!

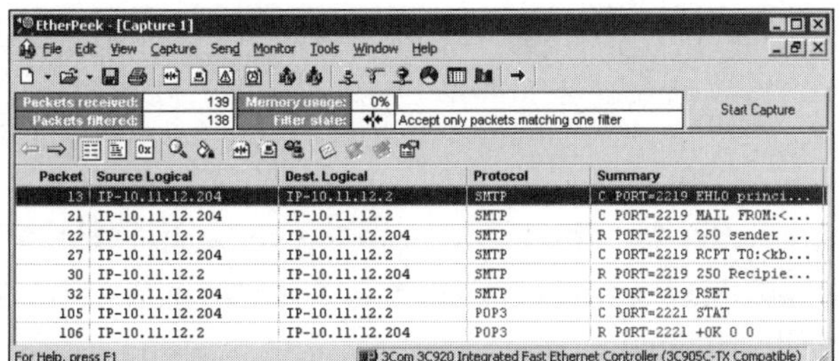

EtherPeek - [Capture 1]
File Edit View Capture Send Monitor Tools Window Help
Packets received: 139
Packets filtered: 138
Memory usage: 0%
Filter state: Accept only packets matching one filter
Start Capture
Packet Source Logical Dest. Logical Protocol Summary
13 IP-10.11.12.204 IP-10.11.12.2 SMTP C PORT=2219 EHLO princi...
21 IP-10.11.12.204 IP-10.11.12.2 SMTP C PORT=2219 MAIL FROM:<...
22 IP-10.11.12.2 IP-10.11.12.204 SMTP R PORT=2219 250 sender ...
27 IP-10.11.12.204 IP-10.11.12.2 SMTP C PORT=2219 RCPT TO:<kb...
30 IP-10.11.12.2 IP-10.11.12.204 SMTP R PORT=2219 250 Recipie...
32 IP-10.11.12.204 IP-10.11.12.2 SMTP C PORT=2219 RSET
105 IP-10.11.12.204 IP-10.11.12.2 POP3 C PORT=2221 STAT
106 IP-10.11.12.2 IP-10.11.12.204 POP3 R PORT=2221 +OK 0 0
For Help, press F1
3Com 3C920 Integrated Fast Ethernet Controller (3C905C-TX Compatible)

Figure 9-16: A sample of what hackers can find with ARP poisoning.

Spoofed ARP replies can be sent to a switch very quickly, which often crashes the switch. The switch reverts to *broadcast mode,* which makes it work like a hub. When this occurs, an attacker can sniff every packet going through the switch without bothering with ARP spoofing.

MAC-address spoofing

MAC-address spoofing tricks the *switch* into thinking you (actually, your computer) are someone else. You simply change your MAC address and masquerade as another user.

You can use this trick to test such access control systems as your IDS, firewall, and even operating-system login controls that check for specific MAC addresses.

UNIX-based systems

In UNIX and Linux, you can spoof MAC addresses with the ifconfig utility. Follow these steps:

1. **While logged in as root, use ifconfig to enter a command that disables the network interface. Insert the network interface number that you want to disable (usually, eth0) into the command, like this:**

   ```
   [root@localhost root]# ifconfig eth0 down
   ```

2. **Enter a command for the MAC address you want to use.**

   Insert the fake MAC address and the network interface number (eth0) into the command again, like this:

   ```
   [root@localhost root]# ifconfig eth0 hw ether new_mac_address
   ```

You can use a more feature-rich utility called MAC Changer (`www.alobbs.com/macchanger`) for Linux systems.

Windows

You can use regedit to edit the Windows Registry, but I like using a neat Windows utility called SMAC (`www.klcconsulting.net/smac`), which makes MAC spoofing a simple process. Follow these steps to use SMAC:

1. **Load the program.**
2. **Select the adapter for which you want to change the MAC address.**
3. **Enter the new MAC address in the New Spoofed MAC Address fields, and click Update MAC.**
4. **Stop and restart the network card with these steps:**
   i. Right-click the network card in Network and Dialup Connections.
   ii. Select Disable, and then right-click again and click Enable for the change to take effect.

   You may have to reboot for this to work properly.
5. **Click Refresh in the SMAC interface.**

   You should see something similar to the SMAC screen capture in Figure 9-17.

To reverse Registry changes with SMAC, follow these steps:

1. **Select the adapter for which you want to change the MAC address.**
2. **Click Remove MAC.**

3. **Stop and restart the network card with these steps:**

   i. Right-click the network card in Network and Dialup Connections.

   ii. Select Disable, and then right-click again and click Enable for the change to take effect.

   You may have to reboot for this to work properly.

4. **Click Refresh in the SMAC interface.**

   You should see your original MAC address again.

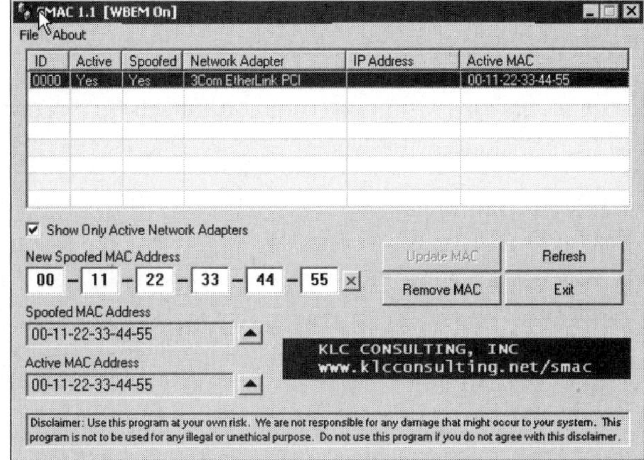

Figure 9-17: SMAC showing a spoofed MAC address.

Countermeasures

A few countermeasures on your network can minimize the effects of a hacker attack against ARP and MAC addresses on your network.

Prevention

You can prevent MAC-address spoofing if your switches can enable port security to prevent automatic changes to the switch MAC address tables.

No realistic countermeasures for ARP poisoning exist. The only way to prevent ARP poisoning is to create and maintain static ARP entries in your switches for every host on the network. This is definitely something that no network administrator has time to do!

Detection

You can detect these two types of hacks through either an IDS or a stand-alone MAC address monitoring utility.

Arpwatch is a UNIX-based program alerts you via e-mail if it detects changes in MAC addresses associated with specific IP addresses on the network.

Denial of service

Denial-of-service (DoS) attacks are among the most common hacker attacks. A hacker initiates so many invalid requests to a network host that it uses all its resources responding to them and ignores legitimate requests.

DoS attacks

The following types of DoS attacks are possible against your network and hosts, and can cause systems to crash, data to be lost, and every user to jump on your case, wondering when Internet access will be restored.

Individual attacks

Here are some common DoS attacks:

- **SYN floods:** The attacker literally floods a host with TCP SYN packets.
- **Ping of Death:** The attacker sends IP packets that exceed the maximum length of 65,535 bytes, which can ultimately crash the TCP/IP stack on many operating systems.
- **WinNuke:** This attack can disable networking on older Windows 95 and NT computers.

Distributed attacks

Distributed DoS (DDoS) attacks have an exponentially greater impact on their victims. The most famous was the DDoS attack against eBay, Yahoo!, CNN, and dozens of other Web sites by the hacker known as MafiaBoy. These are some common distributed attacks:

- **Smurf attack:** An attacker spoofs the victim's address and sends ICMP echo request (ping packets) to the broadcast address. The victim computer gets deluged with tons of packets in response to those echo requests.
- **Trinoo and Tribe Flood Network (TFN) attacks:** Sets of client- and server-based programs launch packet floods against a victim machine, effectively overloading it and causing it to crash.

DoS attacks can be carried out with tools that the hacker either writes or downloads off the Internet. These are good tools to test your network's IDS/IDP and firewalls. You can find programs that allow actual attacks and programs, such as BLADE Software's IDS Informer, that let you send controlled attacks.

Testing

Your first DoS test should be a search for DoS vulnerabilities from a port-scanning and network-analysis perspective.

Don't test for DoS unless you have test systems or can perform controlled tests with the proper tools. Poorly planned DoS testing is a job search in the making. It's like trying to delete data from a network share remotely and hoping that the access controls in place are going to prevent it.

Countermeasures

Most DoS attacks are difficult to predict, but they can be easy to prevent:

- Test and apply security patches as soon as possible for such network hosts as routers and firewalls, as well as for server and workstation operating systems.
- Use IDS and IDP systems to monitor regularly for DoS attacks.

  You can run a network analyzer in *continuous capture* mode if you can't justify the cost of an all-out IDS or IDP solution.
- Configure firewalls and routers to block malformed traffic. You can do this only if your systems support it, so refer to your administrator's guide for details.
- Minimize IP spoofing by either
  - Using authentication and encryption, such as a Public Key Infrastructure (PKI)
  - Filtering out external packets that appear to come from an internal address, the local host (127.0.0.1), or any other private and non-routable address such as 10.x.x.x, 172.16.x.x–172.31.x.x, or 192.168.x.x
- Block all ICMP traffic inbound to your network unless you specifically need it. Even then, you should allow it only in to specific hosts.
- Disable all unneeded TCP/UDP small services (such as echo and chargen).

Establish a baseline of your network protocols and traffic patterns before a DoS attack occurs. That way, you know what to look for. And periodically scan for such potential DoS vulnerabilities as rogue DoS software installed on network hosts.

Work with a *minimum necessary* mentality when configuring your network devices such as firewalls and routers:

- Identify traffic that is necessary for approved network usage.
- Allow the traffic that's needed.
- Deny all other traffic.

General network defenses

Regardless of the specific attacks against your system, a few good practices can help prevent many network problems:

- Stateful inspection on firewalls. This can help ensure that all traffic traversing it is legitimate and can prevent DoS attacks and other spoofing attacks.
- Rules to perform packet filtering based on traffic type, TCP/UDP ports, IP addresses, and even specific interfaces on your routers before the traffic is ever allowed to enter your network.
- Proxy filtering and Network Address Translation (NAT).
- Finding and eliminating fragmented packets entering your network (from Fraggle or other type of attack) via an IDS or IDP system.
- Segmenting and firewalling these network segments:
    - The internal network in general
    - Critical departments, such as accounting, finance, HR, and research

Chapter 10

Wireless LANs

In This Chapter

- Understanding risks of wireless LANs
- Selecting wireless LAN hacking tools
- Hacking against wireless LANs
- Minimizing wireless network security risks

Wireless local area networks (WLANs) — specifically, the ones based on the IEEE 802.11 standard — are increasingly being deployed into both business and home networks. Next to instant messaging and personal video recorders, WLANs are the neatest technology I've used in quite a while. Of course, with any new technology come security issues, and WLANs are no exception. In fact, the 802.11b wireless technology has been the poster child for weak security and network hack attacks for several years running.

WLANs offer a ton of business value, from convenience to reduced network deployment time. Whether your organization allows wireless network access or not, testing for WLAN security vulnerabilities is critical. In this chapter, I cover some common wireless network security vulnerabilities that you should test for. And I discuss some cheap and easy countermeasures you can implement to help ensure that WLANs are not more of a risk to your organization than they're worth.

Understanding the Implications of Wireless Network Vulnerabilities

WLANs are very susceptible to hacker attacks — even more so than wired networks are (discussed in Chapter 9). They have vulnerabilities that can allow a hacker to bring your network to its knees and allow your information to be gleaned right out of thin air. If a hacker comprises your WLAN, you can experience the following problems:

- Loss of network access, including e-mail, Web, and other services that can cause business downtime
- Loss of confidential information, including passwords, customer data, intellectual property, and more
- Legal liabilities associated with unauthorized users

Most of the wireless vulnerabilities are in the 802.11 protocol and within wireless *access points* (APs) — the central hublike devices that allow wireless clients to connect to the network. Wireless clients have some vulnerabilities as well.

Various fixes have come along in recent years to address these vulnerabilities, but most of these fixes have not been applied or are not enabled by default. You may also have employees installing rogue WLAN equipment on your network without your knowledge; this is the most serious threat to your wireless security and a difficult one to fight off. Even when WLANs are hardened and all the latest patches have been applied, you still may have some serious security problems, such as DoS and man-in-the-middle attacks (like you have on wired networks), that will likely be around for a while.

Choosing Your Tools

Several great WLAN security tools are available for both the Windows and UNIX platforms. The UNIX tools — which mostly run on Linux and BSD — can be a bear to configure and run properly if the planets and stars are not properly aligned. The PC Card services in Linux are the trickiest to set up, depending on your type of WLAN card and your Linux version.

Don't get me wrong — the UNIX-based tools are excellent at what they do. Programs such as Kismet (`www.kismetwireless.net`), AirSnort (`airsnort.shmoo.com`), AirJack (`802.11ninja.net/airjack`), and Wellenreiter (`www.wellenreiter.net`) offer many features that most Windows-based applications don't have. These programs run really well if you have all the Linux dependencies installed. They also offer many features that you don't need when assessing the security of your WLAN.

In the spirit of keeping things simple, the tests I outline in this chapter require only Windows-based utilities. My favorite tools for assessing wireless tools in Windows are as follows:

- NetStumbler (`www.netstumbler.com`) for AP discovery and enumeration
- Wireless client management software — such as Orinoco's Client Manager software — for AP discovery and enumeration

- WildPackets' AiroPeek (`www.wildpackets.com`) or your favorite WLAN analyzer for detailed information on wireless hosts, decryption of encrypted traffic, and more
- LANguard Network Security Scanner (`www.gfi.com`) for WLAN enumeration and vulnerability scanning

A case study with Matt Caldwell on hacking wireless networks

Matt Caldwell, shared with me a wild story of a wireless warflying experience — yes, it's wardriving, but in an airplane! Here's his account of what happened.

The Situation

Mr. Caldwell's employer — the state of Georgia — wanted to have the state's wireless networks assessed. The problem with terrestrial wardriving is that it's very slow, so Mr. Caldwell and his team conducted an experiment to determine the most economical way to assess the access points across the state of Georgia, which comprised 47,000 employees and 70 agencies. They knew the location of the buildings and knew they had to visit all of them. As a test, they drove around one building to count the number of access points they detected and concluded that it would take almost six months to assess all the state buildings.

In his spare time, Mr. Caldwell flies single-engine aircraft, and he decided that if the military could gather intelligence via aircraft, so could he! After getting through some political red tape, he and a fellow aviator used duct tape to mount an antenna on a Cessna 172RG (he thanks MacGyver for this idea!). He mounted the antenna at a 90-degree angle from the plane's nose so that he could make notes on the direction of the plot point. By doing some simple math, plus 90 degrees gave them radial on the approximate bearing of the target access point.

The Outcome

As Mr. Caldwell and his colleague climbed above 500 feet, NetStumbler (the wireless assessment software they were using) began chiming over the engine noise with its "bongs." It seemed like every second, a new wireless AP was being discovered. They made their way around downtown Atlanta and detected over 300 unique APs at about 2,000 feet AGL. They proved that warflying can be an effective method of detecting access points and a great statistical-gathering activity. They collected data on 382 APs in less than one hour in the air!

Matt Caldwell's Lessons Learned

- Don't eat a McDonald's double cheeseburger before flying — or at least carry a barf bag!
- Use extra duct tape and a safety rope, or put the antenna in the aircraft.
- Use good software to do triangulation so you don't have to calculate the position manually.
- Seventy percent of the APs detected had no WEP encryption!
- Almost 50 percent of the APs detected had default SSIDs.

Matt Caldwell, CISSP, is founder of and chief security officer for GuardedNet, Inc.

You also need the proper hardware. A good setup I've used is a laptop PC with an Orinoco (formerly made by Lucent, now Proxim) 802.11b PC Card. This card is not only compatible with NetStumbler, but also has an antenna connector that allows you to connect an external antenna. Another bonus is that most wireless security tools are very friendly with the Orinoco card. A lot of security tool support is available for the Prism2 chipset found in wireless cards by Belkin, D-Link, Linksys, and more. Before you purchase a wireless PC Card or PCI adapter, verify what chipset it has to ensure compatibility with the majority of security tools. The SeattleWireless HardwareComparison page (www.seattlewireless.net/index.cgi/HardwareComparison) is a good reference for this type of information.

You can also use a handheld wireless security testing device such as an AirMagnet (www.airmagnet.com) or the Fluke WaveRunner (www.flukenetworks.com). Both devices have their own built-in programs that are great for testing security settings on your WLAN.

An external antenna is also something to consider as part of your arsenal. I have had good luck running tests without an antenna, but your mileage may vary. If you're performing a walk-through of your facilities to test for wireless signals, for example, adding an additional antenna increases your odds of finding legitimate — and, more important, unauthorized APs. You can choose among three main types of wireless antennas:

- **Omnidirectional:** Transmits and receives wireless signals 360 degrees over shorter distances, such as in boardrooms or reception areas. These antennas, also known as dipoles, typically come installed on APs from the factory.
- **Semidirectional:** Transmits and receives directionally focused wireless signals over medium distances, such as down corridors and across one side of an office.
- **Directional:** Transmits and receives highly focused wireless signals over long distances, such as between buildings. This antenna, also known as a high-gain antenna, is the antenna of choice for wireless hackers driving around cities looking for vulnerable APs — an act also known as *wardriving.*

As an alternative to the antennas described in the preceding list, you can use a nifty Pringles-can design. If you're interested in trying this, check out the article at www.oreillynet.com/cs/weblog/view/wlg/448 for details. You can even try other alternatives, such as a pork-and-beans can! A simple Internet search turns up a lot of information on this subject, if you're interested. One site in particular sells a Cantenna kit pretty cheaply at mywebpages.comcast.net/hughpep.

Wireless LAN Discovery

After you have an Internet connection, wireless hardware (a wireless card, at a minimum), and wireless testing software (NetStumbler or similar client management software, at a minimum), you're ready to roll.

Checking for worldwide recognition

The first test requires only the MAC address of your AP and access to the Internet. You're testing to see if someone has discovered your WLAN and posted information about it for the world to see. If you're not sure what your AP's MAC address is, you should be able to view it by using the `arp -a` command in DOS. You may have to ping the access point's IP address first so the MAC address is loaded into your ARP cache. Figure 10-1 shows what this may look like.

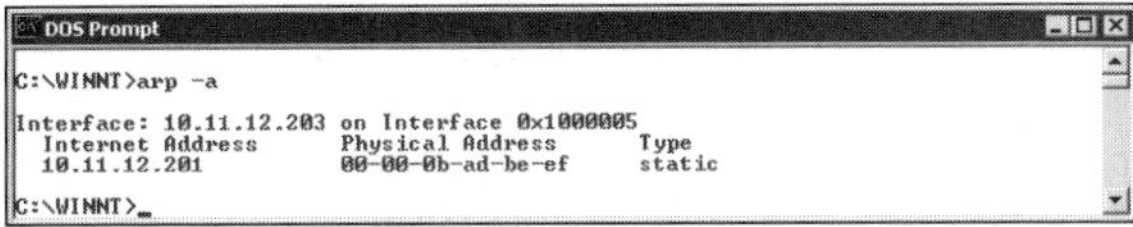

Figure 10-1: Finding the MAC address of an AP using `arp`.

After you have the AP's MAC address, browse to the WiGLE database of WLANs (`www.wigle.net`) to see if your AP is listed. You have to register with the site to perform a database query, but it's worth it. After you select the Query link and login, you see a screen similar to Figure 10-2. You can enter such AP information as geographical coordinates, but the simplest thing to do is enter your MAC address in the format shown.

If your AP is listed, that means that someone has discovered it — most likely via wardriving — and has posted the information for others to see. You need to start implementing the security countermeasures listed in this chapter as soon as possible to keep others from using this information against you! You can also check `www.wifimaps.com` to see if your AP is listed at another WLAN lookup site.

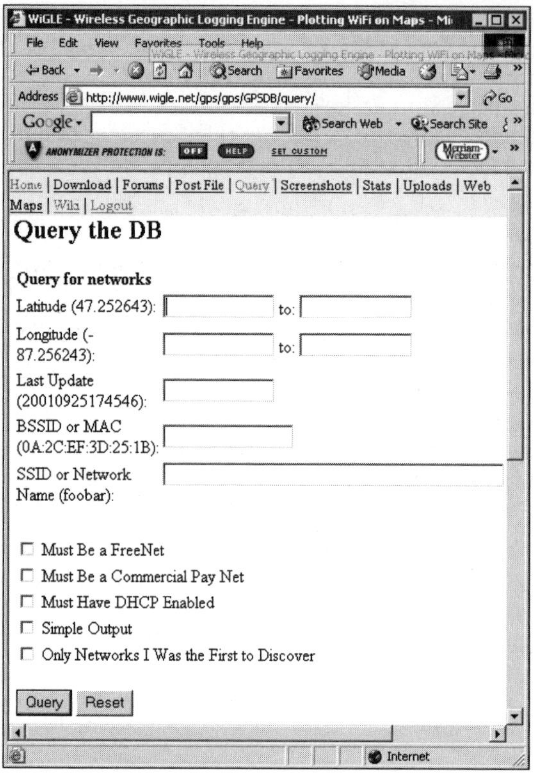

Figure 10-2: Searching for your wireless APs using the WiGLE database.

Scanning your local airwaves

Monitor the airwaves around your building to see what authorized and unauthorized APs you can find. You're looking for the SSID (service set identifier), which is your WLAN's name. If you have multiple WLANs, each one has a network SSID associated with it.

Here's where NetStumbler comes into play. NetStumbler can discover SSIDs and other detailed information about wireless APs, including the following:

- MAC address
- Name
- Radio channel in use
- Vendor name
- Whether encryption is on or off
- RF signal strength (signal-to-noise ratio)

Figure 10-3 shows an example of what you might see when running NetStumbler in your environment. The information that you see here is what others can see. NetStumbler and most other tools work by sending a probe-request signal from the client. Any APs within signal range must respond to with their SSIDs — that is, if they're configured to broadcast their SSIDs.

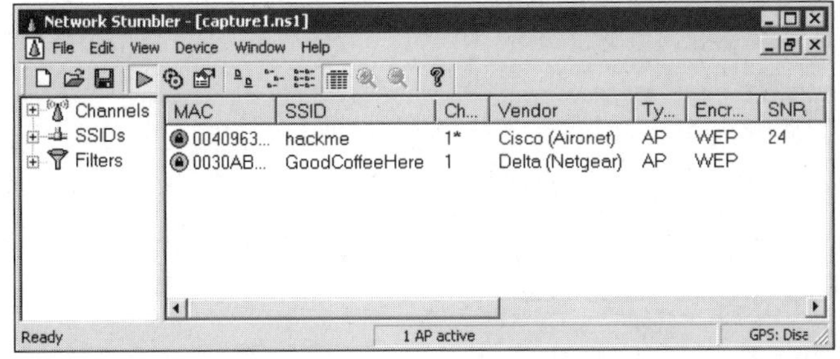

Figure 10-3: NetStumbler displays detailed data on APs.

Kismet — the popular wireless sniffer (network analyzer) for Linux and BSD UNIX — looks not only for probe responses from APs like NetStumbler does, but also for other 802.11 management packets, such as association responses and beacons. This allows Kismet to detect the presence of a WLAN even when probe-response packets are disabled in the AP — something that NetStumbler can't do.

When you're using certain wireless security assessment tools, including NetStumbler and AiroPeek, your adapter may be put in passive monitoring mode. This means you can no longer communicate with other wireless hosts or APs while the program is loaded. Also, some programs require a specialized driver for your wireless card that often disables normal WLAN functionality. If this is the case, you need to roll back (reinstall) the original adapter's driver (supplied by the vendor) to restore the standard functions of your adapter.

The best way to search for APs that are not broadcasting their SSIDs from within Windows is to use a WLAN analyzer such as AiroPeek (my favorite) — which is the sister product of the excellent wired network analyzer EtherPeek — or TamoSoft's CommView for Wi-Fi (`www.tamos.com/products/commwifi`), which I've heard great things about. You can do this by enabling a capture filter on 802.11 management packets, as shown in AiroPeek's options in Figure 10-4.

An ad-hoc mode — a peer-to-peer type setup — in WLANs can allow wireless clients to communicate directly with one another without having to pass through an AP. These types of WLANs operate outside the normal wireless security controls and, thus, can cause serious security issues above and beyond the normal 802.11 vulnerabilities. The best way to detect these rogue networks is to use NetStumbler. You can also use a WLAN analyzer or wireless IDS and search for beacon packets where the ESS field is not equal to 1.

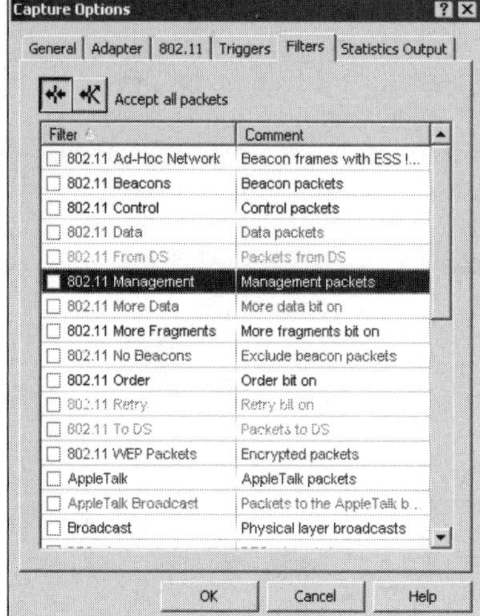

Figure 10-4: AiroPeek detects APs that don't broadcast SSIDs.

Wireless Network Attacks

Various malicious hacks — including various DoS attacks — can be carried out against your WLAN. This includes APs that are forced to reveal their SSIDs during the process of being disassociated from the network and rejoining. In addition, hackers can literally jam the RF signal of an AP — especially in 802.11b and 802.11g systems — and force the wireless clients to reassociate to a rogue AP masquerading as the victim AP. Hackers can create man-in-the-middle attacks by maliciously using tools such as ESSID-jack and monkey-jack and can flood your network with thousands of packets per second by maliciously using packet-generation tools such as Gspoof or LANforge — enough to bring the network to its knees. Even more so than with wired networks, this type of DoS attack is practically impossible to prevent on WLANs.

Various hacking tools for the UNIX platform can perform these types of hacks, including Cqure AP, HostAP, and AirJack. After hackers carry out these types of attacks against your WLAN, they can attempt to capture traffic and penetrate into any systems that attach to it.

You can carry out several — nonmalicious — attacks against your WLAN. The associated countermeasures help protect your network from these vulnerabilities, as well as from the malicious attacks previously mentioned. When testing your WLAN security, look out for the following weaknesses:

- Unencrypted wireless traffic
- Unauthorized APs

- RF signals that are too strong
- Wireless equipment that's easy to access physically
- Default configuration settings

A good starting point for testing is to attempt to attach to your WLAN as an outsider and run a vulnerability-assessment tool, such as LANguard Network Security Scanner. This test enables you to see what others can see on your network, including information on the OS version, open ports on your AP, and even network shares on wireless clients. Figure 10-5 shows the type of information that can be revealed about an AP on your network.

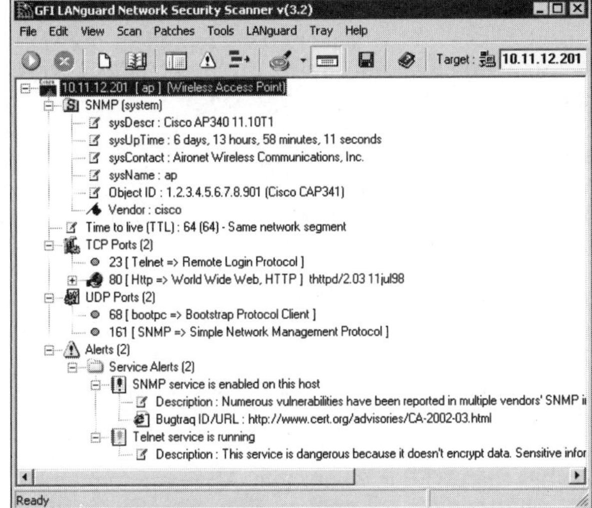

Figure 10-5: A LANguard scan of a potentially vulnerable AP.

Encrypted traffic

Wireless traffic can be captured directly out of the airwaves, making this communications medium susceptible to malicious eavesdropping. Unless the traffic is encrypted, it's sent and received in cleartext just like on a standard wired network. On top of that, the 802.11 encryption protocol, Wired Equivalent Privacy (WEP), has its own weakness that allows hackers to crack the encryption keys and decrypt the captured traffic. This vulnerability has helped put WLANs on the map — so to speak.

WEP, in a certain sense, actually lives up to its name: It provides the privacy equivalent to that of a wired network and then some. However, it was not intended to be cracked so easily. WEP uses a fairly strong symmetric (shared-key) encryption algorithm called RC4. Hackers can observe encrypted wireless traffic and recover the WEP key due to a flaw in how the RC4 initialization vector (IV) is implemented in the protocol. This weakness is due to the fact that the IV is only 24 bits long, which causes it to be repeated every 16.7 million packets — even sooner in many cases, based on the amount of wireless clients entering and leaving the network.

Most WEP implementations initialize WLAN hardware with an IV of 0 and increment it by one for each packet sent. This can lead to the IV's being reinitialized — started over at 0 — approximately every five hours. Given this, WLANs that have a small number of clients transmitting a relatively small rate of wireless packets are normally more secure than large WLANs that transmit a lot of wireless data.

Using various UNIX-based tools such as WEPCrack (`wepcrack.sourceforge.net`), AirSnort (`airsnort.shmoo.com`), and WepAttack (`wepattack.sourceforge.net`), hackers need to collect only a few hours' up to a few days' (depending on how much wireless traffic is on the network) worth of packets to be able to break the WEP key.

A longer key length, such as 128 bit or 192 bit, doesn't make WEP exponentially more difficult to crack. This is because WEP's static key scheduling algorithm requires only that about 20,000 or so additional packets be captured to crack a key for every extra bit in the key length.

Although WEP is crackable, it's still much better than no encryption at all. Similar to the effect that home-security-system signs have on would-be home intruders, a wireless LAN running WEP is not nearly as attractive to a hacker as one without it. The hacker is likely to just move on to easier targets.

You can carry out this attack against your network, but it probably won't prove anything other than WEP is vulnerable. After you implement the WEP countermeasures mentioned in the next section, you can always run some of the WEP cracking tools to ensure that the countermeasures are working.

If you need to use your WLAN analyzer to view traffic as part of your security assessment, you won't be able to see any traffic if WEP is enabled unless you know your WEP key. You can enter your key into your analyzer, but just remember that hackers can do the same thing if they're able to crack your WEP key using one of the tools I mention earlier!

Figure 10-6 shows an example of how you can view protocols on your WLAN by entering your WEP key into AiroPeek via the 802.11 tab in the Capture Options window before you start your packet capture.

Countermeasures

The simplest solution to the WEP problem is to use a VPN for all wireless communications. You can easily implement this in a Windows environment — for free — by enabling PPTP for client communications. You can also use the IPSec support built into Windows, as well as SSH, SSL/TLS, and other proprietary vendor solutions, to keep your traffic secure.

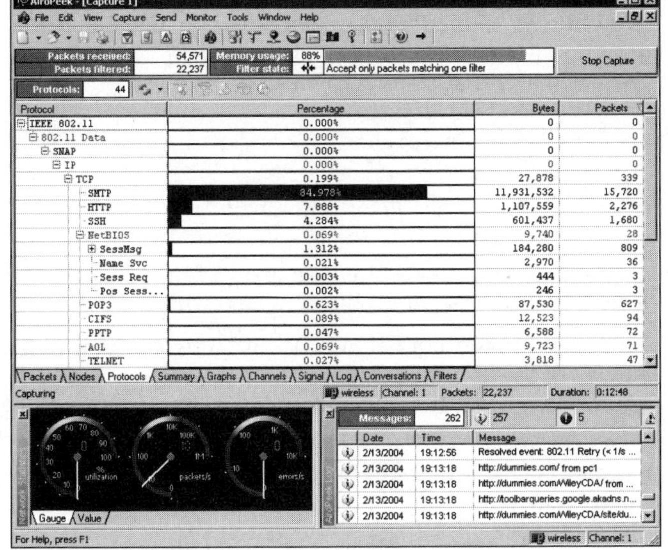

Figure 10-6: Using AiroPeek Client Manager to search for rogue APs.

Newer 802.11-based solutions exist as well. If you can configure your wireless hosts to regenerate a new key dynamically after a certain number of packets have been sent, the WEP vulnerability can't be exploited. Many AP vendors have already implemented this fix as a separate configuration option, so check for the latest firmware with features to manage key rotation. For instance, the proprietary Cisco LEAP protocol uses per-user WEP keys that offer a layer of protection if you're running Cisco hardware.

The wireless industry has come up with a solution to the WEP problem called Wi-Fi Protected Access (WPA). WPA uses the Temporal Key Integrity Protocol (TKIP) encryption system, which fixes all the known WEP issues. WPA requires an 802.1x authentication server, such as a RADIUS server, to manage user accounts for the WLAN. Check with your vendor for WPA updates.

The new 802.11i standard from the IEEE integrates the WPA fixes and more. This standard is an improvement over WPA but is not compatible with older 802.11b hardware, due to its implementation of the Advanced Encryption Standard (AES) for encryption. The workaround for this is to use TKIP, which is backward-compatible with older hardware because it uses the RC4 encryption scheme. Keep an eye out for 802.11i support for your wireless hardware.

Rogue networks

Watch out for unauthorized APs and wireless clients attached to your network that are running in ad-hoc mode.

Using NetStumbler or your client manager software, you can test for APs that don't belong on your network. You can also use the network monitoring features in a WLAN analyzer such as AiroPeek.

Look for the following rogue AP characteristics:

- Odd SSIDs, including the popular default ones *linksys, tsunami, comcomcom,* and *wireless.*
- Odd AP system names — that is, the name of the AP if your hardware supports this feature — not to be confused with the SSID.
- MAC addresses that don't belong on your network. Look at the first three bytes of the MAC address (the first six numbers), which specify the vendor name. You can perform a MAC-address vendor lookup at `coffer.com/mac_find` to find information on APs you're unsure of.
- Weak radio signals, which can indicate that an AP has been hidden away or is on the outside of your building.
- Communications across a different radio channel than what your network communicates on.
- A degradation in network throughput for any WLAN client.

Figure 10-7 shows how you can use AiroPeek's Monitor utility to spot an odd network host (the Netgear system) when you have a Cisco Aironet-only network, or vice versa.

My test network for this example is small compared to what you might see, but you get the idea of how an odd system can stand out.

Don't rely solely on this method. Hackers can spoof their MAC addresses, making them look like Cisco Aironet systems that belong on your network.

Walk around your building or campus to perform this test to see what you can find. Physically look for devices that don't belong — a well-placed AP or WLAN client that's turned off won't show up in your network analysis tools. Search near the outskirts of the building or near any publicly accessible areas. Scope out boardrooms and the offices of upper-level managers for any unauthorized devices. These are places that are typically off-limits but often are used as locations for hackers to set up rogue APs.

Node	Channel	Encryption	Cur. Signal	Max. Signal	Bytes Sent	Bytes Received	Retry Packets	Packets Sent	Packets Received
hackme					0	0		0	0
Aironet:31:0...	1		16	34	1,580,544	39,837,935	444	17,235	44,187
Netgear:A0...	1		50	52	39,628,971	1,767,602	1,317	29,261	43,599
ESSID Unknown					0	0		0	0
BSSID Unknown					0	0		0	0
Ethernet B...	1				0	212,612		0	2,235
01:40:96:F...	1				0	86		0	1
01:40:96:0...	1				0	840		0	14

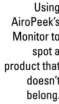

Figure 10-7: Using AiroPeek's Monitor to spot a product that doesn't belong.

WLANs authenticate the wireless devices, not the users. Hackers can use this to their advantage by gaining access to a wireless client via remote-access software such as telnet or SSH or by exploiting a known application or OS vulnerability. After they're able to do that, they potentially have full access to your network.

Countermeasures

The only way to detect rogue APs and hosts on your network is to monitor your WLAN proactively, looking for indicators that wireless clients or rogue APs might exist. But if rogue APs or clients don't show up in NetStumbler or in your client manager software, that doesn't mean you're off the hook. You may also need to break out the WLAN analyzer, wireless IDS, or other network management application.

You can enable MAC-address filtering controls on your AP so that wireless clients must have an authorized MAC address before being allowed to connect. The problem with this countermeasure is that hackers can easily spoof MAC addresses in UNIX by using the `ifconfig` command and in Windows with the SMAC utility, as I describe in Chapter 9. However like WEP, MAC-address-based access controls are another layer of protection and better than nothing at all. If a hacker spoofs one of your MAC addresses, the only way to detect malicious behavior is to spot the same MAC address being used in two or more places on the WLAN.

You may be able to make a couple of configuration changes — depending on your AP — to keep hackers from carrying out these tests against you:

- If possible, increase your wireless beacon broadcast interval to the maximum setting, which is around 65,535 milliseconds (roughly 66 seconds). This can help hide the AP from hackers who are wardriving or walking by your building quickly.

- Disable probe responses to prevent your AP from responding to NetStumbler requests.

Use personal firewall software such as BlackICE — my favorite — (`blackice.iss.net`) or ZoneAlarm (`www.zonelabs.com`) on all client computers to prevent unauthorized remote access to your network.

Physical-security problems

Various physical-security vulnerabilities can result in physical theft, the reconfiguration of wireless devices, and the capturing of confidential information. You should look for the following security vulnerabilities when testing your systems:

- APs mounted on the outside of a building and accessible to the public.
- Poorly mounted antennas — or the wrong types of antennas — that broadcast too strong a signal and that are accessible to the public. You can view the signal strength in NetStumbler or your wireless client manager.

These issues are often overlooked due to rushed installations, improper planning, and lack of technical knowledge, but they can come back to haunt you later.

Countermeasures

Secure APs, antennas, and other equipment in secure closets, ceilings, or other places that are difficult for a would-be intruder to access physically. Terminate your APs outside any firewall or other network perimeter security devices — or at least in a DMZ — whenever possible. If you place the wireless equipment inside your secure network, it can negate any benefits you would get out of your perimeter security devices.

If wireless signals are propagating outside your building where they don't belong, either

- Turn down the transmit power setting of your AP.
- Use a smaller or different antenna (semidirectional or directional) to decrease the signal.

Some basic planning helps prevent these vulnerabilities.

Vulnerable wireless workstations

Wireless workstations have tons of security vulnerabilities — from weak passwords to unpatched security holes to the storage of WEP keys locally. One serious vulnerability is for wireless clients using the Orinoco wireless card. The Orinoco Client Manager software stores encrypted WEP keys in the Windows Registry — even for multiple networks — as shown in Figure 10-8.

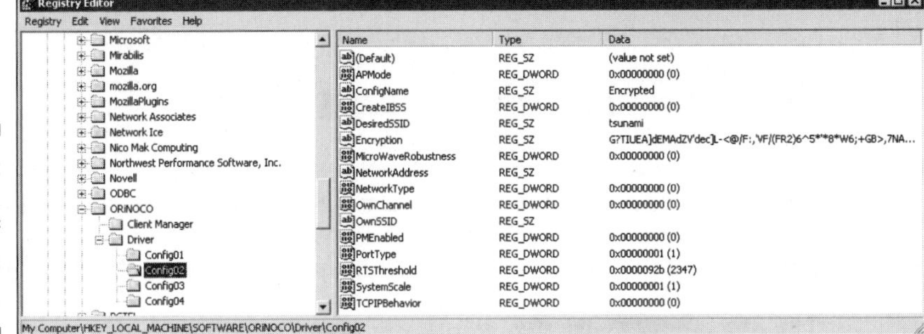

Figure 10-8: Encrypted WEP key of a wireless card.

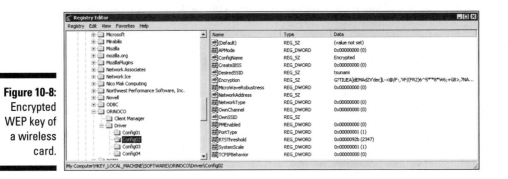

You can crack the key by using the Lucent Orinoco Registry Encryption/Decryption program found at `www.cqure.net/tools.jsp?id=3`. Make sure that you use the `-d` command-line switch and put quotes around the encrypted key, as shown in Figure 10-9. This program comes in handy if you forget what your key is, but it can be used against you as well.

```
DOS Prompt
C:\wireless>lrc -d "G?TIUEA]dEMAdZU'dec]L-<@/F:,'UF/<FR2>6^5*'*8*W6;+GB>,7NA-'ZD
-X&G.H2J/8>M0<JP0XUS1HbU29.Y3>:\3YF_4IRb56"
Lucent Orinoco Registry Encryption/Decryption
Version 0.3
Anders Ingeborn, iXsecurity 2001 <ingeborn@ixsecurity.com>
Hex mode by Don French, 2002 <french_don@yahoo.com>
Input value = G?TIUEA]dEMAdZU'dec]L-<@/F:,'UF/<FR2>6^5*'*8*W6;+GB>,7NA-'ZD-X&G.H
2J/8>M0<JP0XUS1HbU29.Y3>:\3YF_4IRb56
Decrypted key is: wÖwÖ" (or 7799779922 in hex)

C:\wireless>_
```

Figure 10-9: Cracking a WEP key with Lucent Orinoco.

If hackers remotely access a workstation via the Connect Network Registry in regedit, they can obtain these keys, crack them, and be on your network in a jiffy.

Countermeasures

You can implement the following countermeasures on your workstations to keep them from used as entry points into your WLAN.

- Regularly perform vulnerability assessments on your wireless workstations, as well as your other network hosts.
- Apply the latest vendor security patches and enforce strong user passwords.
- Use personal firewalls on these systems to keep malicious intruders off of those systems and out of your network.
- Install antivirus software.
- Consider installing an antispyware application such as PestPatrol.

Default configuration settings

Similar to wireless workstations, wireless APs have many known vulnerabilities. The most common ones are default SSIDs and admin passwords. The more specific ones occur only on certain hardware and software versions that are posted in vulnerability databases and vendor Web sites.

The one vulnerability that stands out above all others is that certain APs, including Linksys, D-Link, and more, are susceptible to a vulnerability that exposes any WEP key(s), MAC-address filters, and even the admin password! All that hackers have to do to exploit this is to send a broadcast packet on UDP port 27155 with a string of `gstsearch`.

To test for this vulnerability, you can use a program called pong. This program sends the broadcast packet automatically and returns any information it discovers. To run pong, follow these steps:

1. **Download the program from** `www.mobileaccess.de/wlan/dl.php/pong_v1.1.zip`**.**
2. **Unzip the program to** `c:\wireless` **(or a similar directory).**
3. **Drop out to a DOS prompt, and enter** pong.

If pong returns *no answer,* as shown in Figure 10-10, you're safe. Otherwise, look out!

DOS Prompt
C:\wireless\pong>pong -r
WLAN exploit program V1.1
Binary gently provided by http://mobileaccess.de/
no answer
C:\wireless\pong>

Figure 10-10: The results you *should* get from pong.

Countermeasures

You can implement some of the simplest and effective security countermeasures for WLANs — and they're all free:

- Make sure that you change default admin passwords, AP names, and SSIDs.
- Disable SSID broadcasting if you don't need this feature. Figure 10-11 shows the SSID setting for a Cisco Aironet AP.
- Disable SNMP if you're not using it.
- Apply the latest firmware patches for your APs and WLAN cards. This countermeasure helps to prevent various vulnerabilities, including the UDP broadcast exploit. If you find that it doesn't, consider using another vendor's wireless products.

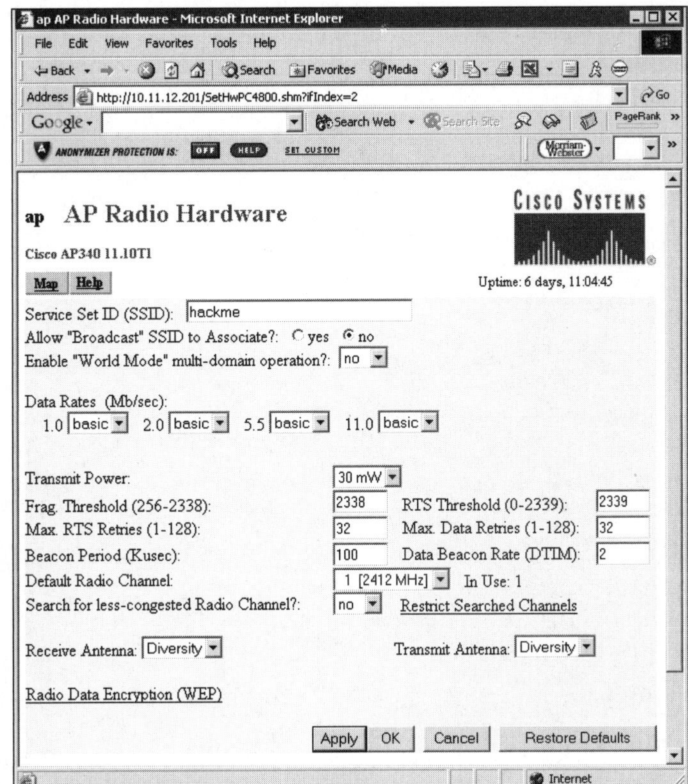

Figure 10-11: Cisco Aironet setting to disable SSID broadcasts.

Part IV
Operating System Hacking

"We take network security very seriously here."

In this part . . .

Now that you're past the network level, it's time to get down to the nitty-gritty — those fun operating systems you use on a daily basis and have come to both love and hate. There's definitely not enough room in this book to cover every operating system version or even every operating system vulnerability, but I certainly hit the important parts — especially the ones that aren't easily fixed with patches.

This part starts out by looking at the most widely used (and picked on) operating system — Microsoft Windows. From Windows NT to Windows Server 2003, I show you some of the best ways to attack and secure these operating systems from the bad guys. This part then takes a look at Linux and its less publicized yet still major security flaws. Many of the hacks and countermeasures I cover can apply to many other flavors of UNIX as well. This part then moves on to the tried-and-true Novell NetWare operating system — perhaps the most secure in this lineup but still not vulnerability-free as many Novell die-hards like to believe. I cover the major issues along with solid countermeasures you can implement to keep your mighty Novell boxes secure and still mostly reboot-free.

Chapter 11

Windows

In This Chapter

- Port scanning a Windows server
- Gleaning Windows information without logging in
- Exploiting common vulnerabilities when logged into Windows
- Minimizing Windows security risks

The Microsoft Windows OS family (with such versions as NT, 2000, XP, and Server 2003) is the most widely used OS in the world. It's also the most widely hacked. Is this because Microsoft doesn't care as much about security as other OS vendors? The short answer is *no.* Sure, numerous security flaws were overlooked — especially in the Windows NT days — but because Microsoft products are so pervasive throughout networks, Microsoft is the easiest vendor to pick on, and often it's Microsoft products that end up in the crosshairs of hackers. This is the same reason that you see so many vulnerability alerts on Microsoft products. The one positive about hackers is that they're driving the requirement for better security!

Many security flaws in the headlines aren't new. They're variants of vulnerabilities that have been around for a long time in UNIX and Linux, such as the RPC vulnerabilities that the Blaster worm used. You've heard the saying "the more things change, the more they stay the same." That applies here, too. Most Windows attacks are prevented if the patches were properly applied. Thus, poor security management is often the real reason Windows attacks are successful, yet Microsoft takes the blame and must carry the burden.

In addition to the password attacks I cover in Chapter 7 and some of the malware attacks I cover in Chapter 14, many other attacks are possible against a Windows-based system. Tons of information can be gleaned from Windows by simply connecting to the system across a network and using tools to pull the information out. Many of these tests don't even require you to be authenticated to the remote system. All hackers need is a Windows computer with a default configuration that's not protected by such measures as a firewall.

When you start poking around on your network, you may be surprised at how many of your Windows-based computers have security vulnerabilities. After you connect to a Windows system and have a valid user name and password (by either knowing it or deriving it from using the password cracking techniques in Chapter 7), you can test other aspects of Windows security.

This chapter shows you how to test for some of the most critical attacks against the Windows OS family and outlines countermeasures to make sure your systems are secure.

Windows Vulnerabilities

Given the general ease of use of Windows, its enterprise-ready Active Directory service, and the feature-rich .NET development platform, many organizations have moved to the Microsoft platform for their networking needs. Many businesses — especially the small to medium-sized ones — depend solely on the Windows OS for network usage. Many large organizations run critical servers such as Web servers and database servers on the Windows platform. If security vulnerabilities aren't addressed and managed properly, they can bring a network or an entire organization to its knees.

When Windows and other Microsoft software are attacked — especially by a widespread Internet-based worm or virus — hundreds of thousands of organizations and millions of computers are affected. Many well-known attacks against Windows can lead to

- Leakage of confidential information, including files being copied and credit card numbers being stolen
- Passwords being cracked and used to carry out other attacks
- Systems taken completely offline by DoS attacks
- Entire databases being corrupted or deleted

When insecure Windows-based systems are attacked, serious things can happen to a tremendous amount of computers around the world.

Choosing Tools

Thousands of Windows hacking and testing tools are available. The key is to find a set of tools that can do what you need and that you're comfortable using.

Many security tools — including some of the tools in this chapter — aren't designed for Windows Server 2003 and newer operating systems but work with them. However, the program documentation sometimes isn't updated to reflect its compatibility. The most recent version of each tool in this chapter is compatible with Windows NT, 2000, and Server 2003.

The more security tools and other power user applications you install in Windows — especially programs that tie into the network drivers and TCP/IP stack — the more unstable Windows becomes. I'm talking about slow performance, blue screens of death, and general instability issues. Unfortunately, often the only fix is to reinstall Windows and all your applications. I've had to rebuild my system once during the writing of this book and a total of three times in the past year. Ah, the memories of those DOS and Windows 3.*x* days when things were much simpler!

Essential tools

Every Windows security tester needs these special tools:

- Nmap (`www.insecure.org`) for UDP and other types of port scanning

  Nmap is an excellent tool for OS fingerprinting.

- Vision (`www.foundstone.com`) for mapping applications to TCP/UDP ports

Free Microsoft tools

You can use the following Windows programs and free security tools that Microsoft provides to test your systems for various security weaknesses.

- Built-in Windows programs (Windows *9x* and later versions) for NetBIOS and TCP/UDP service enumeration:
  - nbtstat for gathering NetBIOS name table information
  - netstat for displaying open ports on the local Windows system
  - net for running various network based commands including viewing of shares on remote Windows systems
- Microsoft Baseline Security Analyzer `www.microsoft.com/technet/security/tools/mbsahome.asp` for testing for missing patches and basic Windows security settings.

- Windows Resource Kits (including some tools that are free for download at www.microsoft.com) for security and OS management.

  You can get specific details about Resource Kit books published by Microsoft Press at www.microsoft.com/learning.

All-in-one assessment tools

The following tools perform a wide variety of security tests including

- Port scanning
- OS fingerprinting
- Basic password cracking
- Detailed vulnerability mappings of the various security weaknesses the tools find on your Windows systems

I recommend any of these comprehensive sets of tools:

- LANguard Network Security Scanner (www.gfi.com)
- QualysGuard (www.qualys.com)

  QualysGuard has very detailed and accurate vulnerability testing.
- Nessus (www.nessus.org)

Task-specific tools

The following tools perform one or two specific tasks. These tools provide detailed security assessments of your Windows systems and insight that you may not otherwise get from all-in-one assessment tools:

- SuperScan (www.foundstone.com) for TCP port scanning and ping sweeps.
- A tool for enumerating Windows security settings. Given the enhanced security of Windows Server 2003, these tools can't connect and enumerate a default install of Windows Server 2003 system like a Windows 2000 or NT system — but you can use these tools nonetheless. It's a good idea to test for vulnerable "non-default" configurations in case the secure default settings have been changed.

  To gather such information as security policies, local user accounts, and shares, your decision may be based on your preferred interface:

- Winfo (`www.ntsecurity.nu/toolbox/winfo`) runs from the Windows command line.
- DumpSec (`www.somarsoft.com`) runs from a graphical Windows interface.
- Walksam (`razor.bindview.com/tools/files/rpctools-1.0.zip`) runs from the Windows command line.

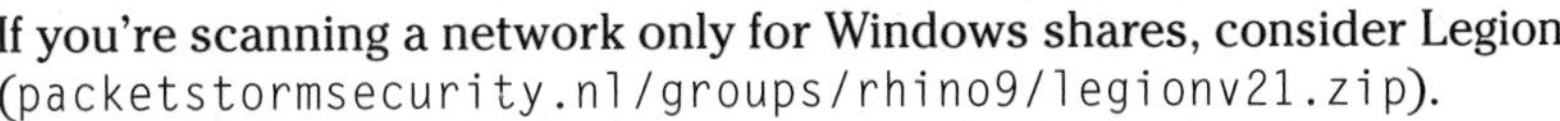

If you're scanning a network only for Windows shares, consider Legion (`packetstormsecurity.nl/groups/rhino9/legionv21.zip`).

- Rpcdump (`razor.bindview.com/tools/files/rpctools-1.0.zip`) for enumerating RPC ports to search for running applications.
- Network Users (`www.optimumx.com/download/netusers.zip`) for gathering Windows login information.

Information Gathering

When you assess Windows vulnerabilities, start by scanning your computers to see what the bad guys can see.

The hacks in this chapter are against the versions of the Windows Server OS (NT, 2000, and Server 2003) from inside a firewall. Unless I point out otherwise, all the tests in this chapter can be run against all versions of the Windows server OS. The attacks in this chapter are significant enough to warrant testing for regardless of your current setup. Your results may vary from mine depending on these factors:

- OS versions
- Security measures, such as patch levels and access controls (such as firewall policies and local Windows security policies)

System scanning

A few straightforward processes can identify weaknesses. Other steps can minimize your vulnerability.

Testing

Start gathering information about your Windows systems by running an initial port scan:

1. **Run basic scans to find which ports are open on each Windows system:**
   - Scan for TCP ports with a port scanning tool, such as SuperScan or Nmap.
   - Scan for UDP ports with a port scanning tool, such as Nmap.
2. **Perform OS enumeration (such as scanning for shares and specific OS versions) by using an all-in-one assessment tool, such as LANguard Network Security Scanner.**
3. **Scan your Windows systems for open ports that could point to potential security vulnerabilities.**

   The tool you use depends on whether you need a basic summary of vulnerable ports or a comprehensive system report:

   - If you need a basic summary of open ports, scan your Windows systems with SuperScan.

     The SuperScan results in Figure 11-1 show several potentially vulnerable ports open on a Windows Server 2003 system, including those for SMTP (port 25), a Web server (port 80), RPC (port 135), and the ever popular — and easily hacked — NetBIOS (ports 139 and 445).

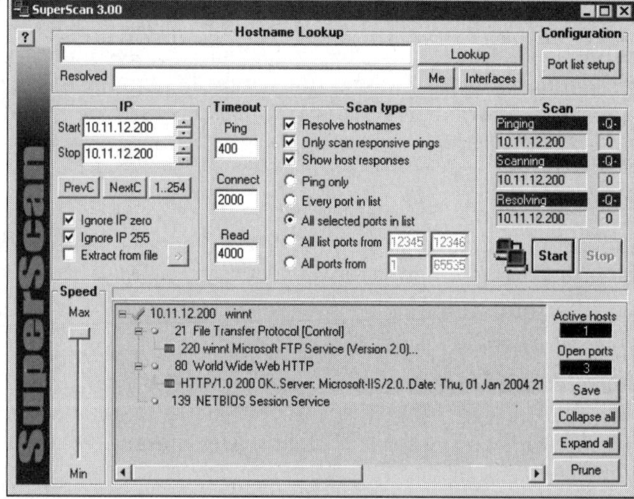

Figure 11-1: Scanning a Windows Server 2003 system with SuperScan.

   - If you need a comprehensive system report, scan your Windows systems with LANguard Network Security Scanner.

     In Figure 11-2, LANguard shows the server version (identified as Windows XP initially and then later as Windows 2003), the system's current date and time setting and system uptime, and the server's domain (PL).

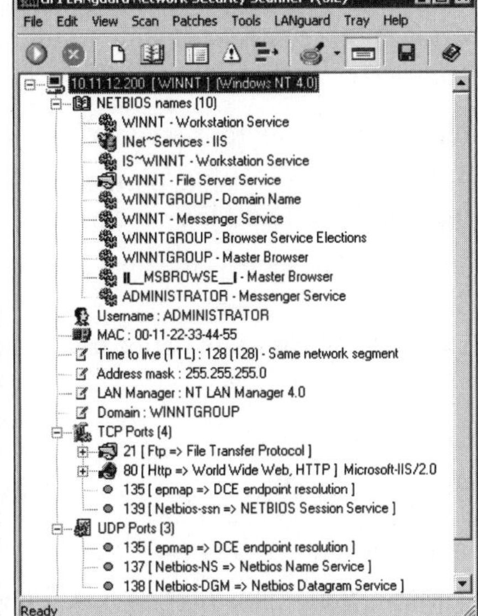

Figure 11-2: Gathering system details with LANguard Network Security Scanner.

4. **You can run Nmap with the** `-O` **option to confirm the OS characteristics — the version information referred to as the *OS fingerprint* — that you found with your scanning tool, as shown in Figure 11-3.**

A hacker can use this information to determine potential vulnerabilities for your system. Make sure you've applied the latest patches and system hardening best practices.

In Figure 11-3, Nmap reports the OS version as Windows .NET Enterprise Server — the original name of Windows Server 2003.

```
C:\nmap>nmap 10.11.12.199 -O

Starting nmap 3.48 ( http://www.insecure.org/nmap ) at 2004-01-01 15:11 Eastern
Standard Time
Interesting ports on win2k3 (10.11.12.199):
(The 1652 ports scanned but not shown below are in state: closed)
PORT     STATE SERVICE
135/tcp  open  msrpc
139/tcp  open  netbios-ssn
445/tcp  open  microsoft-ds
1025/tcp open  NFS-or-IIS
1026/tcp open  LSA-or-nterm
Device type: general purpose
Running: Microsoft Windows 2003/.NET
OS details: Microsoft Windows .NET Enterprise Server (build 3604-3790)

Nmap run completed -- 1 IP address (1 host up) scanned in 9.223 seconds

C:\nmap>_
```

Figure 11-3: Using Nmap to determine the Windows version.

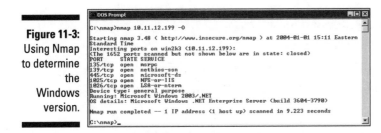

Countermeasures

You can prevent a hacker from gathering certain information about your Windows systems by implementing the proper security settings on your network and on the Windows hosts themselves.

Information

If you don't want anyone gathering information about your Windows systems, you have two options:

- Protect Windows with either of these countermeasures:
  - A firewall that blocks the Windows-specific ports for RPC (port 135) and NetBIOS (ports 137–139 and 445)
  - An intrusion prevention system, such as the host-based BlackICE software
- Disable unnecessary services so that they don't appear when a connection is made

Fingerprinting

You can prevent OS fingerprinting tests by either

- Using a host-based intrusion prevention system
- Denying all inbound traffic with a firewall — this just may not be practical for your needs

NetBIOS

You can gather Windows information by poking around with NetBIOS (Network Basic Input/Output System) functions and programs. NetBIOS allows applications to make networking calls and communicate with other hosts within a LAN.

These Windows NetBIOS ports can be compromised if they're not properly secured:

- **UDP ports for network browsing:**
  - Port 137 (NetBIOS name services)
  - Port 138 (NetBIOS datagram services)
- **TCP ports for Server Message Block (SMB):**
  - Port 139 (NetBIOS session services)
  - Port 445 (runs SMB over TCP/IP without NetBIOS)

Windows NT doesn't support port 445.

Hacks

The following hacks can be carried out on unprotected systems running NetBIOS.

Unauthenticated enumeration

When you're performing your unauthenticated tests, you can gather configuration information about the local or remote systems with either

- All-in-one assessment tools, such as LANguard Network Security Scanner.
- The *nbtstat* program that's built into Windows (nbtstat stands for NetBIOS over TCP/IP Statistics). Figure 11-4 shows information that you can gather from a Windows Server 2003 system with a simple nbtstat query.

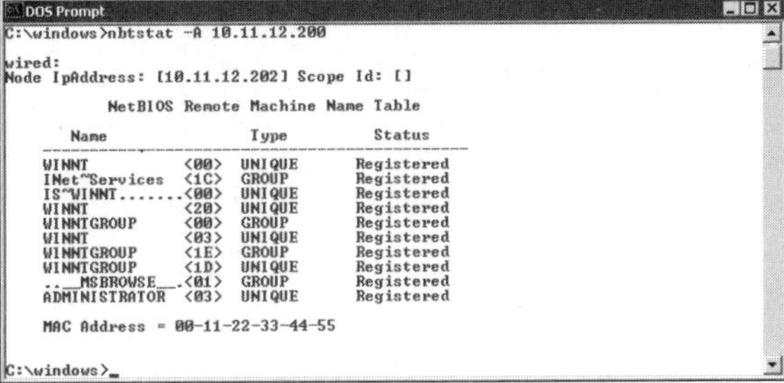
DOS Prompt
C:\windows>nbtstat -A 10.11.12.200
wired:
Node IpAddress: [10.11.12.202] Scope Id: []
NetBIOS Remote Machine Name Table
Name Type Status
WINNT <00> UNIQUE Registered
INet~Services <1C> GROUP Registered
IS~WINNT.......<00> UNIQUE Registered
WINNT <20> UNIQUE Registered
WINNTGROUP <00> GROUP Registered
WINNT <03> UNIQUE Registered
WINNTGROUP <1E> GROUP Registered
WINNTGROUP <1D> UNIQUE Registered
..__MSBROWSE__.<01> GROUP Registered
ADMINISTRATOR <03> UNIQUE Registered
MAC Address = 00-11-22-33-44-55
C:\windows>_

Figure 11-4: Using nbtstat to gather critical Windows information.

nbtstat shows the remote computer's NetBIOS name table, which you gather by using the `nbtstat -A` command. This displays the following information:

- Computer name
- Domain name
- Computer's MAC address

You may even be able to glean the ID of the currently logged user from a Windows NT or Windows 2000 server.

TIP

A GUI utility such as LANguard Network Security Scanner isn't necessary to gather this basic information from a Windows system. The graphical interface offered by commercial software such as this just presents its findings in a prettier fashion!

Shares

Windows uses network shares to *share* out certain folders or drives on the system so other users can access them across the network. Shares are easy to set up and work very well. However, they're often misconfigured, allowing hackers and other unauthorized users to access information they shouldn't be able to get to. You can search for Windows network shares by using the Legion tool. This tool scans an entire range of IP addresses looking for Windows shares. It uses the SMB protocol (TCP port 139) to discover these shares and displays them in a nice graphical fashion sorted by IP address, as shown in Figure 11-5.

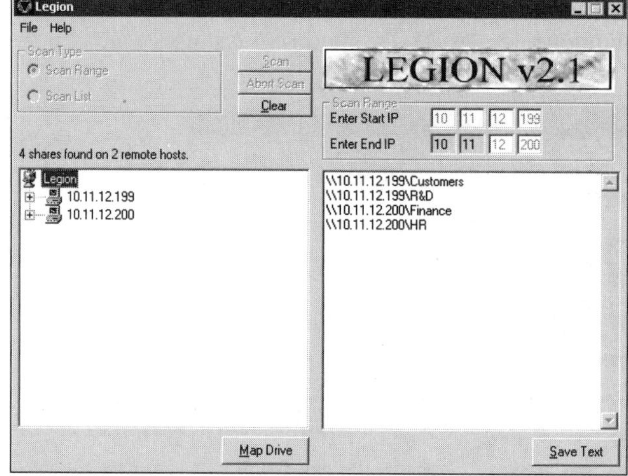

Figure 11-5: Using Legion to scan your network for Windows shares.

The shares displayed in Figure 11-5 are just what hackers are looking for — especially because the share names give hackers a hint at what type of files might be available if they connect to the shares. After hackers discover these shares, they're likely to dig a little further to see if they can browse the files and more within the shares. I cover shares in more detail in the "Share Permissions" section, later in this chapter.

Countermeasures

You can implement the following security countermeasures to minimize NetBIOS attacks on your Windows systems.

Limit traffic

You can protect your Windows systems from NetBIOS attacks by using some basic network infrastructure protection systems as well as some general Windows security best practices:

- If possible, the best way to protect Windows-based systems from NetBIOS attacks is to put them behind a firewall.

  A firewall isn't always effective. If the attack comes from inside the network, a network-perimeter-based firewall won't help.

- If a perimeter-based firewall won't suffice, you can protect your Windows hosts by either
  - Installing a personal firewall such as BlackICE

    This is the simplest and most secure method of protecting a Windows system from NetBIOS attacks.
  - Disabling NetBIOS on your systems.

  This often requires disabling Windows file and printer sharing — which may not be practical in a network mixed with Windows 2000, NT, and even Windows 9*x* systems that rely on NetBIOS for file and printer sharing.

Hidden shares — those with a dollar sign ($) appended to the end of the share name — don't really help hide the share name. Hackers found out long ago that they can easily get around this form of security by obscurity by using the right methods and tools.

Passwords

If NetBIOS network shares are necessary, make strong passwords mandatory.

With the proper tools, hackers can easily crack NetBIOS passwords across the network. NetBIOS passwords aren't case sensitive, so they can be cracked more easily than case sensitive passwords that require both capital and small letters. Chapter 7 explains password security in detail.

RPC

Windows uses remote procedure call (RPC) and DCE internal protocols to

- Communicate with applications and other OSs.
- Execute code remotely over a network.

RPC in Windows uses TCP port 135.

RPC exploits can be carried out against a Windows host — perhaps the best-known being the Blaster worm that reared its ugly head after a flaw was found in the Windows RPC implementation.

Enumeration

Hackers use RPC enumeration programs to see what's running on the host. With that information, hackers can then penetrate the system further.

Rpcdump is my favorite tool for enumerating RPC on Windows systems. Figure 11-6 shows the abbreviated output of Rpcdump run against a Windows 2000 server. Rpcdump found the RPC listeners for MS SQL Server and even a DHCP server running on this host — and this is a hardened Windows 2000 server with all the latest patches running BlackICE intrusion prevention software!

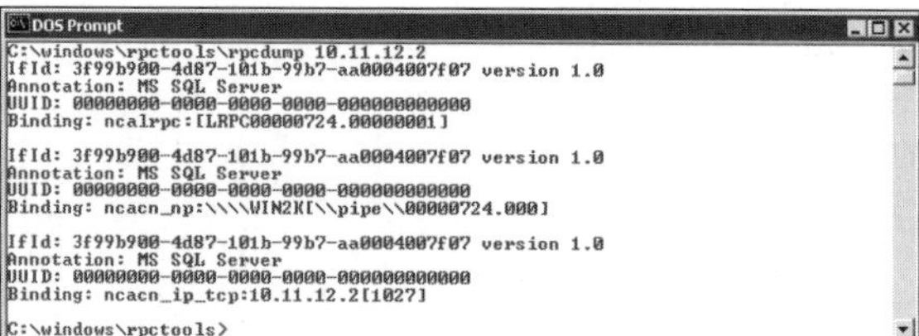

DOS Prompt
C:\windows\rpctools\rpcdump 10.11.12.2
IfId: 3f99b900-4d87-101b-99b7-aa0004007f07 version 1.0
Annotation: MS SQL Server
UUID: 00000000-0000-0000-0000-000000000000
Binding: ncalrpc:[LRPC00000724.00000001]
IfId: 3f99b900-4d87-101b-99b7-aa0004007f07 version 1.0
Annotation: MS SQL Server
UUID: 00000000-0000-0000-0000-000000000000
Binding: ncacn_np:\\\\WIN2K[\\pipe\\00000724.000]
IfId: 3f99b900-4d87-101b-99b7-aa0004007f07 version 1.0
Annotation: MS SQL Server
UUID: 00000000-0000-0000-0000-000000000000
Binding: ncacn_ip_tcp:10.11.12.2[1027]
C:\windows\rpctools>

Figure 11-6: Rpcdump shows RPC-based services.

Countermeasures

The appropriate step to prevent RPC enumeration depends on whether your system has network-based applications, such as Microsoft SQL and Microsoft Outlook:

- Without network-based applications, the best countermeasure is a firewall that blocks access to RPC services (TCP port 135).

  This firewall may disable network-based applications.
- If you have network-based applications, one of these options can reduce the risk of RPC enumeration:
  - If highly critical systems such as Web or database servers need access only from trusted systems, give only trusted systems access to TCP port 135.
  - If your critical systems must be made accessible to the public, make sure your RPC-based applications are patched and configured to run as securely as possible.

Don't try to disable the RPC server within Windows with such "fixes" as Registry hacks. You may end up with a Windows server or applications that stop working on the network, forcing you to reinstall and reconfigure the system.

Null Sessions

A well-known vulnerability within Windows can map an anonymous connection *(null session)* to a hidden share called IPC$ (interprocess communication). This attack method can be used to

- Gather Windows host configuration information, such as user IDs and share names.
- Edit parts of the remote computer's Registry.

Hacks

Although Windows Server 2003 doesn't allow null session connections by default, Windows 2000 Server and NT Server do — and plenty of those systems are still around to cause problems on most networks.

Windows Server 2003 and Windows XP at the desktop are much more secure out of the box than their predecessors. Keep this in mind when it comes time to upgrade your systems.

Mapping

To map a null session, follow these steps for each Windows computer to which you want to map a null session:

1. **Format the basic net command, like this:**

```
net use \\host_name_or_IP_address\ipc$ "" "/user:"
```

   The `net` command to map null sessions requires these parameters:

   - `net` (the built-in Windows *network* command) followed by the `use` command
   - IP address of the system to which you want to map a null connection
   - A blank password and username

     The blanks are why it's called a *null* connection.

2. **Press Enter to make the connection.**

   Figure 11-7 shows an example of the complete command when mapping a null session. After you map the null session, you should see the message `The command completed successfully.`

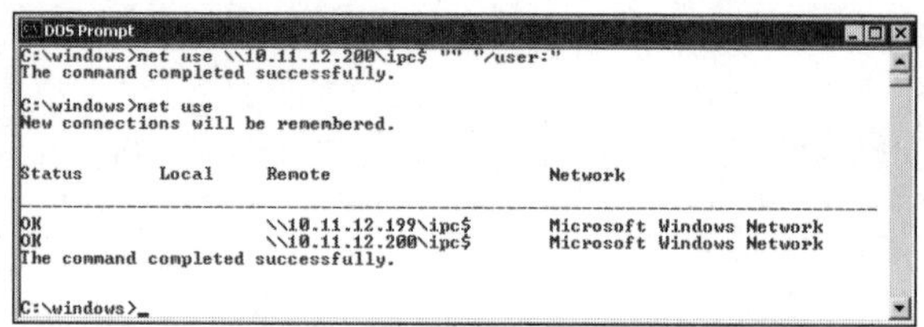

DOS Prompt
C:\windows>net use \\10.11.12.200\ipc$ "" "/user:"
The command completed successfully.
C:\windows>net use
New connections will be remembered.
Status Local Remote Network
OK \\10.11.12.199\ipc$ Microsoft Windows Network
OK \\10.11.12.200\ipc$ Microsoft Windows Network
The command completed successfully.
C:\windows>_

Figure 11-7: Mapping a null session to a Windows 2000 server.

To confirm that the sessions are mapped, enter this command at the command prompt:

```
net use
```

As shown in Figure 11-7, you should see the mappings to the IPC$ share on each computer to which you're connected.

Gleaning information

With a null session connection, you can use other utilities to remotely gather critical Windows information. Dozens of tools can gather this type of information.

You — like a hacker — can take the output of these enumeration programs and attempt (as an unauthorized user) to try such gleaning of information as

- Cracking the passwords of the users found. (See Chapter 7 for more on password cracking.)
- Mapping drives to the network shares.

You can use the following applications for system enumeration against server versions of Windows prior to Server 2003.

Windows Server 2003 is much more secure than its predecessors against such system enumeration vulnerabilities as null session attacks. If the server is in its default configuration, it should be secure; however, you should perform these tests against your Windows Server 2003 systems to be sure.

net view

The `net view` command shows shares that the Windows host has available. You can use the output of this program to see information that the server is advertising to the world and what can be done with it, such as:

- Share information that a hacker can use to attack your systems, such as mapping drives and cracking share passwords.
- Share permissions that may need to be removed, such as the permission for the Everyone group to at least see the share on Windows NT and 2000 systems.

To run net view, enter the following at a command prompt:

```
net view
```

Figure 11-8 shows an example.

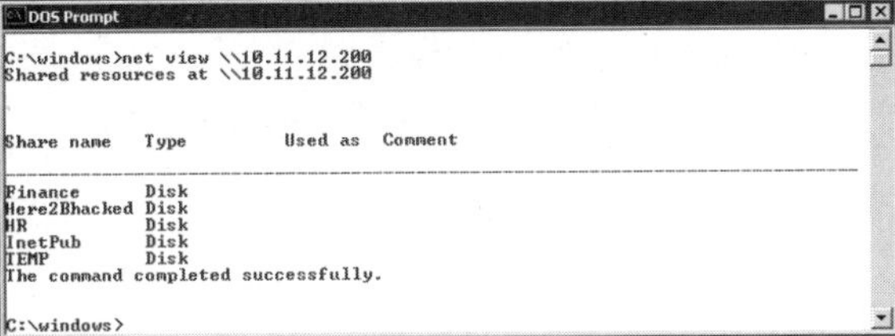

DOS Prompt
C:\windows>net view \\10.11.12.200
Shared resources at \\10.11.12.200
Share name Type Used as Comment
Finance Disk
Here2Bhacked Disk
HR Disk
InetPub Disk
TEMP Disk
The command completed successfully.
C:\windows>

Figure 11-8: `net view` displays drive shares on a remote Windows host.

Configuration and user information

Winfo and DumpSec can gather useful information about users and configuration, such as

- Windows domain to which the system belongs
- Security policy settings
- Local usernames
- Drive shares

Your preference may depend on whether you like graphical interfaces or a command line:

- Winfo (`www.ntsecurity.nu/toolbox/winfo`) is a command-line tool.

  Because Winfo is a command-line tool, you can create batch (script) files that automate the enumeration process. The following is an abbreviated version of Winfo's output of a Windows NT server, but you can glean the same information from a Windows 2000 server:

```
Winfo 2.0 - copyright (c) 1999-2003, Arne Vidstrom
          - http://www.ntsecurity.nu/toolbox/winfo/
SYSTEM INFORMATION:
```

```
 - OS version: 4.0
PASSWORD POLICY:
 - Time between end of logon time and forced logoff: No forced logoff
 - Maximum password age: 42 days
 - Minimum password age: 0 days
 - Password history length: 0 passwords
 - Minimum password length: 0 characters
USER ACCOUNTS:
 * Administrator
   (This account is the built-in administrator account)
 * doctorx
 * Guest
   (This account is the built-in guest account)
 * IUSR_WINNT
 * kbeaver
 * nikki
SHARES:
 * ADMIN$
     - Type: Special share reserved for IPC or administrative share
 * IPC$
     - Type: Unknown
 * Here2Bhacked
     - Type: Disk drive
 * C$
     - Type: Special share reserved for IPC or administrative share
 * Finance
     - Type: Disk drive
 * HR
     - Type: Disk drive
```

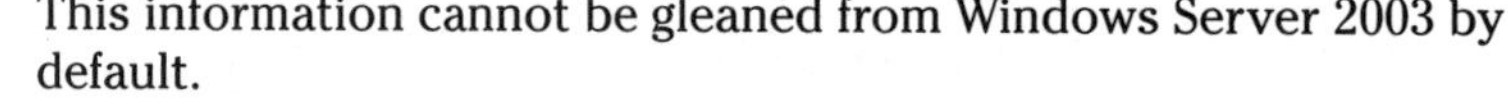

This information cannot be gleaned from Windows Server 2003 by default.

- DumpSec produces Windows configuration and user information in a graphical interface. Figure 11-9 shows the local user accounts on a remote system.

DumpSec can save reports as *delimited files* that can be imported into another application (such as a spreadsheet) when you create your final reports. You can peruse the information for user IDs that don't belong on your system, such as

  • Ex-employee accounts
  • Potential backdoor accounts that a hacker may have created

If hackers get this information, they can attempt to exploit potential weak passwords and log in as those users.

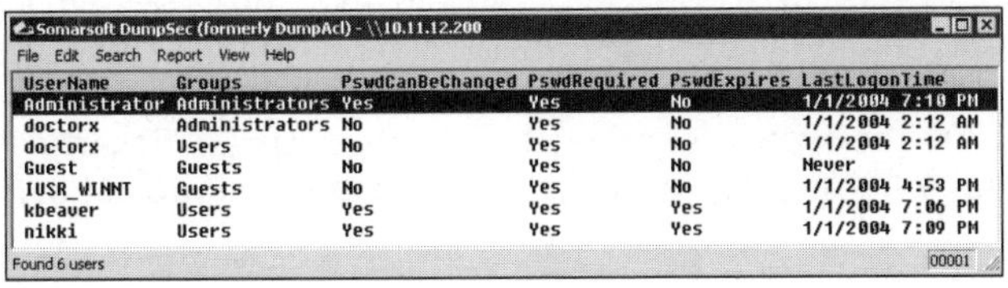

Somarsoft DumpSec (formerly DumpAcl) - \\10.11.12.200

File Edit Search Report View Help

UserName	Groups	PswdCanBeChanged	PswdRequired	PswdExpires	LastLogonTime
Administrator	Administrators	Yes	Yes	No	1/1/2004 7:10 PM
doctorx	Administrators	No	Yes	No	1/1/2004 2:12 AM
doctorx	Users	No	Yes	No	1/1/2004 2:12 AM
Guest	Guests	No	Yes	No	Never
IUSR_WINNT	Guests	No	Yes	No	1/1/2004 4:53 PM
kbeaver	Users	Yes	Yes	Yes	1/1/2004 7:06 PM
nikki	Users	Yes	Yes	Yes	1/1/2004 7:09 PM

Found 6 users 00001

Figure 11-9: DumpSec displays users on a server.

Walksam

Walksam gleans information about Windows users by walking the SAM database through an established null session. Figure 11-10 is an example of its output. This output is obviously similar to the DumpSec output, but the main difference here is that this attack can be scripted to somewhat automate the process.

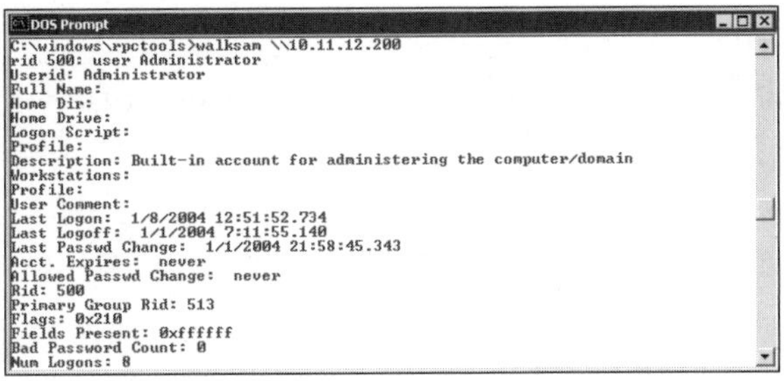

DOS Prompt

```
C:\windows\rpctools>walksam \\10.11.12.200
rid 500: user Administrator
Userid: Administrator
Full Name:
Home Dir:
Home Drive:
Logon Script:
Profile:
Description: Built-in account for administering the computer/domain
Workstations:
Profile:
User Comment:
Last Logon:  1/8/2004 12:51:52.734
Last Logoff:  1/1/2004 7:11:55.140
Last Passwd Change:  1/1/2004 21:58:45.343
Acct. Expires:  never
Allowed Passwd Change:  never
Rid: 500
Primary Group Rid: 513
Flags: 0x210
Fields Present: 0xffffff
Bad Password Count: 0
Num Logons: 8
```

Figure 11-10: User information gathered with Walksam.

Network Users

Network Users (`www.optimumx.com/download/netusers.zip`) can show who has logged into a remote Windows computer. You can see such information as

- Abused account privileges
- Users currently logged into the system

Figure 11-11 shows the history of local logins of a remote Windows 2000 workstation.

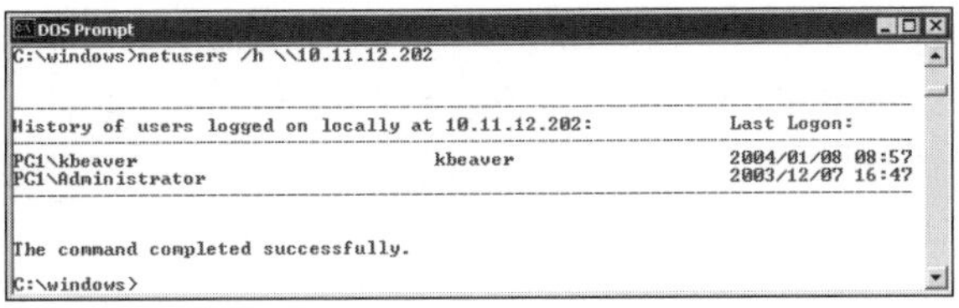

DOS Prompt

```
C:\windows>netusers /h \\10.11.12.202


-----------------------------------------------------------------------------
History of users logged on locally at 10.11.12.202:          Last Logon:
-----------------------------------------------------------------------------
PC1\kbeaver                         kbeaver                  2004/01/08 08:57
PC1\Administrator                                            2003/12/07 16:47
-----------------------------------------------------------------------------


The command completed successfully.

C:\windows>
```

Figure 11-11: The Network Users tool.

This information can help you track who's logging into a system for auditing purposes. Unfortunately, this information can be useful for hackers when they're trying to figure out what user IDs are available to crack. They may even determine the system's daily use if the user IDs are descriptive, such as *backup* (for a backup server) or *devuser* (for a development server).

Countermeasures

You can easily prevent null session connection hacks by implementing one or more of the following security measures.

Secure versions

If it makes good business sense and the timing is right, upgrade to the more secure Windows Server 2003. It doesn't have these vulnerabilities by default.

Blocking NetBIOS

It's absolutely critical that you block NetBIOS on systems that don't need to advertise to the world that it's running and available to be hacked.

- Block NetBIOS on your Windows server by preventing these TCP ports from passing through your network firewall or personal firewall:
  - 139 (NetBIOS sessions services)
  - 445 (runs SMB over TCP/IP without NetBIOS)

    Windows NT doesn't support port 445.

  Although Windows Server 2003 does not have the same null session vulnerability by default as older versions of Windows server operating systems, it's still a good idea to block NetBIOS ports on these systems.
- Disable File and Print Sharing for Microsoft Networks in the Properties tab of the machine's network connection.

Registry

For Windows NT and 2000, you can eliminate this vulnerability by changing the Windows Registry. Depending on the Windows version, you can select one of these security settings:

- **None:** This is the default setting.
- **Rely on Default Permissions (Setting 0):** This setting allows the default null session connections.

- **Do Not Allow Enumeration of SAM Accounts and Shares (Setting 1):** This is the medium security level setting. This setting still allows null sessions to be mapped to IPC$, enabling tools such as Walksam to be able to glean information from the system.
- **No Access without Explicit Anonymous Permissions (Setting 2):** This high security setting prevents null session connections and system enumeration.

The high security setting has a few drawbacks:

- High security creates problems for domain controller communication and network browsing.
- The high security setting isn't available in Windows NT.

Microsoft Knowledge Base Article 246261 covers the caveats of using the high security setting for Restrict Anonymous. It's available on the Web at `support.microsoft.com/default.aspx?scid=KB;en-us;246261`.

Windows 2000

In Windows 2000, you don't have to edit the Registry. You can set local security policy in the Local Policies/Security Options of the Local Security Settings. The security setting is called Additional Restrictions for Anonymous Connections. This setting is referred to as RestrictAnonymous, as shown in Figure 11-12.

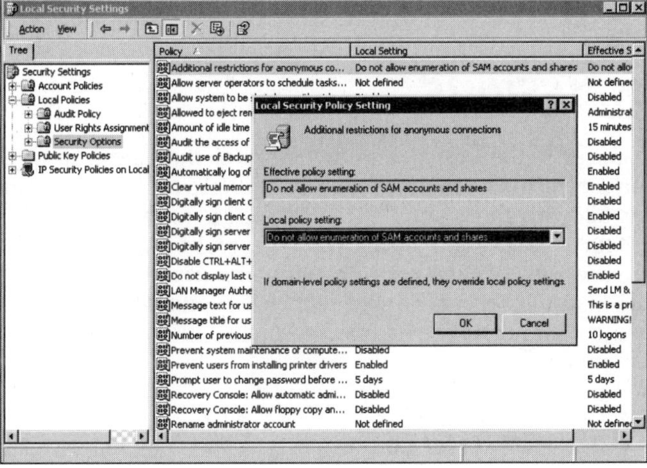

Figure 11-12: Local security policy settings in Windows 2000 to prevent null sessions.

Windows NT

For Windows NT, follow these steps to change the Registry to disable null sessions:

1. **Run either of the following Registry editing programs in Windows:**
   - `regedit.exe`
   - `regedt32.exe`
2. **Make a backup copy of the Registry.**
   - If you're using regedit, select Registry/Export Registry File.
   - If you're using regedt32, select Registry/Save Key.
3. **Browse to the key HKEY_LOCAL_MACHINE\SYSTEM\CurrentControlSet\Control\LSA.**
4. **Right-click in the right window and select New/DWORD Value.**
5. **Enter** RestrictAnonymous **as the name.**
6. **Double-click the RestrictAnonymous key and enter** 1 **as the value.**
7. **Exit the Registry editor (regedit or regedt32).**
8. **Reboot the computer.**

   The new setting takes effect after the system is rebooted.

Share Permissions

Windows *shares* — the available network drives that show up when browsing the network in Network Neighborhood or My Network Places — are often misconfigured, allowing more people to have access to them than they should. This is a security vulnerability that can be exploited by the casual browser, but the implications of a hacker gaining unauthorized access to a Windows system can result in serious consequences, including the leakage of confidential information and even the deletion of critical files.

Windows defaults

The default share permission depends on the Windows system version.

Windows 2000/NT

When creating shares in Windows NT and 2000, the group Everyone is given Full Control access in the share by default for all files to

- Browse files
- Read files
- Write files

Anyone who maps to the IPC$ connection with a null session (as described in the preceding section "Null Sessions") is automatically made part of the Everyone group! This means that remote hackers can automatically gain browse, read, and write access to a Windows NT or 2000 server if they establish a null session.

If share permissions are misconfigured, hackers on the Internet may gain access to these shares on an unprotected system and open, create, and delete files at will!

Windows 2003 Server

In Windows 2003 Server, the Everyone group is given only Read access to shares. This is definitely an improvement over the defaults in Windows 2000 and NT, but it's not the best setting for the utmost security. You still may have situations where you don't even want the Everyone group to have Read access to a share.

Testing

Assessing your share permissions is a good way to get an overall view of who can access what. This testing shows how vulnerable your network shares — and confidential information — can be. You can find shares with default permissions and unnecessary access rights enabled.

The best test for share permissions that shouldn't exist is to log in to the Windows computer and run an enumeration program so you can see who has access to what.

DumpSec

DumpSec shows the share permissions on your servers in a graphical form. You simply connect to the remote computer and select Dump Permissions for Shares in the Report menu. This produces shares labeled as *unprotected,* similar to what's shown in Figure 11-13.

This vulnerability exists in both Windows NT and Windows 2000 servers. Thank goodness Microsoft fixed this default weakness in Windows Server 2003!

Windows workstation security

This chapter focuses on Windows Server OSs (NT, 2000, and Server 2003) with brief mentions of security issues involving Windows workstation OSs (9*x*, Me, and XP). Windows servers are often the most critical servers on a network, but you shouldn't overlook the workstations.

If you're running Windows 95, 98, or Me as the OS for your network workstations, it may be time to upgrade. These three OSs simply aren't made for secure networking. Even the older Windows NT has better security built-in. Why? Because that's how Microsoft designed it. Windows 9*x* and Me were designed for the casual home user — not for networking in a business setting. They support networking such as domain logins and file and printer sharing, but these security measures are easily circumvented. Just try pressing Esc on your keyboard the next time you're presented with a login screen on one of these OSs. The login screen will go away, and you'll have full rights on the system. Your best bet for security and hacker countermeasures is to upgrade these old OSs — and most likely the hardware, too — to the latest and greatest computers running Windows XP Professional or newer.

Although Windows XP is much more secure by default than its older siblings, take a couple more steps to make it as secure as possible:

- Apply the latest patches as described in the section "Windows Update" or by using an automated patch management tool.
- Run LANguard Network Security Scanner and the Microsoft Baseline Security Analyzer to identify any obvious security vulnerabilities, such as weak passwords and autologon.
- Enable the Internet Connection Firewall (ICF). This personal firewall provides a tremendous amount of security over the standard configuration. It blocks all unsolicited inbound traffic unless that traffic is explicitly allowed.
- There are other firewall options as well, such as BlackICE or ZoneAlarm. You may be able to run both ICF and a third-party firewall at the same time, but I don't recommend it for system operation and stability purposes.

To enable ICF on a Windows XP Professional system, perform the following steps:

1. Load the Control Panel and then choose Networking and Internet Connections⇨Network Connections.
2. Right-click on the network adapter on which you want to enable ICF and select Properties.
3. Click the Advanced tab and then select the Protect My Computer or Network by Limiting or Preventing Access to This Computer from the Internet check box.

Supposedly, starting with Windows XP Service Pack 2, ICF (now called Windows Firewall) has many more advanced features such as firewalling being enabled by default, boot-time protection of the system, and support for various security profiles depending on how and where the user is logged in.

LANguard

LANguard Network Security Scanner also shows the share permissions on your servers in a graphical fashion. Figure 11-14 shows an example.

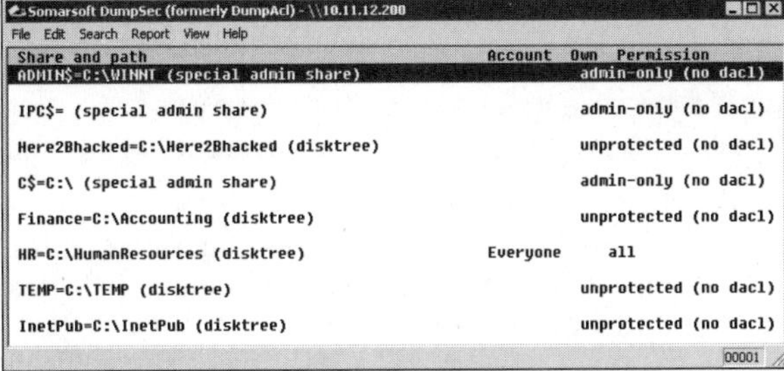

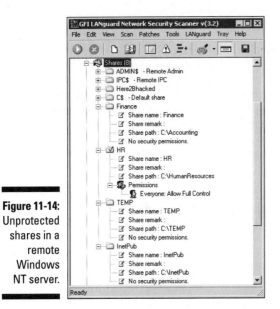

Figure 11-13: Unprotected shares in a Windows NT system.

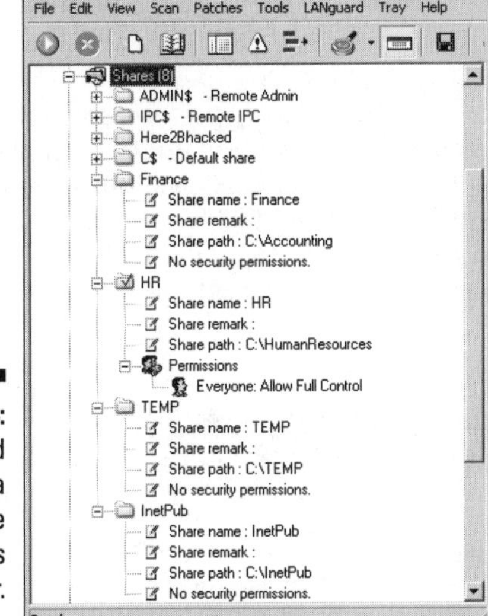

Figure 11-14: Unprotected shares in a remote Windows NT server.

General Security Tests

As part of your ethical hacking, you can run the following security tests to determine other potential weaknesses in your Windows systems.

Windows Update

Windows Update is the simplest way to check for missing Windows patches — especially critical security updates. How you run Windows Update depends on your Windows version:

- If you have Windows 2000, XP, or Server 2003, run Windows Update from the Start menu.
- For Windows NT, browse to `windowsupdate.microsoft.com`. On that page, click Scan for Updates to check your system for any missing patches.

Microsoft has announced plans to stop providing updates for Windows NT. You can't assume that Windows Update will have patches for new security vulnerabilities discovered.

Microsoft Baseline Security Analyzer (MBSA)

Microsoft Baseline Security Analyzer (MBSA) is my preferred method for checking for missing security patches. MBSA is a free utility from Microsoft. MBSA checks Windows NT, 2000, XP, and Server 2003 systems for missing patches and also tests Windows, SQL Server, and IIS for such basic security settings as weak passwords. You can use these tests to identify security weaknesses in your systems. Figure 11-15 shows a sample of the security settings MBSA tests.

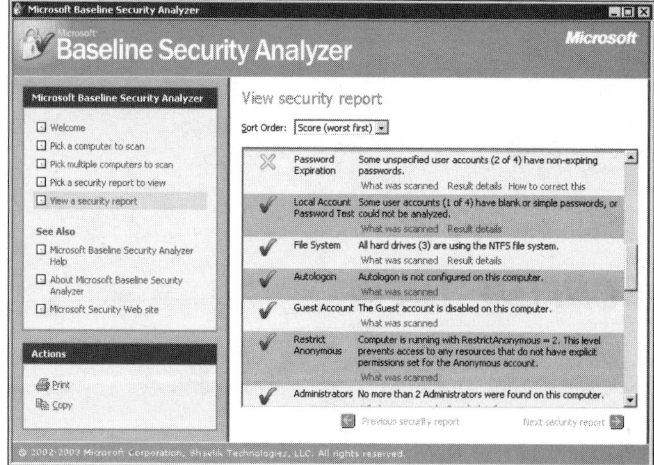

Figure 11-15: Testing basic Windows security settings.

With MBSA, you can scan either

- The local system you're logged into
- Computers across the network, if your currently logged-in user ID exists as an Administrator equivalent on the remote system you're testing

MBSA requires an administrator account on the local machines you're scanning and a manual connection to them.

LANguard

LANguard Network Security Scanner is my favorite feature-rich patch and Windows vulnerability scanning tool. With LANguard, you can

- Test for vulnerabilities and missing patches
- Deploy patches across the network to remote systems

Figure 11-16 shows the depth of information that this program can provide when scanning Windows systems for vulnerabilities and security settings. This type of information is very helpful when testing your own systems — especially if you have a large or complex network.

This information is also very helpful to hackers, especially if they have determined a local user's password. This way, they can authenticate to the system and check to see what patches and security settings are missing.

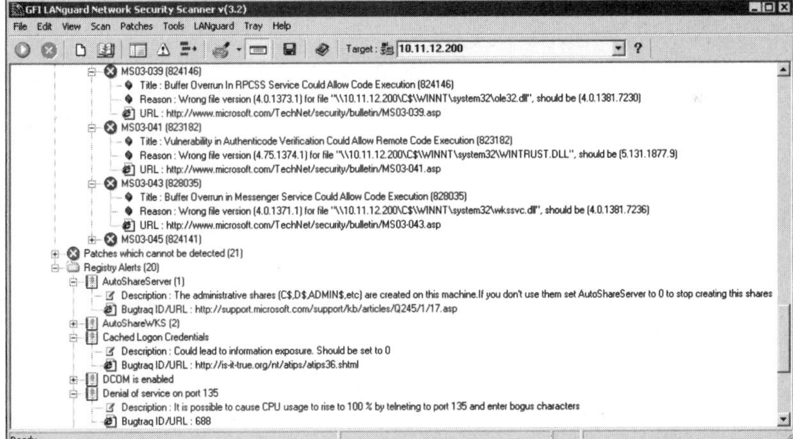

Figure 11-16: Information on missing patches and weak security settings.

It seems like no matter how many times you manually check local security settings and test to ensure that all patches are installed, a program such as LANguard Network Security Scanner or the popular and powerful Hyena (`www.systemtools.com/hyena`) always seems to find security issues you may have overlooked. This is why I recommend that you include an all-in-one assessment tool, such as one of these programs, in your security toolbox.

Chapter 12

Linux

In This Chapter

- Examining Linux hacking tools
- Port-scanning a Linux server
- Gleaning Linux information without logging in
- Exploiting common vulnerabilities when logged into Linux
- Minimizing Linux security risks

Linux — the new darling competitor to Microsoft — is the latest flavor of UNIX that has really taken off in corporate networks. A common misconception is that Windows is the most insecure operating system (OS). However, Linux — and most of its sister variants of UNIX — is prone to the same security vulnerabilities as any other operating system.

Hackers are attacking Linux in droves because of its popularity and growing usage in today's network environment. Because some versions of Linux are *free* — in the sense that you don't have to pay for the base operating system — many organizations are installing Linux for their Web servers and e-mail servers in hopes of saving money. Linux has grown in popularity for other reasons, including the following:

- Abundant resources available, including books, Web sites, and consultant expertise.
- Perception that Linux is more secure than Windows.
- Unlikeliness that Linux will get hit with as many viruses (not necessarily worms) as Windows and its applications do. This is an area where Linux excels when it comes to security, but it probably won't stay that way.
- Increased buy-in from other UNIX vendors, including IBM and Sun Microsystems. Even Novell is rewriting NetWare to be based on the Linux kernel.
- Growing ease of use.

In addition to the password attacks I cover in Chapter 7 and some of the malware attacks I cover in Chapter 14, many other attacks are possible against a Linux-based system. Linux can be tested remotely without being authenticated to the system. With all things being equal (that is, running the latest kernel and having the latest patches applied), it can be more difficult to glean the same amount of information from a Linux host than from a Windows or NetWare host without being logged in. After you log in to Linux with a valid username and password, you can glean a lot of information by running security tests to see how your system might stand up to a malicious internal user or hacker with a valid login.

In this chapter, I show you some critical security issues in the Linux operating system and outline some countermeasures to plug the holes so you can keep the bad guys out. A lot of this information applies to all flavors of UNIX.

I demonstrate the vulnerabilities by using Red Hat Linux versions 7.3 and 8.0, running Linux kernel version 2.4.18. I use Red Hat because it's the most popular and widely used Linux distribution. It's also the Linux that I prefer.

Linux Vulnerabilities

Vulnerabilities and hacker attacks against Linux are affecting a growing number of organizations — especially e-commerce companies and ISPs that rely on Linux for many of their systems. When Linux systems are hacked, the victim organizations can experience the same side effects as if they were running Windows, including:

- Leakage of confidential intellectual property and customer information
- Passwords being cracked
- Systems taken completely offline by DoS attacks
- Corrupted or deleted databases

Choosing Tools

You can use many UNIX-based security tools to test your Linux systems. Some are much better than others. I often find that my Windows-based commercial tools do as good a job as any. My favorites are as follows:

- Windows-based SuperScan (`www.foundstone.com`) for ping sweeps and TCP port scanning
- Nmap (`www.insecure.org`) for OS fingerprinting and more detailed port scanning
- Windows-based LANguard Network Security Scanner (`www.gfi.com`) for port scanning, OS enumeration, and vulnerability testing
- THC-Amap (`www.thc.org/releases.php`) for application version mapping
- Tiger (`ftp.debian.org/debian/pool/main/t/tiger`) for automatically assessing local-system security settings
- Linux Security Auditing Tool (LSAT) (`usat.sourceforge.net`) for automatically assessing local-system security settings
- VLAD the Scanner (`razor.bindview.com/tools/vlad`) to test for the SANS Top 10 Security Vulnerabilities
- QualysGuard (`www.qualys.com`) for OS fingerprinting, port scanning, and very detailed and accurate vulnerability testing
- Nessus (`www.nessus.org`) for OS fingerprinting, port scanning, and vulnerability testing

Thousands of other Linux hacking and testing tools are available. The key is to find a set of tools — preferably as few as possible — that can do the job that you need to do and that you feel comfortable working with.

Information Gathering

You can scan your Linux-based systems and gather information from both outside (if the system is a publicly accessible host) and inside your network.

Scan from both directions so you see what the bad guys can see from both outside and inside the network.

System scanning

Linux services — called *daemons* — are the programs that run on a system and serve up various applications for users.

- Internet services, such as the Apache Web server (httpd), telnet (telnetd), and FTP (ftpd), often give away too much information about the system, such as software versions, internal IP addresses, and usernames. This information can allow a hacker to attack a known weakness in the system.
- TCP and UDP *small services* such as echo, daytime, and chargen, are often enabled by default and don't need to be.

The vulnerabilities inherent in your Linux systems depend on what services are running. You can perform basic port scans to glean information about what's running.

The SuperScan results in Figure 12-1 show many potentially vulnerable services on this Linux system, including RPC, a Web server, telnet, and FTP.

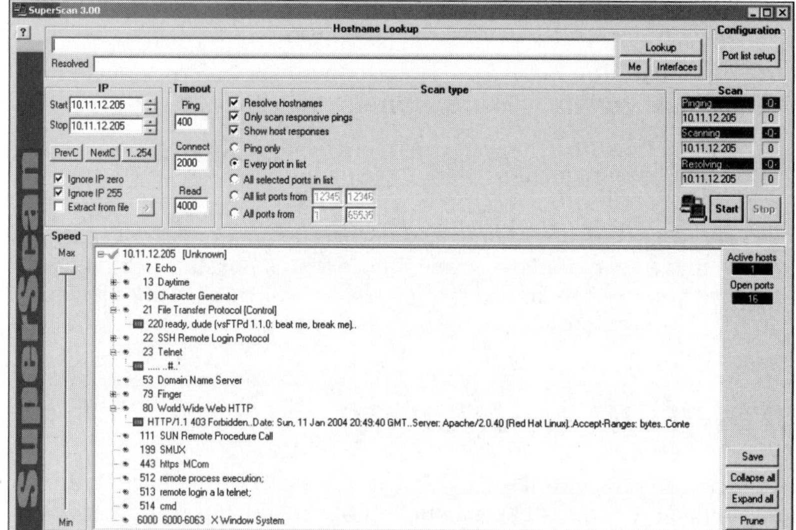

Figure 12-1: Port-scanning a Linux server with SuperScan.

In addition to SuperScan, you can run another scanner, such as Nessus or LANguard Network Security Scanner, against the system to try to glean more information, including

- A vulnerable version of OpenSSH, as shown in Figure 12-2
- The finger information returned by LANguard, as shown in Figure 12-3

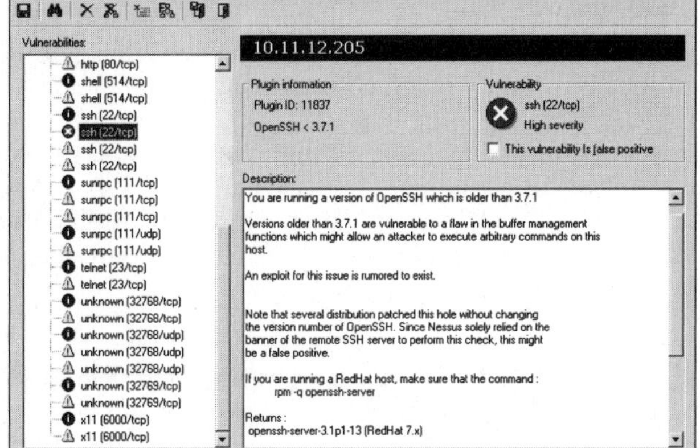

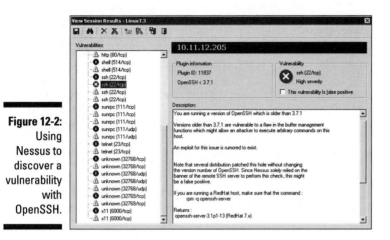

Figure 12-2: Using Nessus to discover a vulnerability with OpenSSH.

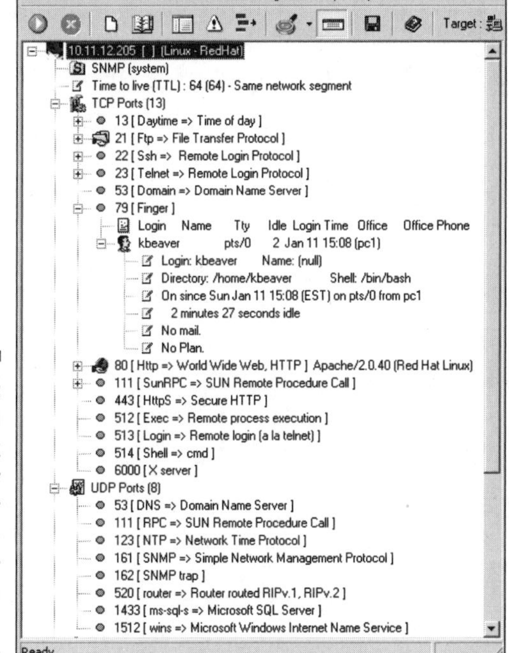

Figure 12-3: LANguard Network Security Scanner gleaning user information via finger.

LANguard even determined that the server is running the Berkeley Software Distribution (BSD) r-services and more in the Alerts section of Figure 12-3. It also displays a description of the potential vulnerability, as well as a link to the CERT Web site, which contains more information about it. Figure 12-3 also shows that LANguard thinks the remote operating system is Red Hat Linux. This information can be handy when you come across unfamiliar open ports.

Figure 12-4 shows various *r-services* and other daemons that network administrators are notorious for running unnecessarily on UNIX–based operating systems. Notice that LANguard points out specific vulnerabilities associated with some of the these services, along with a recommendation to use SSH as an alternative.

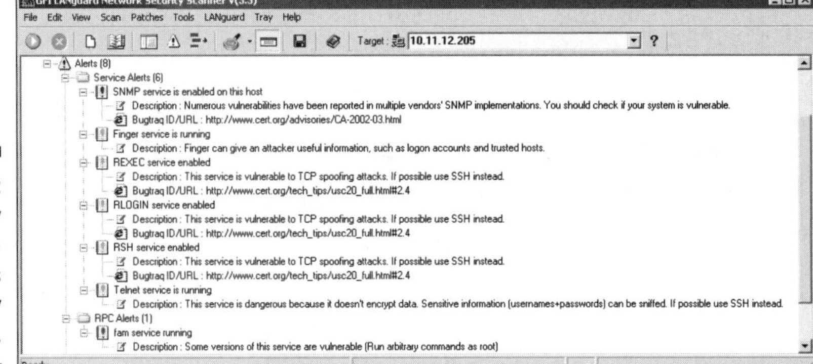

Figure 12-4: Potentially vulnerable r-services found by LANguard.

You can go a step further and find out the exact distribution and kernel version by running an OS fingerprint scan using Nmap, as shown in Figure 12-5.

```
DOS Prompt
C:\nmap>nmap -sV -O 10.11.12.205

Starting nmap 3.48 ( http://www.insecure.org/nmap ) at 2004-01-11 17:27 Ea
Standard Time
Interesting ports on 10.11.12.205:
(The 1639 ports scanned but not shown below are in state: closed)
PORT     STATE SERVICE  VERSION
7/tcp    open  echo
13/tcp   open  daytime
19/tcp   open  chargen?
21/tcp   open  ftp      vsFTPd 1.1.0
22/tcp   open  ssh      OpenSSH 3.4p1 (protocol 1.99)
23/tcp   open  telnet   Linux telnetd
53/tcp   open  domain   ISC Bind 9.2.1
79/tcp   open  finger   Linux fingerd
80/tcp   open  http     Apache httpd 2.0.40 ((Red Hat Linux))
111/tcp  open  rpcbind  2 (rpc #100000)
199/tcp  open  smux     Linux SNMP multiplexer
443/tcp  open  ssl      Microsoft IIS SSL
512/tcp  open  exec?
513/tcp  open  login?
514/tcp  open  shell?
873/tcp  open  rsync?
1241/tcp open  nessus?
6000/tcp open  X11      (access denied)

Device type: general purpose
Running: Linux 2.4.X|2.5.X
OS details: Linux Kernel 2.4.0 - 2.5.20
Uptime 1.605 days (since Sat Jan 10 02:57:27 2004)

Nmap run completed -- 1 IP address (1 host up) scanned in 108.896 seconds
C:\linux>
```

Figure 12-5: Using Nmap to determine the OS kernel version of a Linux server.

The QualysGuard scan of a Linux server shown in Figure 12-6 outlines threats to the system in an informative graphic form that nontechie types — the ones to whom you may be showing the results — just love.

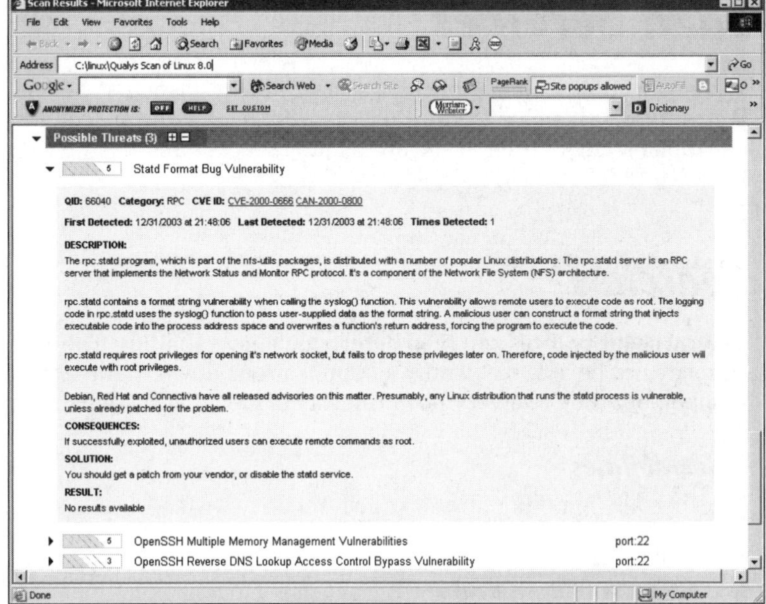

Figure 12-6: Linux threats outlined in a QualysGuard scan.

Countermeasures

Although you can't completely prevent system scanning, you can still implement the following countermeasures to keep the bad guys from gleaning too much information from your systems:

- Protect the systems with either
    - A firewall, such as netfilter/iptables (`www.netfilter.org`).
    - A host-based intrusion-prevention application, such as PortSentry (`sourceforge.net/projects/sentrytools`) now owned by Cisco Systems (`www.psionic.com`) or SNARE (`www.intersectalliance.com/projects/Snare`).

  These security systems are the best way to prevent an attacker from gathering information about your Linux systems.

- Disable the services you don't need, including RPC and such daemons as HTTP, FTP, and telnet. You may very well need some of these daemons and more — just make sure you have a business need for them. This keeps the services from showing up in a port scan and, thus, gives an attacker less incentive to break into your system.
- Make sure the latest software and patches are loaded; if a hacker determines what you're running, the chances of exploitation are reduced.

Unneeded Services

When you know which applications are running — such as FTP, telnet, and a Web server — it's nice to know exactly which versions are running so you can look up any of their associated vulnerabilities and decide whether to just turn them off.

Searches

Several security tools can help determine vulnerabilities. These types of utilities may not be able to identify all applications down to the exact version number, but they're a very powerful way of gleaning system information.

Vulnerabilities

Be especially mindful of these known security weaknesses in a system:

- FTP — especially if it's not properly configured — can provide a way for a hacker to download and access files on your system.
- Telnet is vulnerable to network-analyzer captures of the clear-text user ID and password it uses.
- Old versions of sendmail — the world's most popular e-mail server — have many security issues.

  Make sure sendmail is patched and hardened.
- R-services such as rlogin, rdist, rexecd, rsh, and rcp are especially vulnerable to hacker attacks, as I discuss in this chapter.

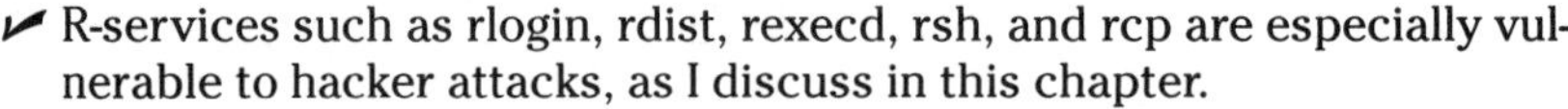

Tools

The following tools can perform more in-depth information gathering beyond port scanning to enumerate your Linux systems and see what the hackers see:

- Nmap can check for specific versions of the services loaded, as shown in Figure 12-7. Simply run Nmap with this command-line switch:

```
-sV
```

- Amap is similar to Nmap, but it has a couple of advantages:
  - Amap is much faster for these types of scans.
  - Amap can detect applications that are configured to run on non-standard ports, such as Apache running on port 6789 instead of its default 80.

  The output of an Amap scan of the localhost (hence, the 127.0.0.1 address) is shown in Figure 12-8. Amap was run with the following options to enumerate some commonly hacked ports:

- `-1` makes the scan run faster.
- `-b` prints the responses in ASCII characters.
- `-q` skips reporting of closed ports.
- `21` probes port.
- `22` probes SSH port.
- `23` probes telnet port.
- `80` probes HTTP port.

- netstat shows the currently running services on a local machine. Enter this command:

```
netstat -anp
```

- List Open Files (lsof) displays processes that are listening and files that are open on the system

  TIP

  To run lsof, enter this command at a Linux command prompt:

```
lsof -i +M
```

Chapter 14 covers more on usage of lsof as well.

```
DOS Prompt
C:\nmap>nmap -sV -T 5 10.11.12.205

Starting nmap 3.48 ( http://www.insecure.org/nmap ) at 2004-01-11 18:58 Eastern
Standard Time
Interesting ports on 10.11.12.205:
(The 1639 ports scanned but not shown below are in state: closed)
PORT     STATE SERVICE  VERSION
7/tcp    open  echo
13/tcp   open  daytime
19/tcp   open  chargen?
21/tcp   open  ftp      vsFTPd 1.1.0
22/tcp   open  ssh      OpenSSH 3.4p1 (protocol 1.99)
23/tcp   open  telnet   Linux telnetd
53/tcp   open  domain   ISC Bind 9.2.1
79/tcp   open  finger   Linux fingerd
80/tcp   open  http     Apache httpd 2.0.40 ((Red Hat Linux))
111/tcp  open  rpcbind  2 (rpc #100000)
199/tcp  open  smux     Linux SNMP multiplexer
443/tcp  open  ssl      Microsoft IIS SSL
512/tcp  open  exec?
513/tcp  open  login?
514/tcp  open  shell?
873/tcp  open  rsync?
1241/tcp open  nessus?
6000/tcp open  X11      (access denied)

Nmap run completed -- 1 IP address (1 host up) scanned in 100.825 seconds

C:\nmap>
```

Figure 12-7: Using Nmap to check application versions.

```
Linux - SecureCRT
File Edit View Options Transfer Script Window Help
[root@localhost amap-4.5]# amap -1 -b -q 127.0.0.1 21-23 80
amap v4.5 (www.thc.org) started at 2004-01-11 18:32:19 - APPLICATION MAP mode

Protocol on 127.0.0.1:80/tcp matches http - banner: HTTP/1.1 403 Forbidden\r\nDate Sun, 11 Jan 2004 2332:
9 GMT\r\nServer Apache/2.0.40 (Red Hat Linux)\r\nAccept-Ranges bytes\r\nContent-Length 2898\r\nConnectior
 close\r\nContent-Type text/html; charset=ISO-8859-1\r\n\r\n<!DOCTYPE HTML PUBLIC "-//W3C//DTD H
Protocol on 127.0.0.1:22/tcp matches ssh - banner: SSH-1.99-OpenSSH_3.4p1\n
Protocol on 127.0.0.1:22/tcp matches ssh-openssh - banner: SSH-1.99-OpenSSH_3.4p1\nProtocol mismatch.\n
Protocol on 127.0.0.1:23/tcp matches telnet - banner:  #'
Protocol on 127.0.0.1:21/tcp matches ftp - banner: 220 ready, dude (vsFTPd 1.1.0 beat me, break me)\r\n53
0 Please login with USER and PASS.\r\n530 Please login with USER and PASS.\r\n

Unidentified ports: none.

amap v4.5 finished at 2004-01-11 18:32:19
[root@localhost amap-4.5]#
Ready   ssh1: 3DES   16, 28   16 Rows, 104 Cols   VT100
```

Figure 12-8: Using Amap to check application versions.

Countermeasures

You can and should disable the unneeded daemons on your Linux systems. This is one of the best ways to keep your Linux system secure. It's like locking the doors and windows in your house — the more you lock, the fewer places an intruder can enter.

Disabling unneeded services

The best method of disabling unneeded services depends on how the daemon is being loaded in the first place. There are several places to do this, depending on the version of Linux you're running.

If you don't need a service running, take the safe route. Turn it off!

inetd.conf

If it makes good business sense — in other words, you don't need it — disable unneeded services by commenting out the loading of daemons you don't need. Follow these steps:

1. **Enter the following command at the command prompt:**

   ```
   ps -aux
   ```

   The process ID (PID) for each daemon, including inetd, is listed on the screen. In Figure 12-9, the PID for the sshd (Secure Shell) daemon is 646.

2. **Copy the PID for inetd from the screen on a notepad.**

3. **Open** `/etc/inetd.conf` **in the Linux text editor vi by entering the following command:**

   ```
   vi /etc/inetd.conf
   ```

4. **When you have the file loaded in vi, enable the insert (edit) mode by pressing I.**

5. **Move the cursor to the beginning of the line of the daemon that you want to disable, such as httpd (Web server daemon), and type** # **at the beginning of the line.**

   This comments out the line and prevents it from loading when you reboot the server or restart inetd.

6. **To exit vi and save your changes, simply press Esc to exit the insert mode, type** :wq, **and then press Enter.**

   This tells vi that you want to write your changes and quit.

7. **Restart inetd by entering this command with the inetd PID:**

   ```
   kill -HUP PID
   ```

```
Linux - SecureCRT
File Edit View Options Transfer Script Window Help
[root@localhost kbeaver]# ps -aux
USER       PID %CPU %MEM   VSZ  RSS TTY      STAT START   TIME COMMAND
root         1  0.0  0.2  1264  460 ?        S    Feb06   0:04 init
root         2  0.0  0.0     0    0 ?        SW   Feb06   0:00 [keventd]
root         3  0.0  0.0     0    0 ?        SW   Feb06   0:00 [kapmd]
root         4  0.0  0.0     0    0 ?        SWN  Feb06   0:00 [ksoftirqd_CPU0]
root         5  0.0  0.0     0    0 ?        SW   Feb06   0:03 [kswapd]
root         6  0.0  0.0     0    0 ?        SW   Feb06   0:00 [bdflush]
root         7  0.0  0.0     0    0 ?        SW   Feb06   0:00 [kupdated]
root         8  0.0  0.0     0    0 ?        SW   Feb06   0:00 [mdrecoveryd]
root        14  0.0  0.0     0    0 ?        SW   Feb06   0:00 [scsi_eh_0]
root        17  0.0  0.0     0    0 ?        SW   Feb06   0:01 [kjournald]
root        73  0.0  0.0     0    0 ?        SW   Feb06   0:00 [khubd]
root       165  0.0  0.0     0    0 ?        SW   Feb06   0:00 [kjournald]
root       407  0.0  0.0     0    0 ?        SW   Feb06   0:00 [eth0]
root       461  0.0  0.2  1324  532 ?        S    Feb06   0:00 syslogd -m 0
root       465  0.0  0.2  1264  432 ?        S    Feb06   0:00 klogd -x
rpc        483  0.0  0.2  1404  524 ?        S    Feb06   0:00 portmap
rpcuser    502  0.0  0.3  1444  728 ?        S    Feb06   0:00 rpc.statd
root       583  0.0  0.2  1256  488 ?        S    Feb06   0:00 /usr/sbin/apmd -p 10 -w 5 -W -P
root       620  0.0  1.2  7732 2332 ?        S    Feb06   1:17 /usr/sbin/snmptrapd -s -u /var/r
named      629  0.0  1.2 10624 2484 ?        S    Feb06   0:00 named -u named
root       646  0.0  0.7  3200 1428 ?        S    Feb06   0:10 /usr/sbin/sshd
root       660  0.0  0.4  1996  916 ?        S    Feb06   0:00 xinetd -stayalive -reuse -pidfil
ntp        674  0.0  0.9  1836 1828 ?        SL   Feb06   0:00 ntpd -U ntp
root       693  0.0  0.2  3196  528 ?        S    Feb06   0:00 rpc.rquotad
root       698  0.0  0.0     0    0 ?        SW   Feb06   0:00 [nfsd]
Ready    ssh1: 3DES    27, 27    27 Rows, 95 Cols    VT100
```

Figure 12-9: Viewing the process IDs for running daemons using `ps -aux`.

chkconfig

If you don't have an `inetd.conf` file, your version of Linux is probably running *xinetd* (`www.xinetd.org`) — a more secure replacement for inetd — to listen for incoming network application requests. You can edit the `/etc/xinetd.conf` file if this is the case. For more information on the usage of xinetd and `xinetd.conf`, enter **man xinetd** or **man xinetd.conf** at a Linux command prompt. If you're running Red Hat 7.0 or later, you can run the `/sbin/chkconfig` program to turn off the daemons you don't want to load.

For example, you can enter the following to disable the snmp daemon:

```
chkconfig --del snmpd
```

You can also enter **chkconfig —list** at a command prompt to see what services are enabled in the `xinetd.conf` file.

The chkconfig program can be used to disable other services, such as FTP, telnet, and Web server.

Access control

TCP Wrappers can control access to critical services that you run, such as FTP or HTTP. This program controls access for TCP services and logs their usage, helping you control access via hostname or IP address and track malicious activities.

You can download it from `www.stanford.edu/group/itss-ccs/security/unix/tcpwrappers.html`.

.rhosts and hosts.equiv Files

Linux — and all the flavors of UNIX — are very file-based operating systems. Practically everything that's done on the system involves the manipulation of files. This is why so many attacks against Linux are at the file level.

Hacks

If hackers can capture a user ID and password by using a network analyzer, or can crash an application and gain root access via a buffer overflow, one thing they look for is what users are trusted by the local system. The `/etc/hosts.equiv` and `.rhosts` files list this information.

.rhosts

The `$home/.rhosts` files in Linux specify which remote users can access the Berkeley Software Distribution (BSD) r-commands (such as rsh, rcp, and rlogin) on the local system without a password. This file is in a specific user's home directory, such as `/home/jsmith`. A `.rhosts` file may look like the this:

```
tribe   scott
tribe   eddie
```

This file allows users Scott and Eddie on the remote-system tribe to login to the local host with the same privileges as the local user. If a plus sign (+) is entered in the remote-host and user fields, any user from any host could log in to the local system. The hacker can add entries into this file by

- Manually manipulating it.
- Running a script that exploits an insecure Common Gateway Interface (CGI) script on a Web-server application that's running on the system.

This configuration file is a prime target for a hacker attack. On most Linux systems I've tested, these files aren't enabled by default. However, a user can create one in his or her home directory on the system — intentionally or accidentally — which can create a major security hole on your system.

hosts.equiv

The `/etc/hosts.equiv` specifies which accounts on the system can access services on the local host. For example, if *tribe* were listed in this file, all users on the tribe system would be allowed access! As with the `.rhosts` file, external hackers can read this file and then spoof their IP address and hostname to gain unauthorized access to the local system. Hackers can also use the names located in the `.rhosts` and `hosts.equiv` files to look for names of other computers to attack.

Countermeasures

Use both of the following countermeasures to prevent hacker attacks against the `.rhosts` and `hosts.equiv` files in your Linux system.

Disabling commands

A good way to prevent abuse of these files is to disable the BSD r-commands altogether. This can be done by either

- Commenting out the lines starting with `shell`, `login`, and `exec` in `inetd.conf`.
- Editing the `rexec`, `rlogin`, and `rsh` files located in the `/etc/xinetd.d` directory. Open each file in a text editor, and change `disable=no` to `disable=yes`, as shown in Figure 12-10.

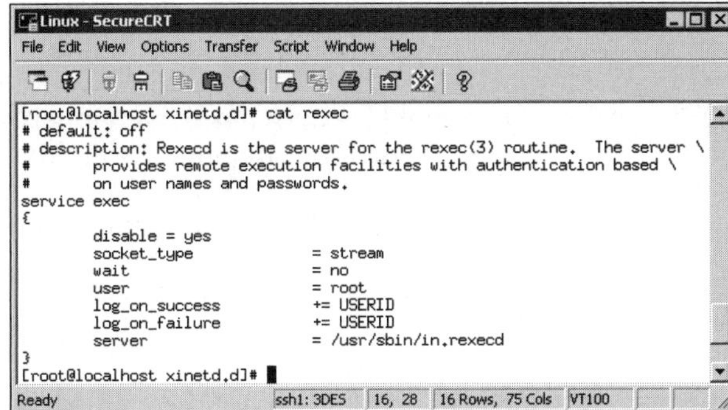

Linux - SecureCRT
File Edit View Options Transfer Script Window Help
[root@localhost xinetd.d]# cat rexec
default: off
description: Rexecd is the server for the rexec(3) routine. The server \
provides remote execution facilities with authentication based \
on user names and passwords.
service exec
{
disable = yes
socket_type = stream
wait = no
user = root
log_on_success += USERID
log_on_failure += USERID
server = /usr/sbin/in.rexecd
}
[root@localhost xinetd.d]#
Ready
ssh1: 3DES
16, 28
16 Rows, 75 Cols
VT100

Figure 12-10: The rexec file showing the disable option.

In Red Hat Linux, you can disable the BSD r-commands with the setup program:

1. Enter **setup** at a command prompt.
2. Select System Services from the menu.
3. Remove the asterisks next to each of the r-services.

Blocking access

A couple of countermeasures can block rogue access of the `.rhosts` and `hosts.equiv` files:

- Block spoofed addresses at the firewall, as I outline in Chapter 9.
- Set the permissions on these files so that only the owners can read them.

- `.rhosts`: Enter this command in each user's home directory:

  ```
  chmod 600 .rhosts
  ```

- `hosts.equiv`: Enter this command in the `/etc` directory:

  ```
  chmod 600 hosts.equiv
  ```

You can also use Tripwire (`www.tripwire.org`) to monitor these files and be alerted when access or changes are made.

NFS

The Network File System (NFS) is used to mount remote file systems (similar to shares in Windows) from the local machine.

Hacks

If NFS was setup improperly or its configuration has been tampered with — namely, the `/etc/exports` file containing a setting that allows the world to read the entire file system — remote hackers can easily obtain remote access and do anything they want on the system. All it takes is a line such as the following in the `/etc/exports` file:

```
/  rw
```

This line basically says anyone can remotely mount the root partition in a read-write fashion. Of course, the following conditions must also be true:

- The NFS daemon (nfsd) must be loaded, along with the portmap daemon that would map NFS to RPC.
- The firewall must allow the nfs traffic through.
- The remote systems that are allowed into the server running the NFS daemon must be placed into the `/etc/hosts.allow` file.

This remote-mounting capability is easy to misconfigure. It's often related to a Linux administrator's not understanding what it takes to share out the NFS mounts and just resorting to the easiest way possible to get it working. After hackers can gain remote access, the system is theirs.

Countermeasures

The best defense against NFS hacking depends on whether you actually need the service running.

- If you don't need NFS, disable it altogether.
- If you need NFS, implement both of the following countermeasures:
    - Filter NFS traffic at the firewall — typically, TCP port 111 if you want to filter all RPC traffic.
    - Make sure that your `/etc/exports` and `/etc/hosts.allow` files are configured properly to keep the world outside your network.

File Permission

In Linux, special file types allow programs to run with the file owner's rights:

- SetUID (for user IDs)
- SetGID (for group IDs)

SetUID and SetGIF are required when a user runs a program that needs full access to the system to perform its tasks. For example, when a user invokes the passwd program to his or her password, the program is actually loaded and run with root or any other user's privileges. This is done so that the user can run the program, and the program can update the password database without root's having to get involved in the process manually.

Hacks

By default, rogue programs that run with root privileges can be easily hidden. A hacker may do this to hide such hacking files as rootkits on the system.

Countermeasures

You can test for these rogue programs by using both manual and automated testing methods.

Manual testing

The following commands can identify SetUID and SetGID programs:

- Programs that are configured for SetUID:

```
find / -perm -4000 -print
```

- Programs that are configured for SetGID:

```
find / -perm -2000 -print
```

- Files that are readable by anyone in the world:

```
find / -perm -2 -type f -print
```

- Hidden files:

```
find / -name ".*"
```

You probably have hundreds of files in each of these categories, so don't be alarmed. When you discover files with these attributes set, you'll need to make sure that they are actually supposed to have those attributes by researching in your documentation, on the Internet, or even by comparing them to a known secure system or data backup.

Keep an eye on your systems to detect any new SetUID or SetGID files that suddenly appear.

Automatic testing

You can use an automated file-modification auditing program to alert you when these types of changes are made. This is what I recommend — it's a lot easier on an ongoing basis.

- A change-detection application, such as Tripwire, can help you keep track of what changed and when.
- A file-monitoring program, such as COPS (`dan.drydog.com/cops`), finds files that have changed in status (such as a new SetUID or removed SetGID).

Buffer Overflows

RPC and other vulnerable daemons are common methods for buffer-overflow attacks. Buffer-overflow attacks are often how the hacker can get in to modify system files, read database files, and more.

Attacks

In a buffer-overflow attack, the hacker either manually sends strings of information to the victim Linux machine or writes a script to do so. These strings contain

- Instructions to the processor to basically do nothing.
- Malicious code to replace the attacked process.

  For example, `exec ("/bin/sh")` creates a shell command prompt.
- A pointer to the start of the malicious code in the memory buffer.

If an attacked application (such as FTP or RPC) is running as root (many programs do), this can give the hacker root permissions in his remote shell.

You can run security-testing tools against your systems to test for buffer overflows, but I don't recommend it, because it can crash your system!

Countermeasures

Three main countermeasures can help prevent buffer-overflow attacks:

- Disable unneeded services.
- Protect your Linux systems with either a firewall or host-based intrusion prevention.
- Enable another access control mechanism, such as TCP Wrappers, that authenticates users with a password.

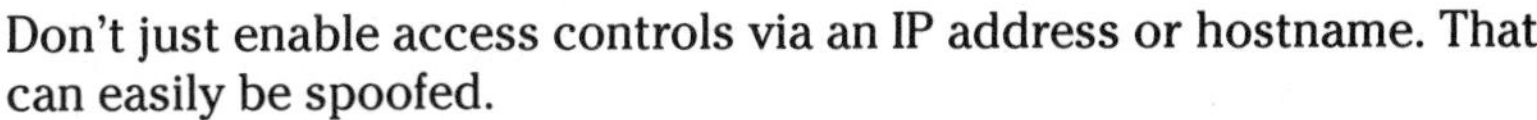

  Don't just enable access controls via an IP address or hostname. That can easily be spoofed.

Always make sure that your systems have been updated with the latest kernel and security patches.

Physical Security

Some Linux vulnerabilities involve the hacker's actually being at the system console.

Hacks

When a hacker is at the system console, anything goes, including rebooting the system (even if no one is logged in) simply by pressing Ctrl+Alt+Del. After the system is rebooted, the hacker can start it up in single-user mode, which allows the hacker to zero out the root password or possibly even read the entire `/etc/passwd` or `/etc/shadow` file.

Countermeasures

Edit your `/etc/inittab` file and remark out (place a # sign in front of) the line that reads `ca::ctrlaltdel:/sbin/shutdown -t3 -r now`, as shown in the last line of Figure 12-11.

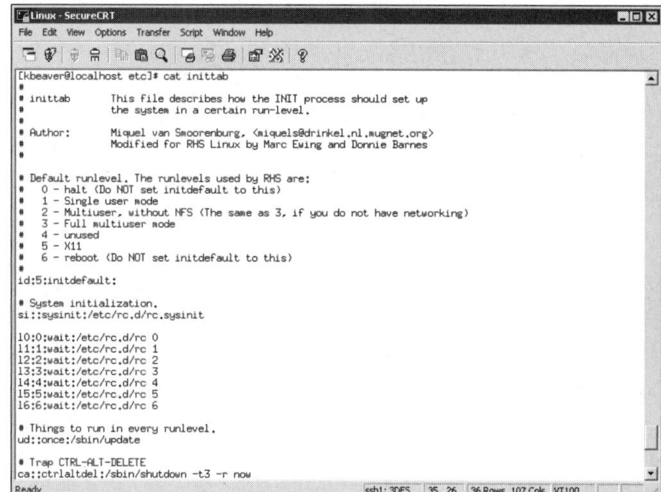

Linux - SecureCRT
File Edit View Options Transfer Script Window Help
[kbeaver@localhost etc]$ cat inittab
#
inittab This file describes how the INIT process should set up
the system in a certain run-level.
#
Author: Miquel van Smoorenburg, <miquels@drinkel.nl.mugnet.org>
Modified for RHS Linux by Marc Ewing and Donnie Barnes
#

Default runlevel. The runlevels used by RHS are:
0 - halt (Do NOT set initdefault to this)
1 - Single user mode
2 - Multiuser, without NFS (The same as 3, if you do not have networking)
3 - Full multiuser mode
4 - unused
5 - X11
6 - reboot (Do NOT set initdefault to this)
#
id:5:initdefault:

System initialization.
si::sysinit:/etc/rc.d/rc.sysinit

l0:0:wait:/etc/rc.d/rc 0
l1:1:wait:/etc/rc.d/rc 1
l2:2:wait:/etc/rc.d/rc 2
l3:3:wait:/etc/rc.d/rc 3
l4:4:wait:/etc/rc.d/rc 4
l5:5:wait:/etc/rc.d/rc 5
l6:6:wait:/etc/rc.d/rc 6

Things to run in every runlevel.
ud::once:/sbin/update

Trap CTRL-ALT-DELETE
ca::ctrlaltdel:/sbin/shutdown -t3 -r now
Ready
ssh1: 3DES
35, 26
36 Rows, 107 Cols
VT100

Figure 12-11: `/etc/inittab` showing the line that allows a Ctrl+Alt+Del shutdown.

If you believe that a hacker has recently gained access to your system either physically or by exploiting a vulnerability such as a weak password or buffer overflow, you can use the *last* program to view the last few logins into the system to check for strange login IDs or login times. This program peruses the `/var/log/wtmp` file and displays the users who logged in last. You can enter `last | head` to view the first part of the file (the first ten lines) if you want to see the most recent logins.

General Security Tests

You can assess critical, and often-overlooked, security issues on your Linux systems, such as the following:

- Misconfigurations or unauthorized entries in the `/etc/passwd` and `/etc/shadow` files
- Password policies
- Users equivalent to root
- Suspicious automated tasks configured in cron
- Signature checks on system binary files
- Checks for rootkits
- Network configuration, including measures to prevent packet spoofing and other DoS attacks
- Permissions on system log files

You can do all these assessments manually — or, better yet, use an automated tool to do it for you! Figure 12-12 shows the initiation of the Tiger security auditing tool, and Figure 12-13 shows a portion of the audit results. Talk about some great bang for no buck with this tool!

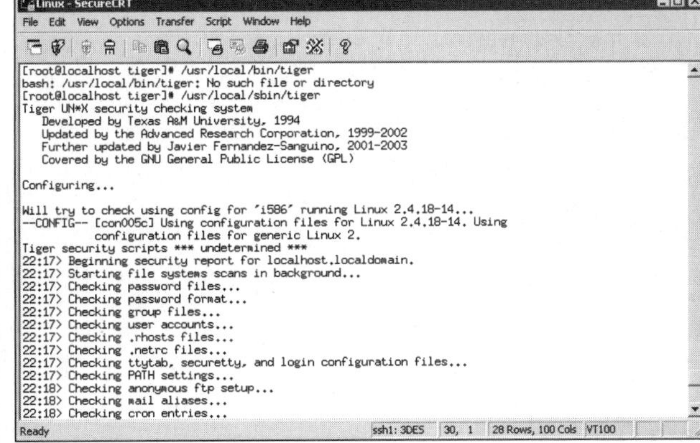

Figure 12-12: Running the Tiger security auditing tool.

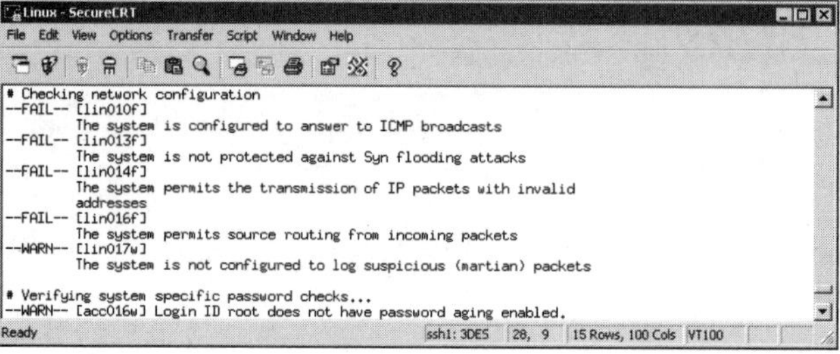

Figure 12-13: Partial output of the Tiger tool.

I like to run the Red Hat–focused Linux Security Auditing Tool (LSAT) in addition to Tiger. It's similar to Tiger, but it also searches for Red Hat Linux-specific security issues.

You can use to test for the SANS Top 20 (`www.sans.org/top20`) Vulnerabilities is VLAD the Scanner by the Bindview Razor security team. A portion of its output is shown in Figure 12-14.

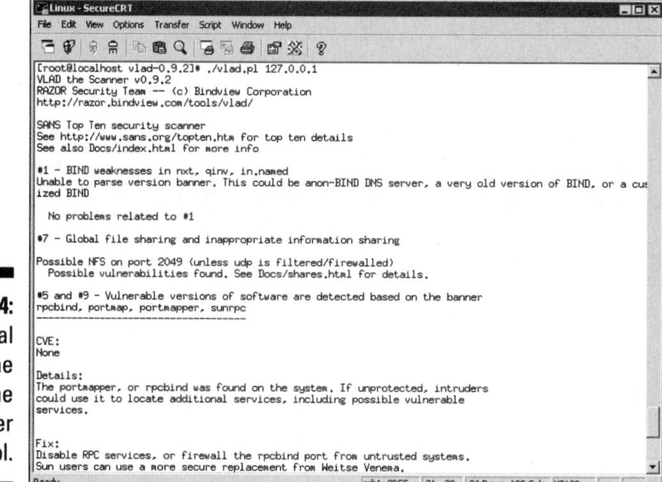

Figure 12-14: Partial output of the VLAD the Scanner tool.

Patching Linux

Ongoing patching is perhaps the best thing you can do to enhance the security of your Linux systems. Regardless of the Linux distribution you use, using a tool to assist in your patching efforts makes your job a lot easier.

Distribution updates

The distribution process is different on every distribution of Linux. You can use the following tools, based on your specific distribution.

Red Hat

You can use the following tools to update Red Hat Linux systems:

- Red Hat Package Manager (RPM), which is the GUI-based application that runs in the Red Hat GUI desktop. It manages those files with a .rpm extension that Red Hat and other freeware and open-source developers use to package their programs.
- up2date, a command-line text-based tool that is included in Red Hat.
- AutoRPM (`www.autorpm.org`).
- The open-source NRH-up2date (`www.nrh-up2date.org`).

Debian

You can use the Debian Package System (dpkg) included with the operating system to update Debian Linux systems.

Slackware

You can use the Slackware Package Tool (pkgtool) tool included with the operating system to update Slackware Linux systems.

SuSE/Novell

SuSE (now owned by Novell) includes the YaST2 Package Manager.

Multiplatform update managers

Commercial tools add nice features over the standard package managers (which I describe in this chapter), such as correlating patches with vulnerabilities and automatically deploying appropriate patches. Commercial tools that can help with Linux patch management include BigFix Patch Manager (`www.bigfix.com`) and SysUpdate (`www.securityprofiling.com`).

Chapter 13

Novell NetWare

In This Chapter

- Selecting NetWare hacking tools
- Port-scanning a NetWare server
- Gleaning NetWare information without logging in
- Exploiting common vulnerabilities when logged into NetWare
- Minimizing NetWare security risks

As much as some of Novell's competitors like to say that NetWare is a thing of the past, it's still alive and kicking quite strongly. There are millions of NetWare users around the world. The organizations running NetWare and other Novell products demand a solid directory-services infrastructure and stable environment.

NetWare administrators — some of the best around — often overlook or deny that NetWare is hackable. This chapter shows you how to test for the most critical NetWare exploits and outlines countermeasures to prevent the problems.

NetWare Vulnerabilities

Novell NetWare has a reputation as one of the most secure operating systems available. This is one reason that you rarely hear of NetWare servers' getting hacked or having new vulnerabilities that crop up constantly. However, NetWare has its security issues. Various NetWare vulnerabilities can be exploited — from NDS (now called *eDirectory*) enumeration to remote password testing to spoofing NetWare packets. Hackers can exploit many of NetWare's vulnerabilities without even logging into the server!

NetWare servers are frequently the most vital servers within a network. They often perform the following functions:

- House critical files
- Store replicas of the eDirectory database for hosting, replicating, and managing such directory-service objects as user IDs, printers, organizational units, and application licenses
- Host e-mail with Novell GroupWise
- Host Web sites and Web applications with such programs as Apache and Tomcat
- Serve as firewalls with Novell BorderManager

Starting with NetWare 7, Novell will release a version of NetWare that's Linux-based. So, if you do a lot of work with NetWare, now's the time to start beefing up on your Linux skills!

Choosing Tools

The following are my favorite NetWare-specific tools — they can offer up everything you need:

- **SuperScan** (`www.foundstone.com`) for port scanning
- **LANGuard Network Security Scanner** (`www.gfi.com`) for port scanning, OS enumeration, and vulnerability testing
- **NCPQuery** (`razor.bindview.com/tools/index.shtml`) for server and eDirectory enumeration
- **Remote** (`packetstormsecurity.nl/Netware/penetration`) for Remote Console password cracking

Make sure that you have the latest version of Novell's Client32 software from `download.novell.com` on your test computer before running these tests.

Getting Started

Although NetWare doesn't have many serious security vulnerabilities (relatively speaking), a few stand out. The hacks in this chapter are against a default installation of NetWare 5.1 from inside the firewall. However, these vulnerabilities and tests apply to most versions of NetWare 4.*x* and newer — the ones running NDS and eDirectory. I also point out a few critical NetWare 3.*x* vulnerabilities.

Patches on your specific systems may have fixed some of these vulnerabilities. If you don't get the exact same results as shown in this chapter, you're probably safe!

If you have the latest Novell-supplied patches on your systems, your systems are likely to be secure. However, the hacks in this chapter are significant, so you should test for them to make sure that your server is safe.

Older versions of NetWare such as 4.2 and 5.0 are being phased out of support. You'll no longer receive security updates for these versions.

Server access methods

You can access a NetWare server in the following four ways — each of which affects how you can test:

- **Not-logged in:** This is a connection where you simply perform port scans or make NCP calls across the network without actually logging in.
- **Logged in:** This connection requires you to log in with a valid bindery or eDirectory user ID and password.

  This is the basic method for accessing standard NetWare services.
- **Web access:** This connection may be available if you're running GroupWise WebAccess e-mail services, various NetWare management tools, or other basic Web-server applications.
- **Console access:** This access method requires you to be either at the server console or using a remote-connectivity product (such as NetWare's built-in rconsole or even a console that shipped with NetWare 3.*x* and earlier systems).

When you finish scanning your NetWare systems for open ports and general information gathering, you can test for common NetWare security vulnerabilities.

Port scanning

Start testing your NetWare systems by performing an initial port scan to check what hackers can see. You can perform these scans in two main ways:

- If the server has a public IP address, scan from outside the firewall, if possible.
- If the server doesn't have a public IP address, you can scan internally on the network.

Hackers can be inside your network, too!

The SuperScan results in Figure 13-1 show several potentially vulnerable ports open on this NetWare server, including FTP and the commonly exploited Echo and Character Generator ports. In addition, the NetWare specific port 524 is NCP (NetWare Core Protocol). NetWare uses this protocol for its internal communications with such hosts as clients and other servers — similar to SMB in Windows.

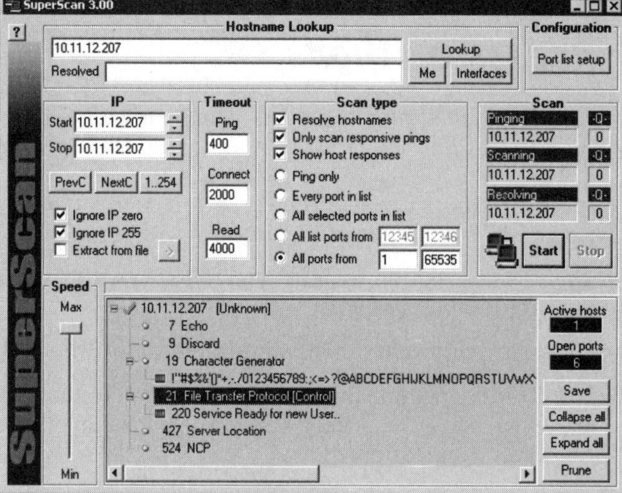

Figure 13-1: Using SuperScan to scan a default installation of NetWare 5.1.

You may also find that GroupWise is running (TCP port 1677), as well as potentially a Web server and other Web-based remote-access ports, such as 80, 443, 2200, 8008, and 8009.

You can also perform a scan with LANguard Network Security Scanner. Using a commercial tool such as this can often provide more details about the systems you're scanning than a basic port scanner. Figure 13-2 shows that it can determine more information about the server, such as the NetWare version and SNMP information. It also tells you what's listening on the open ports without your having to look them up.

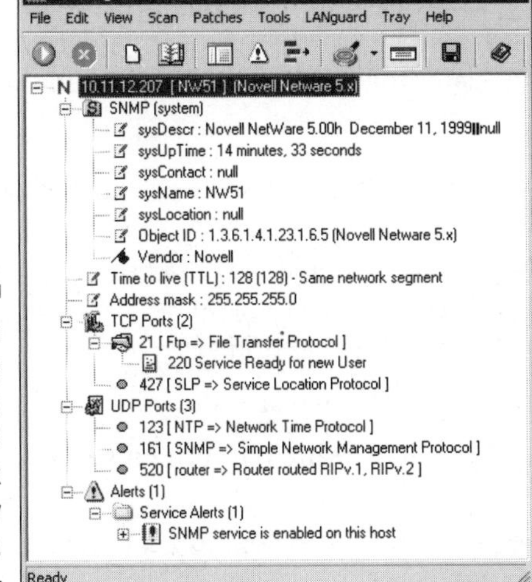

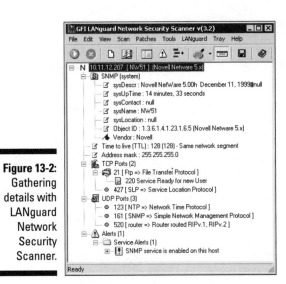

Figure 13-2: Gathering details with LANguard Network Security Scanner.

NCPQuery

You can run NCPQuery with command line options to gather information about your server and directory tree, including the server information shown in Figure 13-3.

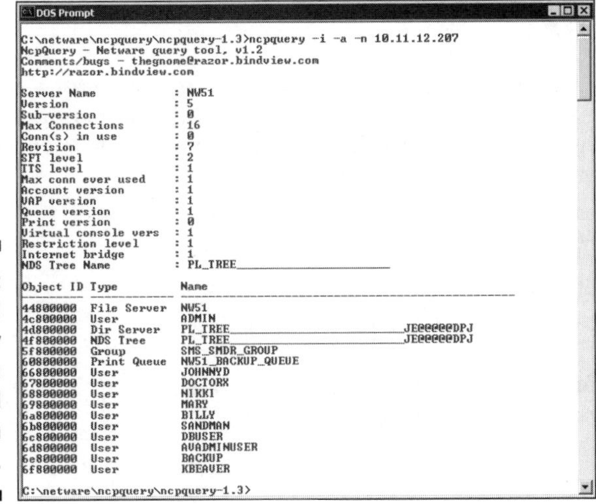

Figure 13-3: Server and eDirectory information gleaned with NCPQuery.

This is a lot of information for a hacker to see without being logged in!

Countermeasures

The following countermeasures can prevent the malicious enumeration of your NetWare systems:

- Installing the latest patches can eliminate many NetWare server vulnerabilities.

  If your NetWare version has been or will be phased out by Novell — meaning that it no longer provides security patches — you should seriously consider upgrading to the latest version.

- Port scanning can be performed with two steps:

  1. Unload any unneeded services, which in turn closes any associated ports.
  2. Place the server behind a firewall to help block outsider attacks.

- Blocking NCP port 524 at the firewall is the only way to disable an NCPQuery type of attack from outside.

  This may not help much for insider attacks. Internal network communications require the NCP port 524 to be available.

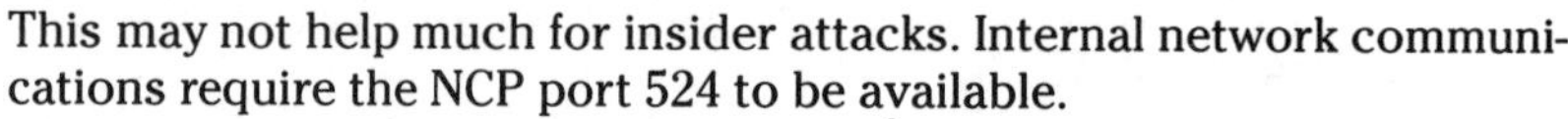

- Use strong passwords for all user IDs in case a hacker discovers an ID and attempts to log in.

Authentication

If a hacker can gather information such as the server, eDirectory, and user ID information, he may be able to exploit a known vulnerability or even try to log in by using the user IDs that he discovered. When he's in, all bets are off, and anything goes. He could

- Log into your network as a regular user.
- Log into your network as admin.
- Obtain physical access to the server console.

It's wise to assume that a hacker could log in as a user or administrator on your NetWare system and test for the worst-case scenario.

Rconsole

One of the most serious NetWare security vulnerabilities is the NetWare Remote Console program (referred to as rconsole). Rconsole is an SPX protocol–based remote-control program similar to telnet and Windows Terminal Services. It gives users full access to the NetWare console if they know the password. rconsole consists of the following:

- The `remote.nlm` and `rspx.nlm` files on the server
- The `rconsole.exe` client program in the `sys:\public` directory
- For rconsole to work, you must load the rspx NLM with one of these methods:
  - Enter `load rspx` at the console.
  - Place it in your `autoexec.ncf` or `ldremote.ncf` file just below your load remote line.

Attacks

Rconsole is vulnerable because its passwords can be easily obtained. The passwords are stored in either clear text or an easily crackable hash format on the server in the `sys:\system\autoexec.ncf` file or `sys:\system\ldremote.ncf` files.

If you encrypt your rconsole passwords, cracking them is simple. The following steps demonstrate how vulnerable the rconsole password really is:

1. **Enter** `load remote` **to load the remote NetWare Loadable Module (NLM) on the server.**
2. **Enter the password you want to use when prompted.**
3. **Enter** `remote encrypt` **and enter your rconsole password again when prompted.**

   The server generates the encrypted password and displays the entire command you need to run on the screen, including the hashed password. It looks similar to the response in Figure 13-4.

   The server may also enter the command into the `ldremote.ncf` file, but it sometimes fails. For simplicity, just enter the `load remote -E password` command manually into your `autoexec.ncf` file. Don't write this password down somewhere that's easily accessible to others.

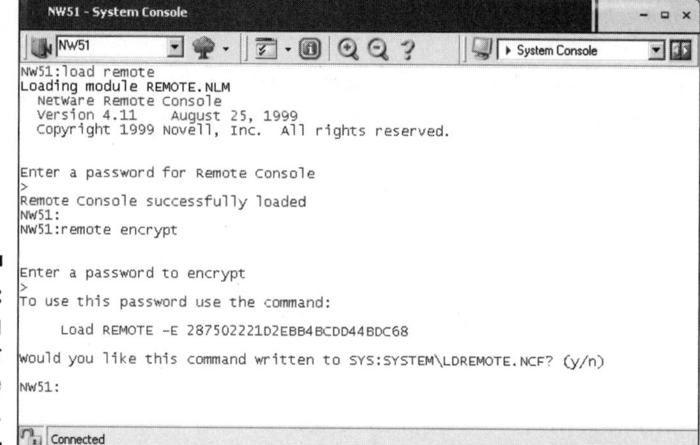

NW51 - System Console
NW51
System Console
NW51:load remote
Loading module REMOTE.NLM
NetWare Remote Console
Version 4.11 August 25, 1999
Copyright 1999 Novell, Inc. All rights reserved.
Enter a password for Remote Console
>
Remote Console successfully loaded
NW51:
NW51:remote encrypt
Enter a password to encrypt
>
To use this password use the command:
Load REMOTE -E 287502221D2EBB4BCDD44BDC68
Would you like this command written to SYS:SYSTEM\LDREMOTE.NCF? (y/n)
NW51:
Connected

Figure 13-4: Encrypting your rconsole password.

Now it's time to try cracking the encrypted rconsole password. For this, I use the remote cracking program — not to be confused with the remote NLM that's part of rconsole.

Simply run the `remote.exe` cracking program against the rconsole password hash that's displayed on the screen (or stored in the server's `autoexe.ncf` or `ldremote.ncf` file). Enter a line like the following at a command prompt:

```
remote password_hash
```

The result is the rconsole password.

You can try the preceding steps against *my* password. Figure 13-4 shows the hash:

```
287502221D2EBB4BCDD44BDC68
```

Anyone using the following three items can even capture the encrypted rconsole password traveling across the wire and decrypt it:

- Network analyzer
- Rcon program (`packetstormsecurity.nl/Netware/penetration/rcon.zip`)
- The steps outlined in the `rconfaq.txt` file at `packetstormsecurity.nl/Netware/audit/rconfaq.zip`

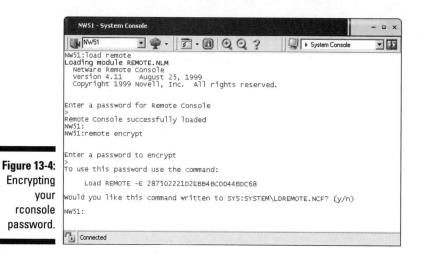

The remote NLM stores its password in server memory. Anyone with console access can go into the NetWare debugger by pressing Shift+Alt+Shift+Esc (yes, you use both Shift keys) on the server keyboard and view it in clear text. The process is explained at `packetstormsecurity.nl/Netware/audit/rconfaq.zip`.

Countermeasures

The following can prevent attacks against NetWare servers running rconsole:

- Don't use rconsole — at least, don't use it on critical NetWare servers. (Does anyone have a server that isn't critical?)
- If you must use rconsole, secure it with one of the following steps for your version of NetWare:
    - In NetWare 4.*x* or earlier, lock your server by using the monitor NLM.
    - With NetWare 5 and newer, load the scrsaver NLM. It displays the fancy text-based NetWare snake and requires a valid NetWare account to unlock.
- Consider using one of these remote NetWare management programs instead of rconsole:
    - Rconj is a Java-based version of rconsole that's able to work over using TCP. It comes with NetWare 5.*x* and later but has limited functionality.

Be sure to patch Rconj if you run it on NetWare 6. Rconj has a known authentication vulnerability when running on NetWare 6 that allows a hacker to gain access without a password.

  - AdRem Software (`www.adremsoft.com`) offers a couple of great rconsole replacements that I highly recommend you check out.
  - AdRem Free Remote Console runs on NetWare 4.*x* SP9 and later servers.

As the name implies, it's free!

AdRem Free Remote Console doesn't encrypt remote-console communications, but it does require a valid NetWare login with a user ID that has console operator privilege (such as admin or equivalent). This adds a level of security that plain old rconsole just can't offer.

  - AdRem sfConsole is a commercial product with a ton of features, including encrypted communications and a Web-based interface.

Server-console access

Physical access to the server console is a hacker's pot of gold. After hackers obtain this access, they can do practically anything they want to with the server. This includes accessing the NetWare debugger to retrieve passwords and potentially other confidential information stored in memory — not to mention crash the server and more.

The following countermeasures help ensure that NetWare console access is minimized to only those who are authorized:

- Physical security is a must. Chapter 6 explains how to secure server rooms.
- Lock the server screen. You can keep the server console secure by either selecting the Lock Server Console option in the monitor NLM or loading the scrsaver NLM.

Intruder detection

Intruder detection is one of the most critical security features built into NetWare. It locks a user account for a specific period of time after a certain number of failed login attempts.

Make sure that intruder detection is enabled on your system. It's *disabled* by default.

Testing

Default settings for intruder detection — after it's enabled — in NetWare 5.1 are shown in Figure 13-5. Chapter 7 details intruder detection.

Try logging in with invalid passwords for several test users — preferably, users from different organizational units (OUs) within eDirectory — to see whether intruder detection is working. Make sure that you type *bad* passwords; blank ones don't seem to work well for this test. Here's how you know whether intruder detection is working:

- If intruder detection is on, you should get a response similar to Figure 13-6.
- If intruder detection is off, you get prompted over and over again for a password.

This is how hackers test whether intrusion detection is enabled on your NetWare server.

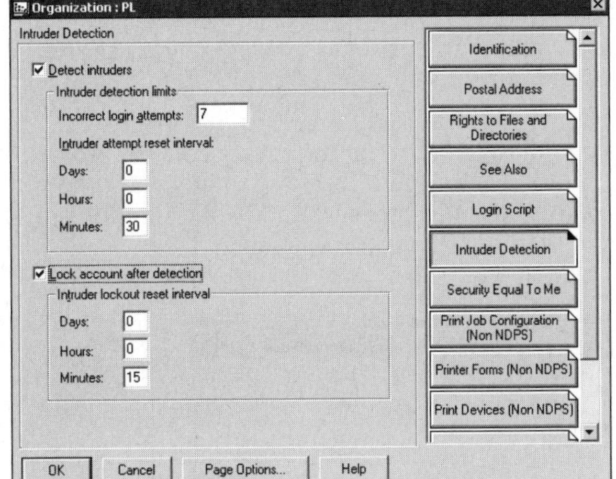

Figure 13-5: Intruder-detection settings in NetWare 5.1.

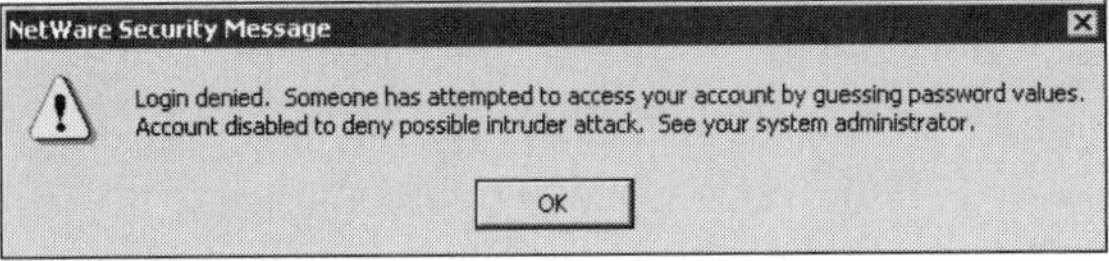

Figure 13-6: A Novell Client32 message.

Countermeasures

You can implement the following countermeasures to ensure that unauthorized logins are minimized and intruder detection is not abused:

- Enable intruder detection as high in the directory tree as possible — preferably, at the uppermost organization level.

  This is one of the best hacking countermeasures you can implement in a NetWare environment.

- Look for evidence that the console NLM was unloaded by searching for entries in the `sys:\etc\console.log` file.
- Consider logging all events to a remote syslog server to help prevent a hacker from tampering with evidence.

Rogue NLMs

If a hacker gains console access to your server, a legitimate yet potentially dangerous NLM can be loaded, which can do bad things to the system.

Testing

The following tests look for rogue NLMs running on your server.

Modules command

You can use the modules command at the server console prompt to view loaded modules. As shown in Figure 13-7, you simply enter the command **modules** at the server-console screen, and it displays a listing of NLMs that are loaded — from first to last in order of loading.

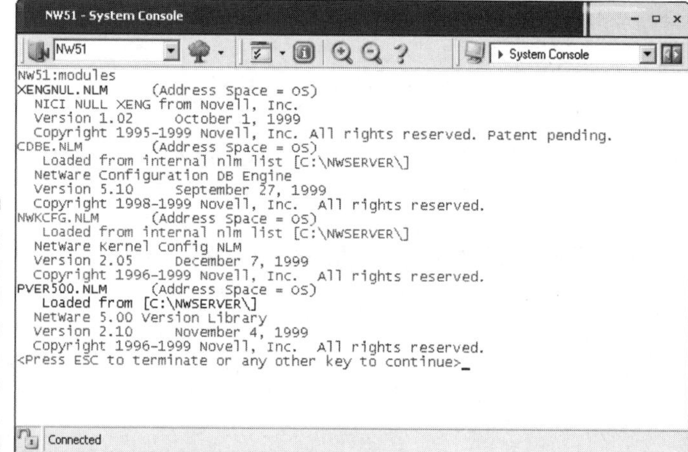
NW51 - System Console
NW51
System Console
NW51:modules
XENGNUL.NLM (Address Space = OS)
NICI NULL XENG from Novell, Inc.
Version 1.02 October 1, 1999
Copyright 1995-1999 Novell, Inc. All rights reserved. Patent pending.
CDBE.NLM (Address Space = OS)
Loaded from internal nlm list [C:\NWSERVER\]
NetWare Configuration DB Engine
Version 5.10 September 27, 1999
Copyright 1998-1999 Novell, Inc. All rights reserved.
NWKCFG.NLM (Address Space = OS)
Loaded from internal nlm list [C:\NWSERVER\]
NetWare Kernel Config NLM
Version 2.05 December 7, 1999
Copyright 1996-1999 Novell, Inc. All rights reserved.
PVER500.NLM (Address Space = OS)
Loaded from [C:\NWSERVER\]
NetWare 5.00 Version Library
Version 2.10 November 4, 1999
Copyright 1996-1999 Novell, Inc. All rights reserved.
<Press ESC to terminate or any other key to continue>_
Connected

Figure 13-7: Viewing loaded applications on a NetWare server.

Look for these NLMs in the modules output. If neither you nor another administrator has loaded the following NLMs, you have a problem:

- Password reset tools:
  - **setpwd**

    This third-party NLM can reset *any* user's password on the server — including admin! It's located at `ftp.cerias.purdue.edu/pub/tools/novell/setpwd.zip`.
  - **setspwd**

    This program resets the supervisor/admin password for NetWare 3.*x* and 4.*x*.
  - **setspass**

    This program resets the supervisor password for NetWare 3.*x* systems.

- **dsrepair:** This built-in NLM can corrupt or destroy eDirectory. It's actually intended to repair and maintain the eDirectory database.
- **netbasic:** This built-in NLM can copy eDirectory files from the hidden `sys:\_netware` directory. It accesses a DOS-like prompt on the server.

Check whether the nwconfig NLM is loaded. This built-in NLM is often used for day-to-day server maintenance, such as installing patches and editing system files. However, a hacker can load it and back up or restore the eDirectory database so that its files can be copied for malicious purposes. You can look to see if the NLM is loaded by either

- Looking at the modules output
- Pressing Ctrl+Esc to view all loaded applications
- Pressing Alt+Esc to toggle through all loaded applications

Many NLMs can load on a NetWare server — especially in the more recent versions. If you have a question about what an NLM does or want to see whether it's valid, you can search on the filename at `www.google.com` or at `support.novell.com` to get more information.

A port scan of the server from another computer can find rogue applications as well.

Tcpcon

The tcpcon NLM shows ports that are listening and connected. Follow these steps to use it:

1. **Enter `load tcpcon` at the server prompt.**
2. **Select Protocol Information from the main menu.**
3. **Select TCP and then TCP Connections to view the TCP ports that are open.**
4. **Select UDP and then UDP Listeners to view the UDP ports that are open.**

   Figure 13-8 shows the TCP ports that are open and listening on this server, including chargen, FTP, and NCP.

If something doesn't look right, it may not be, so investigate the port number further. My favorite port number reference is at `www.iana.org/assignments/port-numbers`, but a simple Google search usually is productive.

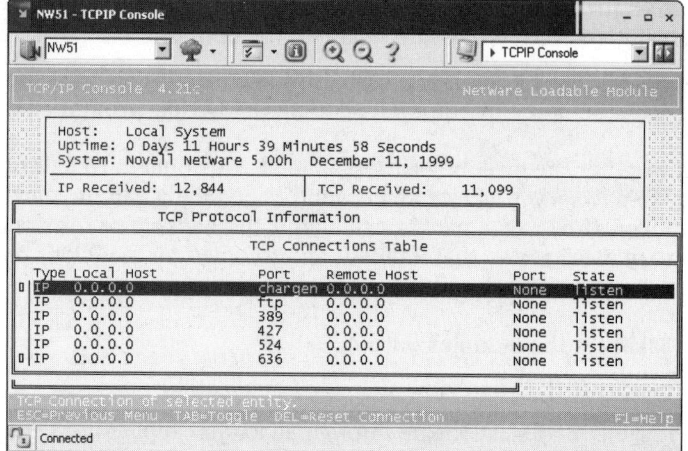

Figure 13-8: Using tcpcon to show open TCP ports on a NetWare server.

Admin utilities

If hackers can successfully log in to a NetWare server or eDirectory, they can use, in malicious ways, some of the great — and free — NetWare admin utilities from JRB Software (`www.jrbsoftware.com`). For example, hackers can

- Run the *downsrvr* program to reboot a NetWare server — most likely at the worst possible time.
- Use the *serv_cmd* program to disable logins, remotely load NLMs, and add bindery contexts to the system.

Countermeasures

The following countermeasures can minimize the chances that malicious NLMs will be running on your servers.

Documentation

The best way to keep track of loaded NLMs is to document, document, and document your server. It's critical to know what's supposed to be loaded on your server at all times.

- For each loaded NLM, you need to know its name, version, and date.

Keeping up-to-date records can get tedious, especially with a large number of servers. Consider purchasing a commercial product — NetServerMon or AdRem Server Manager — to help you manage this task.

- Save and print recent versions of your `startup.ncf` and `autoexec.ncf` files.
- Document — at least, at a high level — your eDirectory structure. You can either
  - Take a screen capture of eDirectory as it looks in NetWare Administrator or ConsoleOne.
  - Run `cx /t /a /r`, and save the output of the program to a text file by entering the following at a command prompt:

```
cx /t /a /r > filename.txt
```

Update your documentation after any system changes are made or any new patches are applied.

Unauthorized logins

To prevent rogue NLMs or remote applications from being loaded or run from a workstation, apply these security measures to your NetWare systems:

- Make strong passwords on *every* NetWare account. I outline minimum password requirements in Chapter 7.
- Secure the server console.
- Enable intruder detection.
- Neutralize dangerous NLMs, such as netbasic. You can either rename them or remove them.

  If you remove dangerous NLMs, make a backup of the files first. You may need them in the future.

Clear-text packets

Most internal LAN traffic — regardless of the operating system in use — travels across the wire in clear text. The clear text can be captured and used against you.

Packet capture

Clear-text packets can be captured with either

- A network analyzer
- Components of the Pandora NetWare hacking suite (`www.nmrc.org/project/pandora`)

Pandora can spoof NCP packets, which can give them admin equivalency on the network after the hacker logs in via a standard user account that he previously compromised. A hacker could log in as a normal user with a weak or blank password and then use Pandora to manipulate NetWare traffic and get admin rights on the network.

Countermeasures

You can easily set up *NCP packet signing* within a NetWare environment. This encrypts and provides proof that a packet actually originated from the sending host. NCP packet signing has four levels, but the level for the utmost security is level 3, which requires packet signatures.

This can slow network traffic and place a larger processing burden on your server. Level-3 packet signing can decrease network performance on busy NetWare servers — sometimes, by more than 50 percent.

The following steps explain how to enable level-3 packet signing:

- Enable level-3 packet signing on the server and at the top of the `autoexec.ncf` file with the following command:

  ```
  set ncp packet signature option=3
  ```

- Enable level-3 packet signing on NetWare clients with these steps:
  1. Right-click your red Novell icon in your Windows system tray.
  2. Select Novell Client Properties and Advanced Settings.
  3. Set the Signature Level to 3 (Required).

In NetWare 3.*x* and earlier, passwords are sent in clear text across the network. For these versions, you can enter the following command on your server and in the `autoexec.ncf` file to help prevent passwords from being captured with a network analyzer:

```
set allow unencrypted passwords=off
```

General Best Practices for Minimizing NetWare Security Risks

Although you can't completely defend NetWare servers against attacks, you can come close, which is more than you can say for other leading operating systems. These NetWare hacking countermeasures can help improve security on your NetWare server above and beyond what I've already recommended.

Rename admin

Rename the admin account. Figure 13-9 shows how this can be done in the Novell ConsoleOne utility.

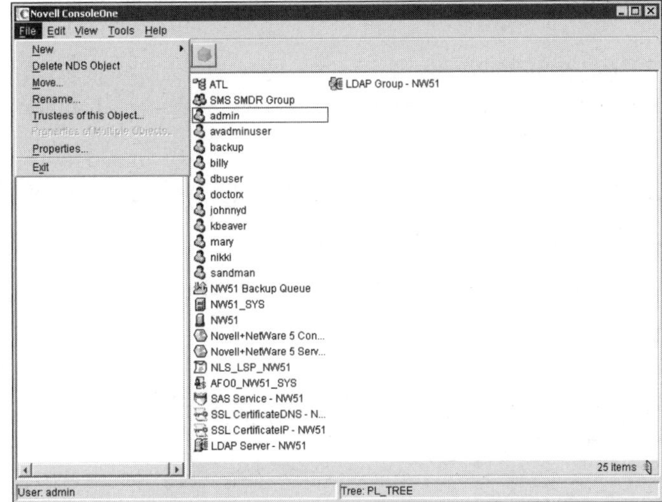

Figure 13-9: Renaming the NetWare admin account with ConsoleOne.

Be careful. Other applications, such as the server backup software, may depend on this ID.

If you rename admin, be sure to edit any backup jobs or startup scripts that depend on the admin account. It's actually best to not use the admin account for these purposes anyway, so this may be a good time to make a change by creating an admin equivalent for each application that's dependent on an admin ID. This can help make your system more secure by reducing the number of places that the admin account is exposed and vulnerable to cracking on the network.

Disable eDirectory browsing

A good way to ward off attacks is to disable Public's right to browse the directory tree in either NetWare Administrator for NetWare 4.*x* or Novell ConsoleOne for NetWare 5.*x* and later. This right is enabled by default to enable users to browse the eDirectory tree easily.

Disabling the Public Browse right or any other eDirectory or file rights can cause problems, such as locking users (including you) out of the network, disabling login scripts, and disabling printing. The potential risk depends on how you configure eDirectory. If you remove Public's Browse right, you can usually grant specific object rights lower in the tree where they're needed to keep everything working. Make sure that you test these types of critical changes before applying them to your production environment.

NetWare Administrator

Follow these steps to disable the Public browse right to eDirectory with NetWare Administrator (`sys:\public\win32\nwadmn32.exe`):

1. **Right-click the Root object in your directory tree.**
2. **Select Trustees of this Object.**
3. **Select the [Public] trustee, as shown in Figure 13-10.**
4. **Uncheck the Browse object right.**

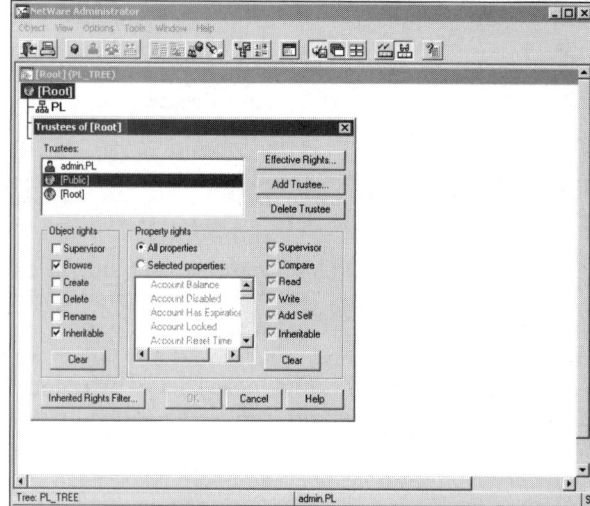

Figure 13-10: The default Browse right for [Public], shown in NetWare Administrator.

Novell ConsoleOne

Follow these steps to disable the Public browse right to eDirectory with Novell ConsoleOne (`sys:\public\mgmt\ConsoleOne\1.2\bin\ConsoleOne.exe`):

1. **Right-click your tree object.**
2. **Select Trustees of this Object.**

3. **Select the [Public] trustee and then click Assigned Rights.**
4. **Uncheck the Browse right, as shown in Figure 13-11.**

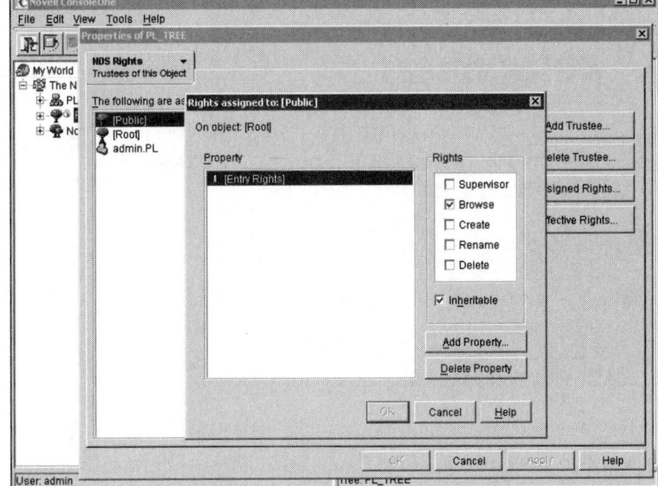

Figure 13-11: The default Browse right for [Public], shown in ConsoleOne.

Removing bindery contexts

Remove any bindery contexts loaded on your server. Bindery contexts are in place in NetWare 4.*x* and later to provide backward compatibility with older clients that need to access the servers as though they're NetWare 3.*x* or earlier servers. This is typically due to either older applications or NetWare clients (such as netx and VLMs) that make bindery calls instead of eDirectory calls.

Removing bindery contexts can help prevent hacker attacks against bindery weaknesses. To disable the bindery context on your server, simply remark out the *set Bindery Context* line in your server's `autoexec.ncf` file.

If you remove your bindery contexts, make sure that no clients or applications depend on NetWare bindery emulation.

System auditing

Turn on system auditing by running the auditcon program at a command prompt. This can help you track down a future intruder by auditing files, volumes, and even the directory tree. It's just good security practice as well. You can get specific instructions on using auditcon for system auditing purposes in the Novell Technical Information Document *How to setup Auditing on your Network* at `support.novell.com/cgi-bin/search/searchtid.cgi?/10068513.htm`.

TCP/IP parameters

In NetWare 5.*x* and above, based on your specific version, you can prevent several types of DoS attacks as shown below by entering the following TCP/IP parameters at the server console:

```
set discard oversized ping packets=on
set discard oversized UDP packets=on
set filter subnet broadcast packets=on
set filter packets with IP header options=on
set ipx netbios replication option=0
set tcp defend land attacks=on
set tcp defend syn attacks=on
```

You can enter the preceding commands into the server's `autoexec.ncf` file so that they load each time the server starts.

Patching

Patch, patch, and patch again! Novell lists the latest patches for the NetWare versions it supports on its Web site:

```
support.novell.com/produpdate/patchlist.html#nw
```

Part V
Application Hacking

"Someone want to look at this manuscript I received on email called, 'The Embedded Virus That Destroyed the Publisher's Servers When the Manuscript Was Rejected'?"

In this part . . .

Well, this book has covered everything from non-technical hacks to network hacks to operating system hacks. One major category is left to cover: the applications that run on top of all of this.

This part first covers malware (you know, those darn viruses, worms, and so on) and malware prevention tools, along with some various countermeasures. Although malware is not particularly an application ethical hackers use (at least try not to use), it still affects everything else done on networks from a security perspective, including messaging systems and Web applications, which are also in this part. This part then takes a look at various messaging hacks and countermeasures affecting e-mail and instant messaging systems. Finally, this part takes a look at common Web application hacks, along with some countermeasures to secure them from the elements.

Chapter 14

Malware

In This Chapter

- Distributing malware
- Testing your systems
- Preventing malware

Malicious software *(malware)* has long been one of the biggest problems computer users face. Viruses and worms have proved to be the biggest nuisances, but these types of malware are ineffective if adequate controls are in place. On the other hand, such types of malware as Trojan horses and rootkits can inflict serious harm against computers and information, and are much harder to defend against.

The implications of testing your own systems with malware attacks — as hackers would do — are similar to some of the social-engineering and physical-security attacks I cover elsewhere in the book. Introducing known malware into your production systems is just not a good idea, considering that your business is at stake. In this chapter, although I cover some benign tests you can run against your systems, I focus on how malware gets onto your systems, how to find and remove it after an infection is found, and what proven countermeasures you can take to increase the odds that malware stays out of your systems.

Implications of Malware Attacks

Malware is one of the greatest threats to the security of your information. Not only do you have to deal with the well-known malware — the ILoveYous and Code Reds of the world — infecting your computers, but also, hackers are constantly developing new ways to wreak havoc on systems. It seems that every month, widespread malware attacks take place around the globe. The more recent attacks are mostly *self-propagating* — which means that they need no user intervention to spread across computer networks and the Internet. These programs attack unpatched software and gullible users opening malicious e-mail attachments

A case study in malware with Ed Skoudis

In this case study, Ed Skoudis, an information-security consultant for International Network Services, shared an experience he had related to malware. Here's his account of what happened.

The situation

Mr. Skoudis and his penetration-testing team were hired by a large financial institution to determine whether they could break into the bank's updated Internet gateway infrastructure. This penetration test focused on the new elements of their infrastructure, including several VPN gateways, firewalls, routers, and a handful of servers. The goal of the test was to search for vulnerabilities and see how deep into the target production network the team could penetrate.

The Web server was where things started to get interesting for Mr. Skoudis and his team. During the test in mid-2003, while scanning all of the target systems for vulnerabilities with the free Nessus tool, the team discovered that the Web server was vulnerable to the WebDAV buffer-overflow exploit. This flaw was originally announced by Microsoft in March 2003, but no one had patched the server for 60 days.

The outcome

Mr. Skoudis and his team were able to execute commands on the machine by *tickling* WebDAV and installed the Netcat tool to create a backdoor. Then they scheduled the Netcat backdoor to restart every 10 minutes, to make sure they could re-enter the system continually if they were ever knocked off. Mr. Skoudis emphasized that penetration testers need to be extremely careful in choosing the type of malware they utilize in their testing regimen. As a side note, he stated that he installs only application-level backdoors that are well understood, like Netcat. In addition, he stressed that penetration testers should not install rootkits or introduce self-replicating code, such as viruses and worms, because they can make a production machine extremely unstable.

With the Netcat backdoor firmly lodged on the target system, the team set up shop on the victim Windows Web server. They installed their scanning tools on this machine, including the Nmap port scanner. Using the conquered Web server as a jump-off point to scan further into the network, the team found another vulnerable system. This time, they discovered a poorly configured Solaris machine on the internal network that allowed SSH access with an easily guessed password. After he and his team compromised the Solaris server, they installed another Netcat backdoor on that system.

With two relatively common flaws — an unpatched Windows Web server and an easily guessed password — Mr. Skoudis and his team managed to gain deep access into the target network. He emphasized the possibility of this type of attack by a not-so-ethical hacker, along with the widespread availability of the malware needed to carry it out, and underscored the importance of having a solid security program. This includes keeping systems patched and educating users and administrators in selecting difficult-to-guess passwords.

Ed Skoudis uses his exceptional technical expertise to perform security assessments, design secure network architectures, and respond to computer attacks for his customers. He is a well-known speaker on issues associated with hacker tools and defenses, and has authored the excellent Prentice Hall books *Malware: Fighting Malicious Code* and *Counter Hack: A Step-by-Step Guide to Computer Attacks and Effective Defenses.*

Most malware attacks — especially the recent ones — exploit well-known vulnerabilities that should've been fixed months before the attacks occur. Unfortunately, the general practice within IT and security is to install patches when people get around to it. This is mostly because people either don't make it a priority to patch or simply can't keep up with all the patches required across all their systems. The hackers know this and take full advantage of it.

The widespread malware attacks that you hear about on the news aren't the ones to worry about. Trojan horses, rootkits, spyware, and other devious programs are the scary ones. These applications can do the following:

- List running processes and applications
- Load and kill running processes and applications
- Capture keystrokes
- Search and copy files
- Steal passwords
- Edit system files
- Turn on Web cams and microphones
- Remotely reboot computers
- Perform practically any administrative function

Bad things can happen if any of these events occurs on your network, including confidential information being stolen, computers being taken offline, and data being deleted.

Types of Malware

Most malware is *platform-specific:* It targets specific operating systems, applications, and vulnerabilities to spread more quickly.

Trojan horses

Trojan horses — named after the infamous Greek wooden horse used to penetrate the city of Troy — are executable files, often transmitted via e-mail, that masquerade as legitimate programs but actually perform malicious acts.

Trojan-horse code works in the background — doing things like deleting information, gathering passwords, and capturing keystrokes — while a legitimate-looking program, such as a screen saver or game, runs in the foreground.

Many Trojans — called *remote-access Trojans,* or *RATs* — set up backdoors on the systems they infect, allowing hackers to access them remotely and control them from across the Internet. Many Trojans aren't detected by antivirus programs. With all things being equal (and antivirus software running), this is the malware you should be afraid of. Some common RATs are NetBus, SubSeven, and Back Orifice.

Viruses

Computer viruses are the best-known malware category. Viruses are programs that are often *self-replicating* — meaning that they can make copies of themselves — and attach to executable files, deleting information and crashing computers whenever a user or other process runs the program. Even PDA viruses exist, some of which drain batteries and call 911 for you — how thoughtful!

Worms

Worms are self-propagating programs that travel around the Internet at lightning speed. They load up in memory, effectively exploit known software vulnerabilities, and often end up crashing the systems.

Rootkits

Rootkits are nasty applications that hackers can use to control a computer *completely,* with the ultimate prize of crashing the system or stealing information. Rootkits are mostly found on UNIX systems but are becoming popular on the Windows platform. Rootkits are sets of programs that either

- Masquerade as typical administrator command-line programs
- Integrate into the *kernel,* or core, of the operating system

Kernel-based rootkits, such as Knark for Linux and the FU rootkit for Windows, tie into the actual operating system. With these programs, hackers can

- Hide system processes and applications from the Windows Task Manager or the process list in UNIX
- Change the group membership of processes and applications so that a malicious program can run as the system, administrator, or root account
- Modify environment variables
- Make programs look like they were run by another user, concealing the hacker's identity in audit logs

Spyware

Spyware programs spy on you and sometimes even capture and transmit confidential information from your computer. They're installed as cookies, Windows Registry entries, and even executables on the local computer.

"Legitimate" spyware that may be installed by an administrator or other person to watch someone's computer usage includes SpectorSoft's eBlaster and Spector Pro, and TrueActive (formerly known as WinWhatWhere).

These programs are extremely powerful and capture video screen shots, turn on the local microphone, track Web browsing, and even forward copies of e-mails sent and received to a third-party address. Powerful *and* scary!

Adware is similar to spyware but a little less intrusive. It tracks Internet usage and pulls targeted ads to specific users, based on their habits.

Built-in programming interfaces

Programming interfaces built into operating systems can be used maliciously:

- **Java applets** are programs written in the Sun Microsystems programming language. Although these programs run in a *sandbox* — or safe area — to ensure that the local system is not compromised by malicious code, they can still cause security problems.
- **Microsoft .NET applications** are programs written based on the new application framework from Microsoft. Like Java applets, these programs have their own playpen that helps ensure that malicious code is not executed.
- **ActiveX controls** are Microsoft-based programs that everyone loves to hate. ActiveX controls can be executed with minimal effort in such applications as Internet Explorer, Outlook, and other Microsoft programs.

Their control over a computer can potentially cause serious harm to a computer system and its stored information.

- **VBScripts** are scaled-down versions of Microsoft's Visual Basic programming language. Similar to ActiveX controls, these scripts can wreak havoc on local data.

  Many of the common malware programs traversing the Internet today are VBScripts.

- **Windows Script Host (WSH)** is a script processor built into Windows — similar to DOS batch files — that can be used to perform malicious acts.
- **JavaScript programs,** which are similar to ActiveX and VBScripts, are written in Netscape's scripting language. They can cause computers harm if users willingly run them within Web browsers and e-mails.

Not all applications written in these programming interfaces are malicious. Many legitimate programs are used every day that run just fine and don't do any harm.

Logic bombs

A *logic bomb* is a program — often, an automated script using regular network administration tools — that is scheduled to run when it's triggered by a certain event, such as someone's logging in, or run on a specific date or time, such as two weeks after an employee is let go.

Logic bombs are a common way for disgruntled employees to seek revenge on their former employers. Some logic bombs have destroyed entire databases of information, including the famous logic bomb planted by Tim Lloyd at Omega Engineering a few years back. This program erased all the information from the company's NetWare server, putting a stop to its manufacturing processes. This event resulted in $10 million in damages to the company, and ultimately, 80 employees got laid off.

Security tools

Your own security tools can be used against you. This includes the following tools:

- Vulnerability scanners, such as Nessus and even the tried-and-true Netcat tool, can place backdoors in your systems.
- Network analyzers, including the ARP poisoning tools ettercap and dsniff.

- The DOS debug program that still ships with Windows.
- The NetWare debugger backdoor.

  You access the backdoor by pressing Shift+Alt+Shift+Esc all at the same time (using both Shift keys) at the server console.

How Malware Propagates

Some time back — practically forever, in computer time — most malware propagated via floppy disks. In 1981, the first computer virus was released: the Apple II Elk Cloner virus. In 1986, the first virus that affected the Microsoft/Intel platform — the Brain virus — was released. Both of these viruses were floppy-disk–based, but neither packed the punch that many viruses have come to inflict on their victims since that time.

Some of the first malware exploited vulnerabilities in computer hardware and software architectures — like what happens today. These old-fashioned viruses spread very slowly by today's standards. It could take months and sometimes years for a few thousand systems to be infected. What's different about today's malware? It's the method of propagation. The Internet allows malware to spread around the world quickly. Malware can affect hundreds of thousands of systems within a few weeks, as happened with the Code Red and Nimda worms, or within a few minutes, as we saw with the Slammer/Sapphire worm. Hackers from anywhere in the world can try penetrating your systems — at their convenience.

Automation

Automated attacks are the wave of the future for malware. The Internet is not going away. In fact, more systems are going online — more users, more hackers, and a greater number of applications are emerging that can be affected. This includes Web services; peer-to-peer (P2P) software, such as instant messaging (IM); and other file-sharing technologies, such as Gnutella, Kazaa, Morpheus, and mobile-device applications that run on PDAs and cell phones.

E-mail

The most common malware attack channel is through e-mail. A hacker simply attaches a virus or Trojan horse to an e-mail — often, through an automated mechanism — and sends the message to unsuspecting users. This process is automated with self-propagating worms making an attack even easier. The text of the e-mail says, "See the attached note" or "Check out this game." Many gullible users open the attachment, thinking it's something that will brighten up their day. Instead, it's malware looking to copy or delete local files and often glean e-mail addresses from the user's address book to send itself on to other users. If antivirus software is missing, outdated, or disabled at the time, this can spell bad news for the computer or network.

Hacker backdoors

Malware is propagated on computer systems by hackers compromising a host from across the network or Internet, obtaining administrator or root access by exploiting a known vulnerability and then installing the malware to their heart's content. They can set up backdoors, giving them remote access so they can come back and play in the future.

Many of these infections go unnoticed indefinitely, usually until the network administrator suspects that something strange is going on, or the system crashes, or information gets stolen or erased.

Testing

You can carry out various tests to check for malware infections on your network, as described in the following sections.

Vulnerable malware ports

You should look for Trojan ports when assessing your systems. Here are some common ones to look out:

- 31337, 54320, and 54321 (Back Orifice and Back Orifice 2000)
- 12345 and 12346 (NetBus)
- 1243 and 27374 (SubSeven)

When testing, look for computers listening on these ports. These port numbers can usually be changed in most malware applications, so don't rely on these completely.

Two great Web sites I refer to a lot when I want to see how a particular piece of malware works are the following:

- `www.simovits.com/trojans/trojans.html` is a comprehensive listing of Trojan horses.
- PestPatrol's catalog of pests at `research.pestpatrol.com/PestInfo/pestdatabase.asp`.

Manual assessment

It helps to know your systems — what software is installed and what services are running. Document your baseline environment, if you haven't already, by using the same methods I describe in this chapter.

If you suspect that one of your systems may be infected by malware, or you want to see which applications are loaded on your system, there are tools and techniques you can use. The key here is to search for things that just don't look right.

Windows

Because most malware affects Windows, there are various tests specific to that platform you can carry out to test for malware infections.

Odd file names

If you're unsure what a specific file does or want more details on file-format and header information, you have a couple of options for information:

- Check Wotsit's Format at `www.wotsit.org` for information on file formats and headers.
- Search for the filename in Google with both Web and Groups searches.

Netstat

Run `netstat -an` at a command prompt.

- The `a` option displays all connections and listening ports.
- The `n` option displays IP addresses and port numbers in numeric form to make them easier to read.

You see something similar to the following list:

```
Active Connections
Proto  Local Address          Foreign Address        State
TCP    0.0.0.0:80             0.0.0.0:0              LISTENING
TCP    0.0.0.0:135            0.0.0.0:0              LISTENING
TCP    0.0.0.0:445            0.0.0.0:0              LISTENING
TCP    10.11.12.202:139       0.0.0.0:0              LISTENING
TCP    10.11.12.202:1044      208.215.179.139:80     CLOSE_WAIT
TCP    10.11.12.202:2099      10.11.12.204:139       ESTABLISHED
TCP    10.11.12.202:2100      10.11.12.2:139         TIME_WAIT
UDP    0.0.0.0:445            *:*
UDP    10.11.12.202:137       *:*
UDP    10.11.12.202:138       *:*
```

The preceding example shows several Microsoft NetBIOS networking ports (135, 137, 138, 139, and 445) and an HTTP connection in progress (port 80). The NetBIOS connections may be questionable, but I've actually initiated those connections, so I trust that they're legitimate.

Look for connections to the following ports to scope out possible malware or other hacker behavior in progress:

- NetBIOS ports
- Common malware ports
- Ports that can indicate malicious behavior, including telnet (TCP port 23) and FTP sessions that shouldn't be occurring (TCP ports 20 and 21)

Port mapping

A port-mapper program shows which applications are actually connected to the specific open ports.

My favorite port mapper is a free tool called Vision by Foundstone (`www.foundstone.com`). I recommend this tool for your toolbox.

Figure 14-1 shows the detailed information that Vision can provide. Ports 12345 and 12346 are mapped to `c:\temp\Patch.exe`. That's the NetBus server executable — yikes!

Task Manager

Press Ctrl+Alt+Del to load the Windows Task Manager and see whether any strange applications or processes are loaded.

Many strange-looking processes are legitimate. Make sure that you know what you're dealing with, so you don't stop a legitimate program. A quick Google search on the filename usually provides enough information. Just because it's not there doesn't mean it's not loaded, though, because some processes, such as the FU rootkit for Windows, have the ability to hide themselves.

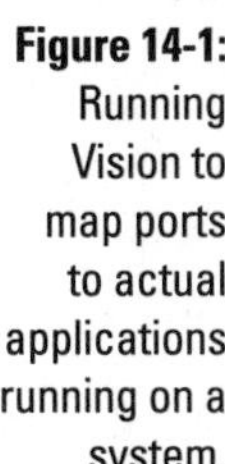

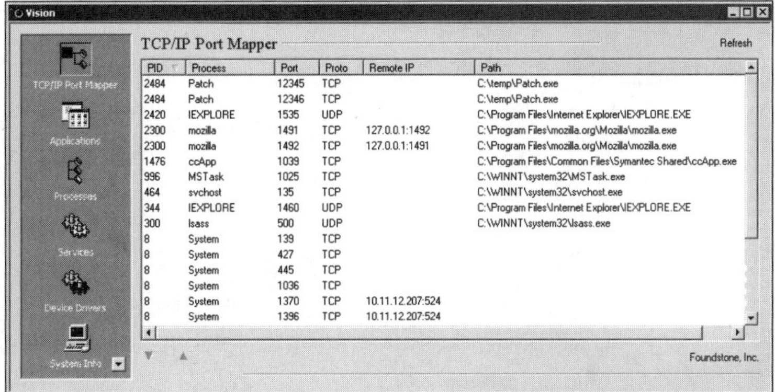

Figure 14-1: Running Vision to map ports to actual applications running on a system.

Net use

You can run `net use` at a command prompt to see what drives are mapped to external systems. Look for drive mappings that should not be there.

Registry

Look in your Windows Registry under the following `HKEY_LOCAL_MACHINE` (HKLM) keys for strange-looking applications that are loading. This is a common place for malware to be initiated upon startup.

```
HKLM\SOFTWARE\Microsoft\Windows\CurrentVersion\Run
HKLM\Microsoft\Windows\CurrentVersion\RunOnce
HKLM\SOFTWARE\Microsoft\Windows\CurrentVersion\RunOnceEx
```

Startup files

Check your Windows startup folder and files such as `autoexec.bat` and `config.sys` in the root directory of the C: drive for any applications that don't belong. Unknown programs can signal that a rogue application is configured to start every time the computer boots.

Linux

For your Linux-based systems, you can run various tests to find out more about what's running on your systems.

netstat

Run `netstat -at` to view active network connections.

Figure 14-2 shows that a Web server and SSH server are running with two computers connected to these services. In addition, you see that the X11 service for X Window along with the domain service (DNS), sunrpc, and SMTP service for e-mail. Check these types of things before a suspected attack occurs so that you know what belongs and what doesn't.

```
Linux - SecureCRT
File Edit View Options Transfer Script Window Help
[root@localhost sbin]# netstat -at
Active Internet connections (servers and established)
Proto Recv-Q Send-Q Local Address               Foreign Address         State
tcp        0      0 *:32768                     *:*                     LISTEN
tcp        0      0 localhost.localdo:32769     *:*                     LISTEN
tcp        0      0 *:sunrpc                    *:*                     LISTEN
tcp        0      0 *:http                      *:*                     LISTEN
tcp        0      0 *:x11                       *:*                     LISTEN
tcp        0      0 10.11.12.205:domain         *:*                     LISTEN
tcp        0      0 localhost.locald:domain     *:*                     LISTEN
tcp        0      0 *:ssh                       *:*                     LISTEN
tcp        0      0 localhost.localdom:rndc     *:*                     LISTEN
tcp        0      0 *:1241                      *:*                     LISTEN
tcp        0      0 localhost.localdom:smtp     *:*                     LISTEN
tcp        0      0 *:https                     *:*                     LISTEN
tcp        0      0 10.11.12.205:http           pc2:1235                TIME_WAIT
tcp        0      0 10.11.12.205:http           pc2:1234                TIME_WAIT
tcp        0      0 10.11.12.205:http           pc2:bvcontrol           TIME_WAIT
tcp        0     20 10.11.12.205:ssh            pc1:1853                ESTABLISHED
[root@localhost sbin]#
Ready    ssh1: 3DES   20, 24   20 Rows, 81 Cols   VT100
```

Figure 14-2: Running netstat in Linux shows the network connections.

lsof

The lsof utility lists open files, as shown in Figure 14-3, so you can check for strange connections. This is similar to the Vision program for Windows.

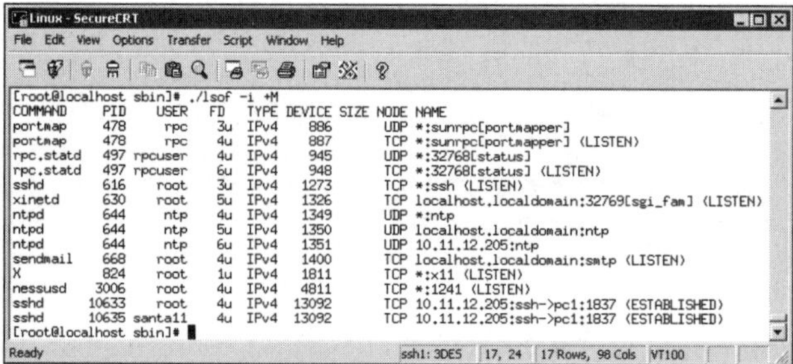

Linux - SecureCRT
File Edit View Options Transfer Script Window Help
[root@localhost sbin]# ./lsof -i +M
COMMAND PID USER FD TYPE DEVICE SIZE NODE NAME
portmap 478 rpc 3u IPv4 886 UDP *:sunrpc[portmapper]
portmap 478 rpc 4u IPv4 887 TCP *:sunrpc[portmapper] (LISTEN)
rpc.statd 497 rpcuser 4u IPv4 945 UDP *:32768[status]
rpc.statd 497 rpcuser 6u IPv4 948 TCP *:32768[status] (LISTEN)
sshd 616 root 3u IPv4 1273 TCP *:ssh (LISTEN)
xinetd 630 root 5u IPv4 1326 TCP localhost.localdomain:32769[sgi_fam] (LISTEN)
ntpd 644 ntp 4u IPv4 1349 UDP *:ntp
ntpd 644 ntp 5u IPv4 1350 UDP localhost.localdomain:ntp
ntpd 644 ntp 6u IPv4 1351 UDP 10.11.12.205:ntp
sendmail 668 root 4u IPv4 1400 TCP localhost.localdomain:smtp (LISTEN)
X 824 root 1u IPv4 1811 TCP *:x11 (LISTEN)
nessusd 3006 root 4u IPv4 4811 TCP *:1241 (LISTEN)
sshd 10633 root 4u IPv4 13092 TCP 10.11.12.205:ssh->pc1:1837 (ESTABLISHED)
sshd 10635 santa11 4u IPv4 13092 TCP 10.11.12.205:ssh->pc1:1837 (ESTABLISHED)
[root@localhost sbin]#
Ready
ssh1: 3DES
17, 24
17 Rows, 98 Cols
VT100

Figure 14-3: Using the lsof utility to look for potential malware applications that are loaded.

ps

The ps utility displays running processes, as shown in Figure 14-4. You can check for strange applications that don't look right.

This is why it helps to know what's supposed to be loaded!

Startup files

Check your Linux startup files (such as `inetd.conf` and `xinetd.conf`) for any applications that don't belong. Unknown programs can signal that a rogue application is configured to start every time the computer boots.

```
[root@localhost sbin]# ps -aux
USER       PID %CPU %MEM   VSZ  RSS TTY      STAT START   TIME COMMAND
root         1  0.0  0.2  1264  460 ?        S    Dec07   0:05 init
root         2  0.0  0.0     0    0 ?        SW   Dec07   0:00 [keventd]
root         3  0.0  0.0     0    0 ?        SW   Dec07   0:00 [kapmd]
root         4  0.0  0.0     0    0 ?        SWN  Dec07   0:00 [ksoftirqd_CPU0]
root         5  0.0  0.0     0    0 ?        SW   Dec07   0:06 [kswapd]
root         6  0.0  0.0     0    0 ?        SW   Dec07   0:00 [bdflush]
root         7  0.0  0.0     0    0 ?        SW   Dec07   0:00 [kupdated]
root         8  0.0  0.0     0    0 ?        SW   Dec07   0:00 [mdrecoveryd]
root        14  0.0  0.0     0    0 ?        SW   Dec07   0:00 [scsi_eh_0]
root        17  0.0  0.0     0    0 ?        SW   Dec07   0:01 [kjournald]
root        73  0.0  0.0     0    0 ?        SW   Dec07   0:00 [khubd]
root       165  0.0  0.0     0    0 ?        SW   Dec07   0:00 [kjournald]
root       456  0.0  0.2  1324  532 ?        S    Dec07   0:00 syslogd -m 0
root       460  0.0  0.2  1264  432 ?        S    Dec07   0:00 klogd -x
rpc        478  0.0  0.2  1404  528 ?        S    Dec07   0:00 portmap
rpcuser    497  0.0  0.3  1444  728 ?        S    Dec07   0:00 rpc.statd
root       578  0.0  0.2  1256  488 ?        S    Dec07   0:00 /usr/sbin/apmd -p 10 -w 5 -W -P /et
root       616  0.0  0.7  3200 1428 ?        S    Dec07   0:05 /usr/sbin/sshd
root       630  0.0  0.4  1996  916 ?        S    Dec07   0:00 xinetd -stayalive -reuse -pidfile /
ntp        644  0.0  0.9  1836 1828 ?        SL   Dec07   0:00 ntpd -U ntp
root       668  0.0  1.1  4960 2224 ?        S    Dec07   0:02 sendmail: accepting connections
smmsp      678  0.0  1.0  4776 2000 ?        S    Dec07   0:00 sendmail: Queue runner@01:00:00 for
root       688  0.0  0.2  1300  428 ?        S    Dec07   0:00 gpm -t ps/2 -m /dev/mouse
root       697  0.0  0.3  1432  620 ?        S    Dec07   0:00 crond
xfs        728  0.0  1.6  4432 3232 ?        S    Dec07   0:00 xfs -droppriv -daemon
daemon     746  0.0  0.2  1292  524 ?        S    Dec07   0:00 /usr/sbin/atd
root       772  0.0  0.2  1244  388 tty1     S    Dec07   0:00 /sbin/mingetty tty1
```

Figure 14-4: Running the ps utility to display running processes.

Network card

Determine whether someone or some malware has placed the machine's network card into promiscuous mode, indicating the use of a network analyzer. Enter this line at the command prompt:

```
ifconfig -a | grep PROMISC
```

If the return value is not empty, an interface is running in promiscuous mode.

You can enter this command into a cron job that runs every few hours that can alert you if one is found.

Antivirus software testing

For starters, check whether your antivirus software is actually working.

Before you begin testing your antivirus software, make sure that you have the latest virus software engine and signatures loaded.

You have a couple of safe options for checking the effectiveness of your antivirus software, as described in the following two sections. This is by no means a comprehensive method of testing your malware-protection mechanisms, but it serves as a good, safe start.

Eicar test string

Eicar is a European-based malware think tank that has worked in conjunction with malware vendors to provide this basic system test. The eicar test string is transmitted in the body of an e-mail or as a file attachment so that you can see how your server and workstations respond. You basically access this file — which contains the following 68-character string — on your computer to see whether your antivirus or other malware software detects it:

```
X5O!P%@AP[4\PZX54(P^)7CC)7}$EICAR STANDARD-ANTIVIRUS-TEST-FILE!$H+H*
```

You can download a text file with this string from www.eicar.org/anti_virus_test_file.htm. Several versions of the file are available on this site. One version is a zip file. I recommend testing with this file to make sure that your antivirus software can detect malware within compressed files.

When you run this test, you may see results similar to Figure 14-5 from your antivirus software.

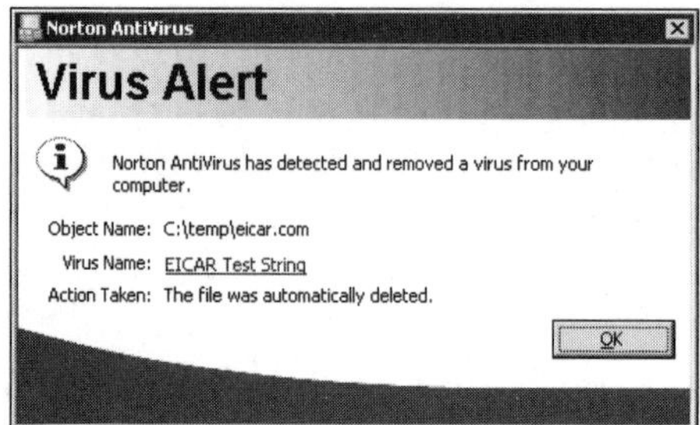

Figure 14-5: Using the eicar test string to test antivirus software.

GFI's Email Security Testing Zone

A freebie at www.gfi.com/emailsecuritytest is a good e-mail malware test to run against your server and clients. This series of tests sends e-mails with malicious-like scripts in such programming languages as Visual Basic and ActiveX to check exactly what gets through your e-mail system. These aren't malicious tests — just tests that *should* invoke your antivirus software or other protective measures on your e-mail server or gateway if your software is configured and working correctly.

Network scanning

Use Nmap, SuperScan, or your favorite port-scanning tool to check for abnormal ports open on your network hosts.

Some connections that show as open aren't necessarily accurate and dependable. You may need to investigate unknown ports on the systems further by using a port-mapping tool such as Vision for Windows or lsof for Linux, as described previously in this chapter.

Using SuperScan, you may find the following results in a quick network scan:

```
* - 10.10.1.1  fs1
      |___ 12345 Win95/NT Netbus backdoor
* - 10.10.1.2  [Unknown]
* - 10.10.1.4  laser
* + 10.10.1.204  PC100
      |___ 12345 Win95/NT Netbus backdoor
* + 10.10.1.209  DQ
      |___ 12345 Win95/NT Netbus backdoor
```

You can also use Nmap to find specific malware ports, as shown in Figure 14-6.

```
DOS Prompt
C:\nmap>nmap -p 1-65535 10.11.12.204

Starting nmap 3.48 ( http://www.insecure.org/nmap ) at 2003-12-15 11:15 Eastern
Standard Time
Interesting ports on pc2 (10.11.12.204):
(The 65529 ports scanned but not shown below are in state: closed)
PORT      STATE SERVICE
135/tcp   open  msrpc
139/tcp   open  netbios-ssn
445/tcp   open  microsoft-ds
1025/tcp  open  NFS-or-IIS
12345/tcp open  NetBus
12346/tcp open  NetBus

Nmap run completed -- 1 IP address (1 host up) scanned in 220.056 seconds
```

Figure 14-6: Nmap results showing the NetBus server listening on ports 12345 and 12346.

During a recent incident response project that I was on, I found dozens of computers listening on TCP port 12345 — the default port of the NetBus Trojan! Needless to say, I was quite concerned. After some poking around, I discovered that NetBus had not infested the network, as it originally appeared. It was the OfficeScan NT antivirus product by Trend Micro that was listening on that port — who would've thought? Major lesson learned.

I recommend scanning your entire network for spyware with PestPatrol Auditor's Edition (`www.pestpatrol.com`) or a similar program. Figure 14-7 shows the results of a stand-alone PestPatrol scan on the local computer; it found NetBus and several spyware cookies. PestPatrol detects spyware, adware, Trojans, and some rootkits.

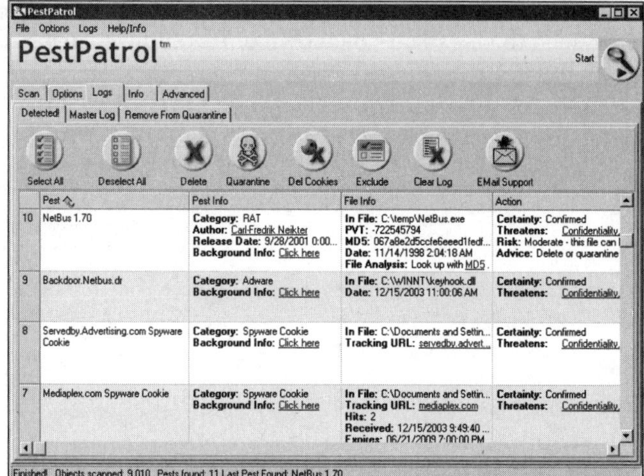

Figure 14-7: Sample results from a PestPatrol scan.

Every time I run a full scan on my system, tools are called *suspect,* and my software — antivirus software especially — tends to "clean up" those tools for me. I must either replace my security tools from backup or download and install them again. If any of your security tools or security testing software may look like malware on your computer, either

- Keep backup copies of the original installation files.
- Have your malware-protection software skip the files or directories where your security tools are installed.

Of course, if an infection is suspected — and periodically, such as once a month, even when infections aren't suspected — run your antivirus software against all the computers on your network. Another tool to double-check your systems is McAfee's AVERT Stinger (`vil.nai.com/vil/stinger`). This standalone antivirus executable checks for several dozen of the latest common malware items and known variants of each.

Behavioral-analysis tools

For a neat set of tests to find whether your Windows-based systems are susceptible to behavioral-based malware attacks — that is, attacks that don't match a specific signature, but perform a function such as writing to the local hard drive — check out the demos at the Finjan Software Test Center at `www.finjan.com/mcrc/sec_test.cfm`. These tests — which include "malicious" executables, JavaScript, ActiveX, and Visual Basic — safely show you just what can happen without the proper malware protection in place on your systems.

In my testing, few antivirus and personal firewall applications actually detected any wrongdoings when running these tests. The scripting tests require you to grant permission to load the scripts — many users just do this automatically!

Malware Countermeasures

You can implement various countermeasures to prevent malware attacks against your systems, as described in the following sections.

General system administration

Security countermeasures within your organization can help prevent attacks:

- Your first and foremost goal should be to keep hackers and malware out of your systems in the first place. If you perform the other countermeasures and system-hardening best practices mentioned throughout this book and referenced in Appendix A, you're on your way.
- Create an incident-response plan. The FedCIRC Incident Handling Checklists at `www.fedcirc.gov/incidentResponse/IHchecklists.html` is a good place to start.

  No matter what measures you have in place to protect your systems from malware infections, you'll probably be attacked sometime. Plan ahead so you don't have to make critical decisions under pressure.
- Before deploying networkwide any programs downloaded from the Internet, test and analyze the programs for malicious behavior on isolated systems.
- Use malware-protection software (such as antivirus, spyware protection, and Trojan testers).

  Two guidelines can increase the effectiveness of your protection:

  - Load the software on the layers of your network wherever possible, including on firewalls, content-filtering servers, e-mail gateways/ firewalls, e-mail servers, and e-mail clients.

  - Use different malware-protection applications (from multiple vendors) or a program that combines the scanning engines of several antivirus vendors in one fell swoop, such as Antigen from Sybari Software (`www.sybari.com/home`).

- Apply the latest software patches — especially critical security updates.
- Back up critical systems regularly. This could include performing the following:
  - Image or other backup that can be restored quickly in the event of a serious infection
  - Copies and MD5 or SHA checksums of critical executables in case you need to restore or compare existing ones for authenticity
  - Emergency repair disks for critical systems in case of a malware infection
- Enable heuristics protection in your antivirus software, if possible, to help detect behavioral anomalies that need to be blocked or cleaned.
- Never rely on digitally signed code — such as ActiveX controls that Internet Explorer downloads and prompts you to load — to run properly on your systems. Digital signatures on this code verify only that it came from a trustworthy source — not how it actually behaves when it's loaded.
- Don't just disable such application interfaces as ActiveX, Windows Script Host, JavaScript, and Java without a good reason.

  All these programming interfaces have some legitimate uses. Applications can stop working if these interfaces are disabled haphazardly. If the other security controls I mention here are in place, your systems should be pretty secure from malware written in these languages. You want to find a good balance between security and usability for your users so that security doesn't get in the way of people doing their jobs.
- Make sure that a firewall is always in place on your network. Use it to look for
  - Suspicious ports in use (or trying to be used)
  - Heavy traffic patterns that can signal a malware infection
- Use IDS and IDP systems to stop potential malware infections in their tracks when they try to enter your network.
- Run a rootkit-detection application:
  - Rkdet (`vancouver-Webpages.com/rkdet`) for Linux checks for someone installing a rootkit or other malware on your systems.
  - chkrootkit (`www.chkrootkit.org`) tests after the fact for over 50 different installed rootkits on many popular flavors of UNIX.

E-mails

In addition to the preceding security countermeasures, you can implement several e-mail–specific malware-protection measures:

- Make it policy for users not to open unsolicited e-mails and any attachments — especially those from unknown senders.
- Plan for users who ignore or forget about the policy of leaving unsolicited e-mails and attachments unopened.

  These automatic technical measures can help prevent malware from infecting user systems:

  - At the server or e-mail gateway, filter e-mails that have executable attachments, such as `.com`, `.exe`, `.pif`, `.scr`, and `.vbs`. The File Extension Source at `filext.com` has information about more than 8,500 file types.
  - *Always* run antivirus software wherever it can be installed — at the handheld, desktop, and server levels, if possible.
  - Run antivirus software at the server or gateway levels, if possible.

  Make sure that encrypted files and emails can be protected against malware.

  - Encryption won't keep malware out of files or e-mails. You'll just have encrypted malware within the files or e-mails.
  - Encryption keeps your server or gateway antivirus from detecting the malware until it reaches the desktop.

Files

You must perform regular malware protective maintenance on your file systems. The following countermeasures will help:

- Periodically scan all possible systems on your network, and enable real-time malware protection that can't easily be disabled by users.

  Scan all files — not just executable ones — to help prevent unknown malware issues.
- Consider changing file associations for potentially malicious executables, such as `com`, `.exe`, `.pif`, `.scr`, and `.wsh`.

  For example, you can change the Windows Script Host file associations to something like Notepad.exe in case they're ever launched. That way, Notepad will load the file instead of the Windows Script Host engine.

Chapter 15

Messaging Systems

In This Chapter

- Attacking e-mail systems
- Assailing instant messaging
- Securing your servers and clients

Messaging systems — those e-mail and instant messaging (IM) applications that we depend on — are often hacked within a network. Why? Well, from my experience, messaging software — both at the server and client level — is vulnerable because network administrators forget about securing these systems, believe that antivirus software is all that's needed to keep trouble away, and ignore the existing security vulnerabilities.

In this chapter, I show you how to test for common e-mail and instant-messaging issues. I also outline key countermeasures to help prevent these hacks against your systems.

Messaging-System Vulnerabilities

E-mail and instant-messaging applications are hacking targets on your network. In fact, e-mail systems are some of the most targeted. Given the proliferation and business value of instant messaging and other P2P applications, attacks against networks launched via instant-messaging channels will be at least as common as e-mail attacks.

A ton of vulnerabilities are inherent in messaging systems. The following factors can create weaknesses:

- Security is rarely integrated into software development.
- Convenience and usability often outweigh the need for security.
- Many of the messaging protocols were not designed with security in mind — especially those developed several decades ago, when security wasn't nearly the issue it is today.

Many hacker attacks against messaging systems are just minor nuisances; others can inflict serious harm on your information and your organization's reputation. The hacker attacks against messaging systems include these:

- Transmitting malware (as I describe in Chapter 14)
- Crashing servers
- Obtaining remote control of workstations
- Capturing and modifying confidential information as it travels across the network
- Perusing e-mails in e-mail databases on servers and workstations
- Perusing instant-messaging log files on workstation hard drives
- Gathering messaging trend information, via log files or a network analyzer, that can tip off the hacker about conversations between people and organizations
- Gathering internal network configuration information, such as hostnames and IP addresses

Hacker attacks like these can lead to such problems as lost business, unauthorized — and potentially illegal — disclosure of confidential information, and loss of information.

E-Mail Attacks

The following e-mail attacks exploit the most common e-mail security vulnerabilities I've seen. The good news is that you can eliminate or minimize most of them to the point where your information is not at risk. You may not want to carry out all these attacks against your e-mail system — especially during peak traffic times — so be careful!

Some of these attacks require the basic hacking methodologies: gathering public information, scanning and enumerating your systems, and attacking. Others can be carried out by sending e-mails or capturing network traffic.

E-mail bombs

E-mail bombs can crash a server and provide unauthorized administrator access. They attack by creating DoS conditions against your e-mail software and even your network and Internet connection by taking up so much bandwidth and requiring so much storage space.

A case study in e-mail hacking with Thomas Akin

In this case study, Thomas Akin, a well-known expert in e-mail systems and forensics, shared with me an experience in e-mail hacking. Here's his account of what happened.

The situation

Mr. Akin was involved in a case where a client's e-mail system was blacklisted for sending hundreds of thousands of spam e-mails. The client spent two weeks reconfiguring its e-mail server in an attempt to stop the spam e-mails from going through the system. The client looked at every technical possibility — including making sure that the server was not an open SMTP relay — but nothing worked. Over 100,000 spam e-mails a day were being sent through the company. After losing several customers because the company couldn't send them any e-mails, the company called Mr. Akin to see whether he could help.

Mr. Akin first checked to see whether the e-mail system was acting as an open relay, but it was not. Because the e-mail system wasn't misconfigured, there shouldn't have been any reason for blacklisting the client. Then he reviewed the spam e-mail headers, expecting to see a standard spoofed e-mail. Instead, after reviewing the headers, he saw that they *were* coming from the company's e-mail system. Not only that, but they were also originating from a reserved IP address — an address that isn't even allowed on the Internet.

Momentarily stumped, Mr. Akin looked at the text of the e-mail messages themselves. "One time only!" "Buy me now!" "Best deal ever!" This is the standard spam nonsense, except that these e-mails were signed by Laura and John (names disguised to protect the guilty). Not only that, Laura and John listed their phone numbers so potential customers could contact them easily — 555-1234. How nice of them!

The outcome

A quick search online turned up a phone-number match to a Laura and John living in East Bumble, USA. Bingo! It turned out that John was a former employee and that his dial-up account had not been disabled when he was fired from the company. A quick glance at the log files showed that the "john" account had used the company's dial-up access during the exact times the spam e-mails were sent out. The company immediately disabled the account, and the spam e-mails stopped.

Even though the spamming was stopped, the company was desperate to know how the e-mails were being sent through its system. The dial-up account should have allowed only limited access through a menu system — not full access to the organization's network. After some research, Mr. Akin determined that John had bypassed the dial-up's menu system and was using a program called slirp to turn his internal dial-up connection into a full Internet connection. Because John was dialing into the company's modem bank, the e-mail system saw him as an internal user, letting him send e-mail to anyone and anywhere he wanted. The company quickly reviewed all dial-up accounts and found that over two dozen accounts were still active and being used by former employees!

Thomas Akin is the founding director of the Southeast Cybercrime Institute at Kennesaw State University. He is a CISSP, holds several networking certifications, and is a member of Mensa.

Attachments

An attacker can create an attachment-overloading attack by sending hundreds or thousands of e-mails with very large attachments.

Attacks

Attachment attacks may have a couple of different goals:

- The whole e-mail server may be targeted for a complete interruption of service with these failures:
    - Storage overload

      Multiple large messages can quickly fill the total storage capacity of an e-mail server. If the messages aren't automatically deleted by the server or manually deleted by individual user accounts, the server will be unable to receive new messages.

      This can create a serious DoS problem for your e-mail system, either crashing it or requiring you take your system offline to clean up the junk that has accumulated. A 100MB file attachment sent ten times to 80 users can take 80GB of storage space. Yikes!
    - Bandwidth blocking

      An attacker can crash your e-mail service or bring it to a crawl by filling the incoming Internet connection with junk. Even if your system automatically identifies and discards obvious attachment attacks, the bogus messages eat resources and delay processing of valid messages.
- An attack on a single e-mail address can have serious consequences if the address is for a really important user or group.

Countermeasures

These countermeasures can help prevent attachment-overloading attacks:

- Limit the size of either e-mails or e-mail attachments. Check for this option in e-mail server configuration options (such as those provided in Novell GroupWise and Microsoft Exchange), e-mail content filtering, and e-mail clients.

  This is the best protection against attachment overloading.
- Limit each user's space on the server. This denies large attachments from being written to disk. Limit message sizes for inbound and even outbound messages if you want to prevent a user from launching this attack inside your network. I've found 10MB to 20MB to be good limits.

Consider using FTP or HTTP instead of e-mail for large file transfers. By doing so, you can store one copy of the file on a server and have the recipient download it on his or her own. This can help keep message store sizes at a minimum.

Connections

A hacker can send a huge amount of e-mails simultaneously to addresses on your network. These connection attacks can cause the server to give up on servicing any inbound or outbound TCP requests. This can lead to a complete server lockup or a crash, often resulting in a condition where the attacker is allowed administrator or root access to the system!

Attacks

This attack is often carried out in spam attacks, which are covered later in this chapter.

Countermeasures

Many e-mail servers allow you to limit the number of resources used for inbound connections, as shown in the Number of SMTP Receive Threads option for Novell GroupWise in Figure 15-1. It can be next to impossible to completely stop an unlimited amount of inbound requests. However, you can minimize the impact of the attack. This setting limits the amount of server processor time, which can help prevent a DoS attack.

Figure 15-1: Limiting the number of resources to handle inbound messages.

Even in large companies, there's no reason that thousands of thousands of inbound e-mail deliveries should be necessary within a short time period.

Some e-mail servers, especially UNIX-based servers, can be programmed to deliver e-mails to a daemon or service for automated functions. If DoS protection isn't built into the system, a hacker can crash both the server and the application that receives these messages.

Autoresponders

An interesting attack I've seen is to find two or more users on the same or different e-mail systems that have autoresponder configured. Autoresponder is that annoying automatic e-mail response you often get back from random users when you're subscribing to a mailing list. A message goes to the mailing-list subscribers, and then users have their e-mail configured to automatically respond back, saying they're out of the office or, worse, on vacation. This is a great way to tell thousands of people that your house and belongings are possibly available for taking — but I digress.

Attacks

An autoresponder attack is a pretty easy hack. Many unsuspecting users and e-mail administrators never know what hit them! The hacker sends each of the two (or more) users an e-mail from the other simply by masquerading as that person (an easy hack I outline in this chapter). This attack can create a never-ending loop that bounces thousands of messages back and forth between users. This can create a DoS condition by filling either the user's individual disk space quota on the e-mail server or the e-mail server's entire disk space.

Countermeasures

The best countermeasure for an autoresponder attack is to make it policy that no one sets up an autoresponder message. Those messages are too annoying to be of value anyway, right?

Prevent e-mail attacks as far out on your network perimeter as you can. The more traffic or malicious behavior you keep off your e-mail servers and clients, the better.

Automatic e-mail security

You can implement the following countermeasures as an additional layer of security for your e-mail systems.

Tarpitting

Tarpitting detects inbound messages destined for unknown users. If your e-mail server supports tarpitting, it can help prevent spam or DoS attacks against your server. If a predefined threshold is exceeded — say, more than ten messages — the tarpitting function effectively blocks traffic from the sending IP address for a period of time.

E-mail firewalls

E-mail firewalls and content-filtering applications (such as CipherTrust's IronMail and NetIQ's MailMarshal, respectively) can prevent various e-mail attacks. These tools protect practically every aspect of an e-mail system.

Perimeter protection

Although not e-mail–specific, many firewall, IDS, and IDP systems can detect various e-mail attacks and shut off the attacker in real time. This can come in handy during an attack at an inconvenient time.

Banners

One of the first orders of business for a hacker when hacking an e-mail server is performing a basic banner grab to see whether he can tell what e-mail server software is running. This is one of the most critical tests to find out what the world knows about your SMTP, POP3, and IMAP servers.

Gathering information

Figure 15-2 shows the banner displayed on an e-mail server when a basic telnet connection is made on port 25 (SMTP). To do this, at a command prompt, simply enter **telnet ip_or_hostname_of _your_server 25**. This brings up a telnet session on TCP port 25.

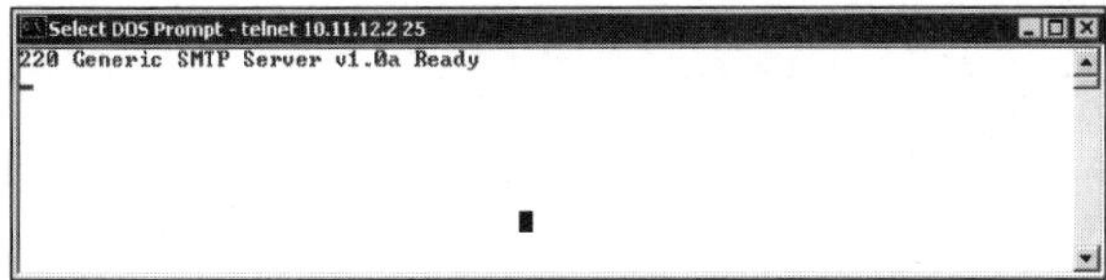

Figure 15-2: An SMTP banner showing server-version information.

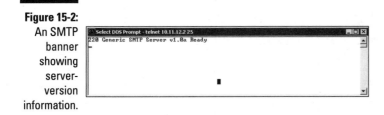

In Figure 15-2, it's pretty obvious what e-mail software type and version the server is running. This information can give hackers some ideas about possible attacks, especially if they search a vulnerability database for known vulnerabilities of that software version. Figure 15-3 shows the same e-mail server with its SMTP banner changed from the default (okay, the previous one was, too) to disguise such information as the e-mail server's version number.

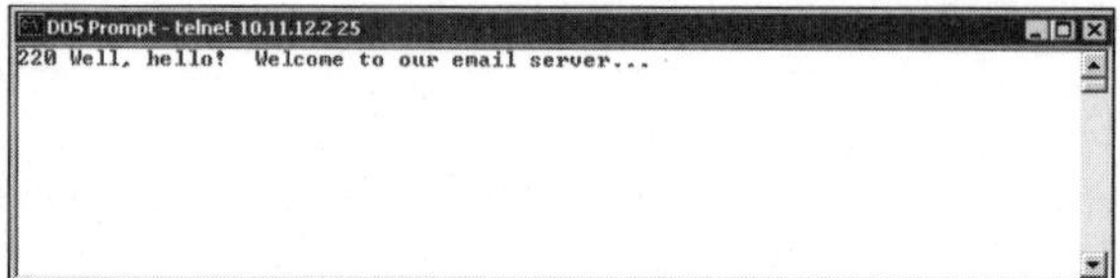

Figure 15-3: An SMTP banner that disguises the version information.

You can gather information on POP3 and IMAP e-mail services as well by telnetting to either port 110 (POP3) or port 143 (IMAP).

If you've changed your default SMTP banner, don't think that no one can figure out the version. One Linux-based tool called smtpscan (`www.greyhats.org/outils/smtpscan`) determines e-mail server version information based on how the server responds to malformed SMTP requests. Figure 15-4 shows the results from smtpscan against the same server shown in Figure 15-3. It detected the product and version number of the e-mail server!

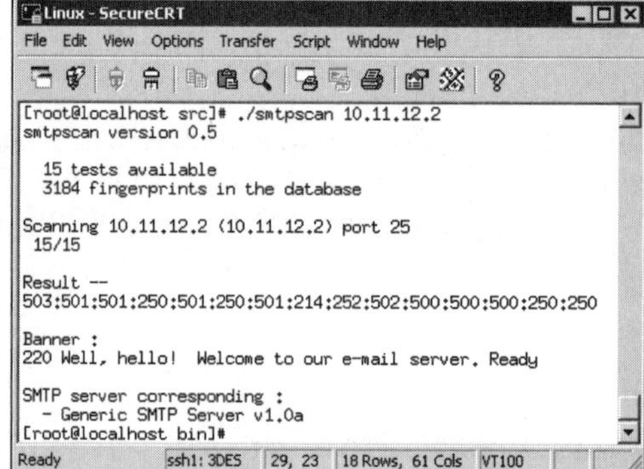

Figure 15-4: smtpscan gathers version info when the SMTP banner is disguised.

Countermeasures

There isn't a 100 percent secure way of disguising banner information. I suggest these banner security tips for your SMTP, POP3, and IMAP servers:

- Change your default banners to cover up the information.
- Make sure that you're always running the latest software patches.
- Harden your server as much as possible by using well-known best practices from such resources as SANS (`www.sans.org`), NIST (`csrc.nist.gov`), National Security Agency Security Recommendation Guides (`www.nsa.gov/snac/index.html`), and *Network Security For Dummies,* by Chey Cobb (Wiley Publishing, Inc.).

SMTP attacks

Some hacker attacks exploit weaknesses in the Simple Mail Transfer Protocol (SMTP). This e-mail communications protocol — which is over 20 years old — was designed for functionality, not security.

Account enumeration

A clever way that hackers can verify whether e-mail accounts exist on a server is simply to telnet to the server on port 25 and run the VRFY command. The VRFY — short for verify — command makes a server query to check whether a specific user ID exists. Spammers often automate this method to perform a *directory harvest attack* (DHA). It's a way of gleaning valid e-mail addresses from a server or domain so hackers know who to send spam messages.

Attacks

Figure 15-5 shows how easy it is to verify an e-mail address on a server with the VRFY command enabled. Scripting this attack can test thousands of e-mail address combinations.

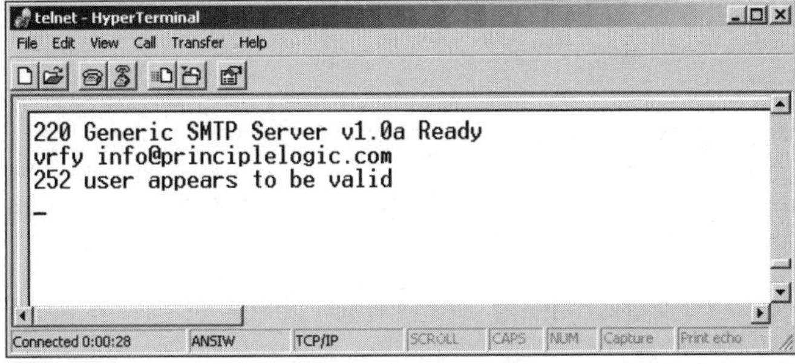

Figure 15-5: Using VRFY to verify that an e-mail address exists.

The SMTP command EXPN — short for expand — may allow attackers to verify what mailing lists exist on a server as well. You can simply telnet to your e-mail server on port 25 and try EXPN on your system if you know of any mailing lists that may exist. Figure 15-6 shows what this result may look like. It's simple to script this attack and test thousands of mailing-list combinations.

You may get bogus information from your server when performing these two tests. Some SMTP servers don't support the VRFY and EXPN commands, and some e-mail firewalls simply ignore them or return false information.

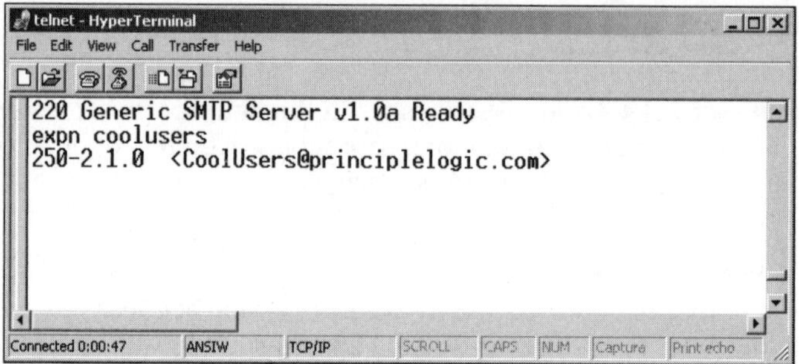

Figure 15-6: Using EXPN to verify that a mailing list exists.

Countermeasures

The best solution for preventing this type of e-mail account enumeration depends on whether you need to enable the VRFY and EXPN commands:

- Disable VRFY and EXPN unless you need your remote systems to be able to gather user and mailing-list information from your server.
- If you need VRFY and EXPN functionality, check your e-mail server or content filtering documentation for the ability to limit these commands to specific hosts on your network or the Internet.

Relay

SMTP relay lets users send e-mails through external servers. Open e-mail relays are one of the greatest problems on the Internet. Spammers and hackers can use an e-mail server to send spam or attack through e-mail under the guise of the unsuspecting open-relay owner.

Keep in mind the following key points when checking your e-mail system for SMTP-relay weaknesses:

- Test your e-mail server by using more than one tool or testing method. Multiple tests minimize any errors or oversights.
- Test for open relay from outside your network. If you test from the inside, you may get a false positive, because outbound e-mail relaying may be configured and necessary for your internal e-mail clients.

Automatic testing

Here are a couple of easy ways to test your server for SMTP relay:

- Free online tools.

  One of my favorite online tools is located at `www.abuse.net/relay.html`. You can perform the anonymous test without entering your e-mail address — unless you're an abuse.net member. It immediately displays the test results in your browser.

- Other Windows-based tools, such as Sam Spade for Windows. Figure 15-7 shows how you can run an SMTP Relay check on your e-mail server. Figure 15-8 contains the results of this test on my test server, showing that relaying is enabled.

Some SMTP servers accept inbound relay connections and make it look like relaying works. This isn't always the case, because the filtering may take place behind the scenes. Check whether the e-mail actually made it through by checking the account you sent the test relay message to.

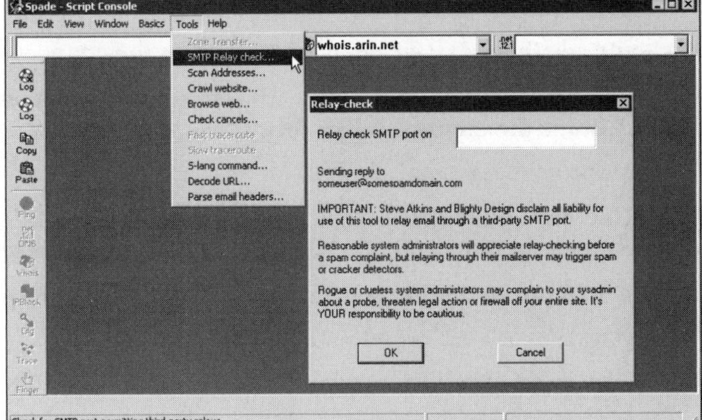

Figure 15-7: SMTP relay check tool in Sam Spade for Windows.

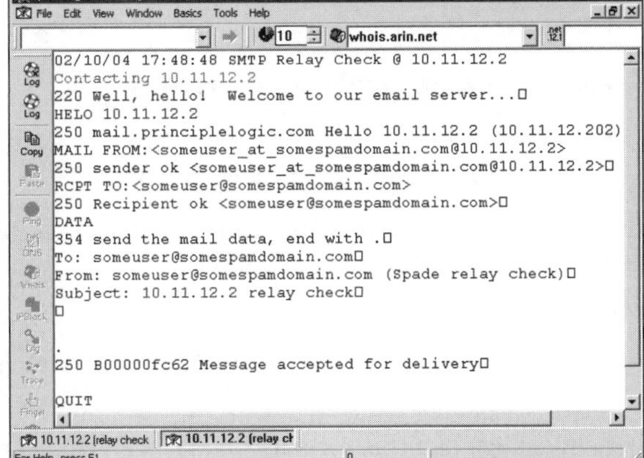

Figure 15-8: Positive results from testing for an open SMTP relay.

Manual testing

You can manually test your server for SMTP relay by telnetting to the e-mail server on port 25. Follow these steps:

1. **Telnet to your server on port 25.**

   You can do this two ways:

   - Use your favorite graphical telnet application, such as HyperTerminal (which comes with Windows) or SecureCRT (`www.vandyke.com`).
   - Enter the following command at a Windows or UNIX command prompt:

   ```
   telnet mailserver_address 25
   ```

   To see what's entered, you may have to enable local echoing of characters in your telnet program, such as Hyper Terminal.

   You should see the SMTP welcome banner when the connection is made.

2. **Enter a command to tell the server, "Hi, I'm connecting from this domain." Enter the command like this:**

   ```
   helo yourdomain.com
   ```

   After each command in these steps, you should receive a different-numbered message, like `999 OK`. You can ignore these messages.

3. **Enter a command to tell the server your e-mail address, like this:**

   ```
   mail from:yourname@yourdomain.com
   ```

4. **Enter a command to tell the server who to send the e-mail to, like this:**

   ```
   rcpt to:yourname@yourdomain.com
   ```

5. **Enter a command to tell the server that the message body is to follow, like this:**

   ```
   data
   ```

6. **Enter the following text as the body of the message:**

   ```
   A relay test
   ```

7. **End the command with a period on a line by itself.**

   This marks the end of the message. After you enter this final period, your message will be sent if relaying is allowed.

8. **Check for relaying on your server:**

   - Look for a message like *Relay not allowed* to come back from the server.

     If you get a message like this returned, SMTP relaying is not allowed on your server.

You may get this message after you enter the rcpt to: command.

- If you don't receive a message back from your server, check your inbox for the relayed e-mail.

  If you receive the test e-mail you sent, SMTP relaying is enabled on your server.

Countermeasures

You can implement the following countermeasures on your e-mail server to disable or at least control SMTP relaying:

- Disable SMTP relay on your e-mail server. If you don't know whether you need SMTP relay, you probably don't. You can enable SMTP relay for specific hosts if needed.

  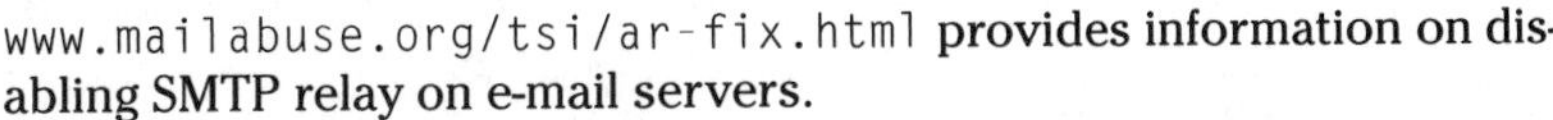

  `www.mailabuse.org/tsi/ar-fix.html` provides information on disabling SMTP relay on e-mail servers.
- Enforce authentication, if your e-mail server allows it. You may be able to require such authentication methods as password authentication or an e-mail address that matches the e-mail server's domain. Check your e-mail server and client documentation for details on setting up this type of authentication.

E-mail header disclosures

If your e-mail client and server are configured with typical defaults, a malicious hacker may find critical pieces of information:

- Internal IP address of your e-mail client machine (maybe the entire IP addressing scheme)
- Software versions of your client and server and their vulnerabilities
- Hostname

Testing

Figure 15-9 shows the header information revealed in a test e-mail I sent to my free Web account. As you can see, it shows off quite a bit of information about my e-mail system.

- The third Received line discloses my system's hostname, IP address, server name, and e-mail client software version.
- The X-Mailer line displays the Microsoft Outlook version I used to send this message.

X-Apparently-To:	my~secret~account!@yahoo.com via someone_else's_ip_address; Wed, 04 Feb 2004 09:39:49 -0800
Return-Path:	<kbeaver@principlelogic.com>
Received:	from someone_else's_ip_address (EHLO ISP_email_server) (someone_else's_ip_address) by Yahoo_email_server with SMTP; Wed, 04 Feb 2004 09:39:48 -0800
Received:	from my_email_server ([ip_address]) by ISP_email_server (InterMail vM.5.01.06.05 201-253-122-130-105-20030824) with ESMTP id <20040204173942.FYWC1950.ISP_email_server@my_email_server> for <my~secret~account!@yahoo.com>; Wed, 4 Feb 2004 12:39:42 -0500
Received:	from MY HOST NAME (Not Verified[10.11.12.211]) by my_email_server with Generic SMTP Server v1.0a id <B00000f611>; Wed, 04 Feb 2004 12:39:35 -0500
Message-ID:	<000801c3eb46$258927a0$800101df >
From:	"Kevin Beaver" <kbeaver@principlelogic.com> Add to Address Book
To:	my~secret~account!@yahoo.com
Subject:	See my headers?
Date:	Wed, 4 Feb 2004 12:40:38 -0500
MIME-Version:	1.0
Content-Type:	multipart/alternative; boundary="----=_NextPart_000_0005_01C3EB1C.1762FA00"
X-Priority:	3
X-MSMail-Priority:	Normal
X-Mailer:	Microsoft Outlook Express 6.00.2800.1158
X-MimeOLE:	Produced By Microsoft MimeOLE V6.00.2800.1165
Content-Length:	661

Figure 15-9: Critical information revealed in e-mail headers.

Countermeasures

The best countermeasure to prevent information disclosures in e-mail headers is to configure your e-mail server/gateway/firewall to rewrite your e-mail headers, either changing the information shown or removing it altogether. Check your e-mail server documentation to see whether this is an option.

If full-fledged header rewriting is not available, you may at least be able to prevent the sending of some critical information, such as server software version numbers and internal IP addresses.

Capturing traffic

E-mail traffic can be captured with a network analyzer or an e-mail packet sniffer and reconstructor.

Mailsnarf is an e-mail packet sniffer and reconstructor. It's part of the dsniff package. You can get dsniff from `www.monkey.org/~dugsong/dsniff` (UNIX variants) or `www.datanerds.net/~mike/dsniff.html` (Windows).

If traffic is captured, a hacker can do one of the following:

- Compromise one host and potentially have full access to another adjacent host, such as your e-mail server.
- Exploit known security vulnerabilities in e-mail server, e-mail client, and software.

Malware

E-mail systems are regularly attacked by such malware as viruses and worms.

- E-mail is one of the best ways for malware to propagate. Chapter 14 covers malware.
- Hackers often compromise systems by running e-mail services that aren't being used or that need to be updated.

General best practices for minimizing e-mail security risks

The following countermeasures help keep messages as secure as possible.

Software solutions

The right software can neutralize many threats:

- Use malware-protection software on the e-mail server — better, the e-mail gateway — to prevent malware from reaching e-mail clients.
- Apply the latest operating system and e-mail application security patches consistently and after any security alerts are released.
- If it makes good business sense, encrypt messages. You can use S/MIME or PGP to encrypt sensitive messages or use e-mail encryption at the desktop level or the server or e-mail gateway. (You can use SSL/TLS between your e-mail client and server via POP3S or IMAPS or between your e-mail gateway and remote e-mail gateways. I prefer to implement encryption between gateways so that the user doesn't have to be involved.)

It's best not to depend on your users to encrypt messages. Use an enterprise solution to encrypt messages.

Operating guidelines

Some simple operating rules can keep your walls high:

- Put your e-mail server behind a firewall, preferably in a DMZ that's on a different network segment from the Internet and from your internal LAN.
- Disable unused protocols and services on your e-mail server.
- Run your e-mail server on a dedicated server, if possible, to help keep hackers out of other servers and information if the server is hacked.
- Log all transactions with the server in case you need to investigate malicious use in the future.

- If your server doesn't need e-mail services running (SMTP, POP3, and IMAP), disable them — immediately.
- For Web-based e-mail such as Microsoft's Outlook Web Access (OWA), properly secure your Web-server application and operating system by using the hardening resources I mention throughout this book.
- If you're running sendmail — especially an older version — consider running a secure alternative, such as Postfix or qmail.

Instant Messaging

The hottest new technology taking networks by storm is instant messaging (IM). Although IM offers a lot of business value, some serious security issues are associated with it. This is especially true if it's not managed properly and end users are free to install, configure, and use it in any way they want.

Vulnerabilities

IM has several critical security vulnerabilities, including the following:

- Name hijacking, allowing a hacker to assume the identity of an IM user
- Launching a DoS attack on an IM client, allowing the attacker to take remote control of the computer
- Capturing internal IP address information (similar to the way it's disclosed in e-mail headers)
- Transferring malware, including viruses and malicious Trojan horses

You can remedy most of these vulnerabilities by applying the latest software patches and keeping antivirus signatures up to date. However, two IM vulnerabilities are susceptible to malicious attack, so they deserve a little more discussion. These affect most of the popular IM clients, including AOL Instant Messenger (AIM) and ICQ. These vulnerabilities are just problems with file sharing and log files, but these weaknesses can make all the difference in the world when it comes to securing your network.

Sharing network drives

The biggest problem with IM clients is the ability to share files. This feature may be pretty neat for home users or others with stand-alone computers, but it can pose a real security risk to your network and information. Practically every IM client gives users the ability to share both local and network files. Figure 15-10 shows an example of file sharing configured in AIM.

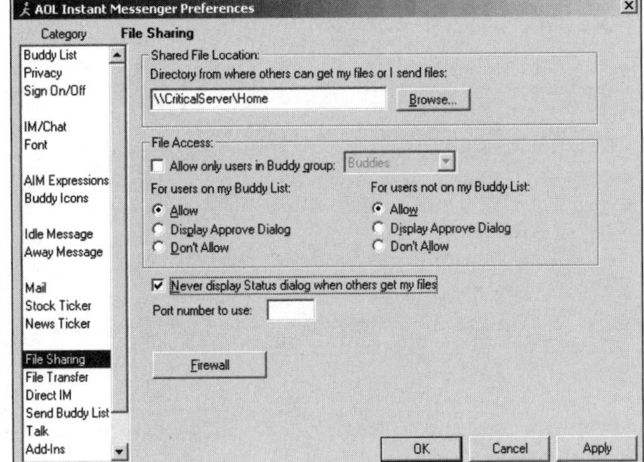

Figure 15-10: File-sharing options under end-user control.

Once untrained or careless users share your network drives via their IM clients, they've just granted potentially anyone on their IM network permission to view and copy those files. Figure 15-11 shows a sample of what you can see over the AIM network.

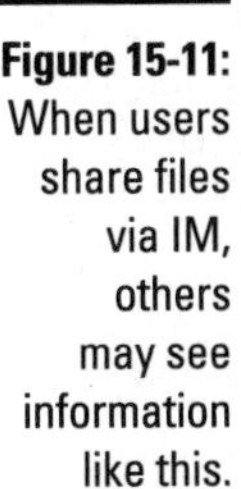

Figure 15-11: When users share files via IM, others may see information like this.

Figure 15-12 shows some AIM File Transfer settings that can allow any remote user to place files on your network — malware and all!

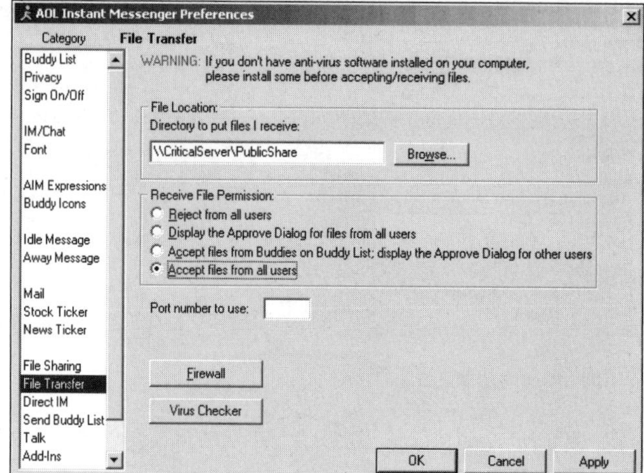

Figure 15-12: Options to receive files in AOL Instant Messenger.

If you know of IM users on your network, follow these steps to assess the security of their software and configuration:

1. **Determine IM clients that are running on your network.**

   You can detect IM software with

   - Manual inspection of the local workstation
   - A third-party workstation hardware and software inventory program
   - A network analyzer that shows IM traffic. For instance, you can use Ethereal to capture and display various types of IM protocols, such as AOL Instant Messenger (AIM protocol), ICQ (ICQ protocol), and MSNMS (MSN Messenger).

2. **Install the IM clients on your own system.**

   Avoid creating your own security holes: Download and install the latest client versions, and don't enable file sharing.

3. **Find your network's IM users.**

   You can identify IM users by either looking up users with a directory search in the IM client (many IM clients publish this information by default) or asking users for their handles for all their IM clients.

4. **For each user, check settings to see whether they're sharing files.**

   It's often just a simple right-click on their IM handle within the IM software to copy files to and from their system.

Log files

Many IM clients can log all IM conversations. Some clients log all conversations by default. Have users enabled logging and inadvertently shared their log files with the world? It's a smoking gun for a hacker to use! Figure 15-13 shows part of an ICQ conversation stored in communications gobbledygook in a log file found in the `c:\Program Files\ICQ` folder.

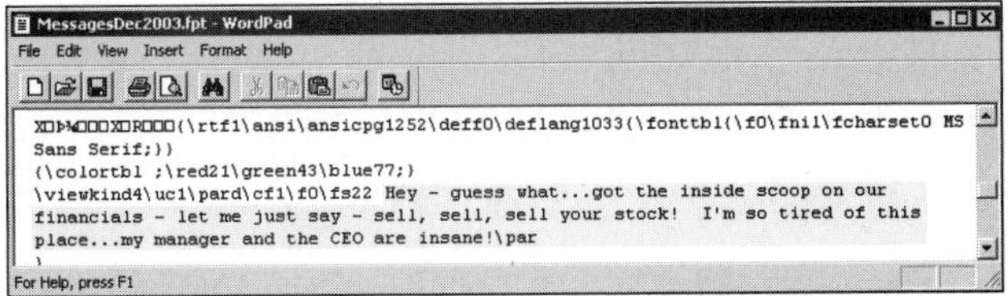

Figure 15-13: IM log files revealing juicy information.

Countermeasures

IM vulnerabilities can be difficult to detect, because most rogue IM software is desktop-based. If you have a large network, checking every computer for these vulnerabilities is pretty much impossible. Spot checks can be inaccurate, because every desktop and every user can be different.

Even if you disallow IM — or any messaging software — on your network, users always install it. If you implement these countermeasures, you're better prepared to protect your users from themselves and hackers.

Detecting IM traffic

In addition to a network analyzer, you can detect IM traffic by using the following tools:

- IM traffic-detection tools from Akonix (`www.akonix.com`) work like a network analyzer.
- Rogue Aware (`www.akonix.com/products/rogueaware.asp`) is a free tool. As shown in Figure 15-14, Rogue Aware detects such traffic on the network as IM and other P2P communications (such as Kazaa and Gnutella) and file sharing on the network. I recommend that you check it out and use this tool as part of your ethical hacking toolkit. Ideally, you install it on a computer that's connected to a monitor port on a switch or a hub adjacent to your firewall to ensure that you see all the traffic.

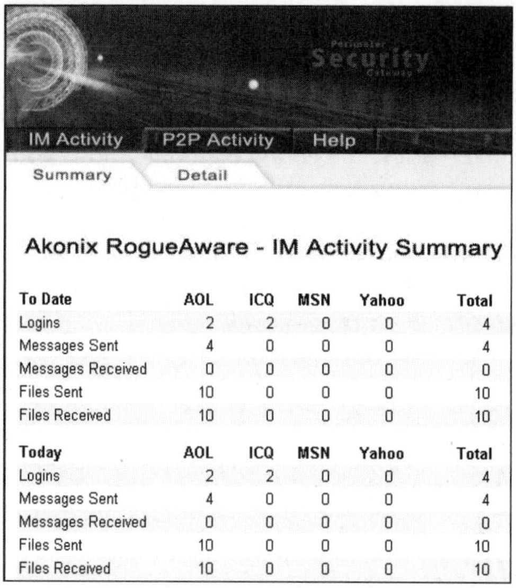

IM Activity P2P Activity Help

Summary Detail

Akonix RogueAware - IM Activity Summary

To Date	AOL	ICQ	MSN	Yahoo	Total
Logins	2	2	0	0	4
Messages Sent	4	0	0	0	4
Messages Received	0	0	0	0	0
Files Sent	10	0	0	0	10
Files Received	10	0	0	0	10
Today	**AOL**	**ICQ**	**MSN**	**Yahoo**	**Total**
Logins	2	2	0	0	4
Messages Sent	4	0	0	0	4
Messages Received	0	0	0	0	0
Files Sent	10	0	0	0	10
Files Received	10	0	0	0	10

Figure 15-14: Akonix Rogue Aware detects IM logins and file sharing.

- Akonix's Enforcer and L7 Enterprise are commercial utilities that have more functionality. Other vendors offer similar solutions, such as FaceTime Communications (`www.facetime.com`) and IM Logic (`www.imlogic.com`). If you can justify the cost — which is relatively easy — I recommend that you check these products out.
- Desktop auditing utilities can show you which applications are installed and their specific settings. Such products as Ecora's Enterprise Auditor (`www.ecora.com/ecora/products/enterprise_auditor.asp`), Microsoft's Systems Management Server (`www.microsoft.com/smserver/default.asp`) and some lower-end shareware tools can offer this type of functionality.

Maintenance and configuration

In addition to the tools listed in the previous section, you can implement these IM hacking countermeasures:

- **User behavior:**
  - Have a policy banning or limiting the usage of all P2P software.
  - Instruct users not to open file attachments or configure their IM software to share or receive file attachments.
  - Instruct users to keep their buddy lists private and not share their information.

- **System configuration:**
  - Change default IM software installation directories to help eliminate automated attacks.
  - Apply all the latest IM software patches.
  - Ensure that the latest antivirus software and personal-firewall software is loaded on each instant-messaging client.
  - Ensure that proper file and directory access controls are in place to effectively give your users the minimum necessary rights for their jobs. This countermeasure helps keep prying eyes out if someone can exploit an IM vulnerability.
  - If you allow IM on your network for business purposes, consider standardizing an enterprise-based IM application such as Jabber or Lotus Sametime. These applications have more-robust and manageable security options, which can ensure control.

Chapter 16

Web Applications

In This Chapter

- Attacking Web applications
- Countering application hacking

Web applications, like e-mail, are common hacker targets because they're everywhere and often open for anyone to poke around in. Basic Web sites used for marketing, contact information, document downloads, and so on are a common target for hackers — especially the script-kiddie types — to deface. However, for criminal hackers, Web sites that store valuable information, like credit-card and Social Security numbers, are especially attractive. This is where the money is, so to speak.

Why are Web applications so vulnerable? The general consensus is they're vulnerable because of poor software development and testing practices. Sound familiar? It should, because this is the same problem that affects operating systems and practically all computer systems. This is the side effect of relying on software compilers to perform error checking, lack of user demand for higher-quality software, and emphasizing time-to-market instead of security and stability.

This chapter presents Web application hacks to check on your systems. You can test for literally thousands of vulnerabilities, but I focus on the ones I see most often. I also outline countermeasures to help minimize the chances that a hacker can carry out these attacks against your Web applications.

Web-Application Vulnerabilities

Hacker attacks against insecure Web applications — via Hypertext Transfer Protocol (HTTP) — make up the majority of all Internet-related attacks. Most of these attacks can be carried out even if the HTTP traffic is encrypted (via HTTPS or HTTP over SSL) because the communications medium has nothing to do with these attacks. The security vulnerabilities actually lie within either the Web applications themselves or the Web server and browser software that the applications run on and communicate with.

Many attacks against Web applications are just minor nuisances or may not affect confidential information or system availability. However, some attacks can wreak havoc on your systems. Whether the Web attack is against a basic brochureware site or against the company's most critical customer server, these attacks can hurt your organization.

Choosing Your Tools

Freeware and commercial tools can help ensure that your tests are comprehensive and minimize your testing time. All these tools basically work the same way, with such capabilities as scanning for script vulnerabilities, testing for invalid user input, and viewing critical files.

My favorite tools are Nikto (`www.cirt.net/code/nikto.shtml`), Nessus (`www.nessus.org`), and SPI Dynamics' WebInspect (`www.spidynamics.com`). These certainly are not the only tools available. It's still a young market for commercial tool vendors, so keep your eyes peeled for emerging products.

Insecure Login Mechanisms

Many Web sites require users to login before they can do anything with the application. These login mechanisms often do not handle incorrect user IDs or passwords gracefully. They often divulge too much information that a hacker can use to gather valid user IDs and passwords.

Testing

To test for insecure login mechanisms, browse to your application and login in the following ways:

- Using an invalid user ID with a valid password
- Using an valid user ID with an invalid password
- Using an invalid user ID and password

After you enter this information, the Web application probably responds with a message like `Your user ID is invalid` or `Your password is invalid`. The Web application may also return a generic error message, such as `Your user ID and password combination is invalid` and, at the same time, return different error codes in the URL for invalid user IDs and invalid passwords, as shown in Figures 16-1 and 16-2.

Case study in hacking Web applications with Caleb Sima

In this case study, Caleb Sima, a well-known penetration-testing expert, shared an experience performing a Web-application security test. Here's his account of what happened.

The Situation

Mr. Sima was hired to perform a Web-application penetration test to assess the security of a well-known financial Web site. Equipped with nothing more than the URL of the main financial site, Mr. Sima set out to find what other sites existed for the organization and began by using Google to search for possibilities. He initially ran an automated scan against the main servers to discover any low-hanging fruit. This scan provided information on the Web-server version and some other basic information, but nothing that proved useful without further research. And while Mr. Sima performed the scan, neither the IDS nor the firewall noticed any of his activity! Then he issued a request to the server on the initial Web page, which returned some interesting information. The Web application appeared to be accepting many parameters, but as he continued to browse the site, he noticed that the parameters in the URL stayed the same. He decided to delete all the parameters within the URL to see what information the server would return when queried. The server responded with an error message describing the type of application environment.

Next, Mr. Sima performed a Google search on the application that resulted in some detailed documentation. He found several articles and tech notes within this information that showed him how the application worked and what default files might exist. In fact, the server had several of these default files. He used this information to probe the application further. He quickly discovered internal IP addresses, as well as what services the application was offering. Now that he knew exactly what version the admin was running, he wanted to see what else he could find.

Mr. Sima continued to manipulate the URL from the application by adding & characters within the statement to control the custom script. This allowed him to capture all source codes files! He noted some interesting filenames, including `VerifyLogin.htm`, `ApplicationDetail.htm`, `CreditReport.htm`, and `ChangePassword.htm`. Then he tried to connect to each file by issuing a specially formatted URL to the server. The server returned a *User not logged in* message for each request and stated that the connection must be made from the intranet.

The Outcome

Mr. Sima knew where the files were located and was able to sniff the connection and determine that the `ApplicationDetail.htm` file set a cookie string. With little manipulation of the URL, he hit the jackpot! This file returned client information and credit cards when a new-customer application was being processed. `CreditReport.htm` allowed him to view customer credit-report status, fraud information, declined-application status, and a multitude of other sensitive information. The lesson to be learned: Hackers can utilize many types of information to break through Web applications. The individual exploits in this case study were minor, but when combined, they resulted in severe vulnerabilities.

Caleb Sima was a charter member of the X-Force team at Internet Security Systems and the first member of the Penetration Testing team. He went on to co-found SPI Dynamics (`www.spidynamics.com`) and become its CTO, as well as director of SPI Labs, the application-security research and development group within SPI Dynamics.

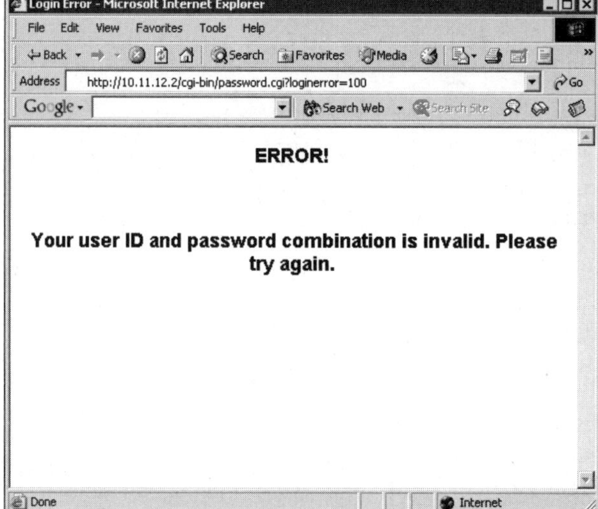

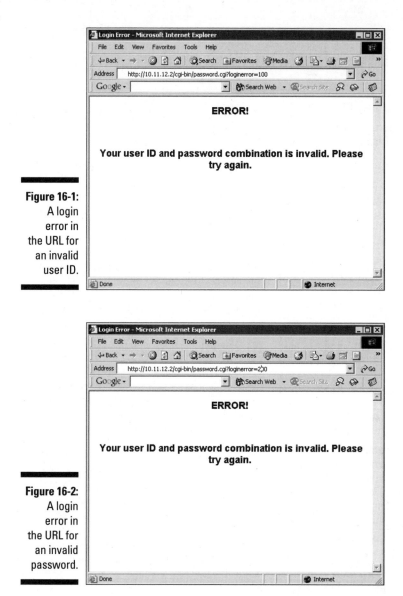

Figure 16-1: A login error in the URL for an invalid user ID.

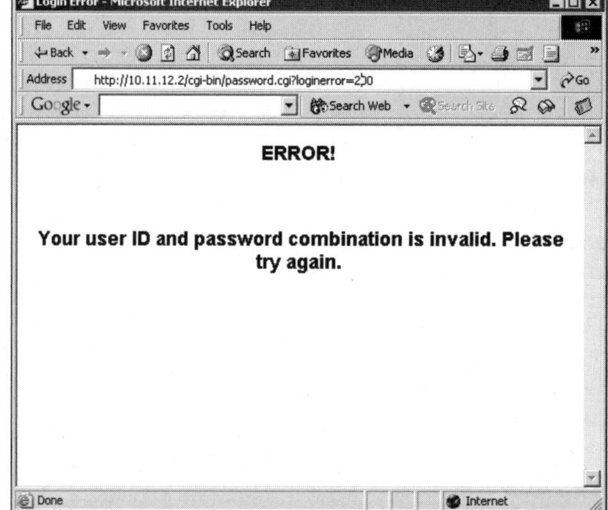

Figure 16-2: A login error in the URL for an invalid password.

In either case, this is bad news, because the application is telling you not only which parameter is invalid, but also which one is *valid.* This means that the hackers now know either a good user name or password — their work has been cut in half! If they know the username (which usually is easier to guess), they can simply write a script to automate the password-cracking process, and vice versa. They can also use a remote Web login-cracking tool, such as Brutus (`www.hoobie.net/brutus`), to attempt to break in, using a preconfigured file with user IDs and passwords, or even use it to perform brute-force attacks.

Countermeasures

You can implement the following countermeasures to prevent hackers from attacking weak login systems in your Web applications:

- Any login errors that are returned to the end user should be as generic as possible, saying something like `Your user ID and password combination is invalid.`
- The application should never return error codes in the URL that differentiate between an invalid user ID and invalid password, as shown in Figures 16-1 and 16-2.

If a URL message must be returned, the application should keep it as generic as possible. Here's an example:

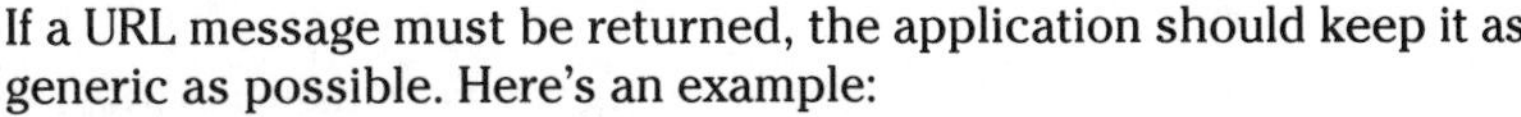

```
www.your_Web_app.com/login.cgi?success=false
```

This URL message may not be as convenient to the user, but it helps hide the mechanism and the behind-the-scenes actions from a hacker.

Directory Traversal

A directory traversal is a really basic attack, but it can turn up interesting information about a Web site. This attack is basically browsing a site and looking for clues about the server's directory structure.

Testing

Perform the following tests to determine information about your Web site's directory structure.

robots.txt

Start your testing with a search for the Web server's `robots.txt` file. This file tells search engines which directories not to index. Thinking like a hacker, you may deduce that the directories listed in this file may contain some information that needs to be protected. Figure 16-3 shows a `robots.txt` file that gives away information.

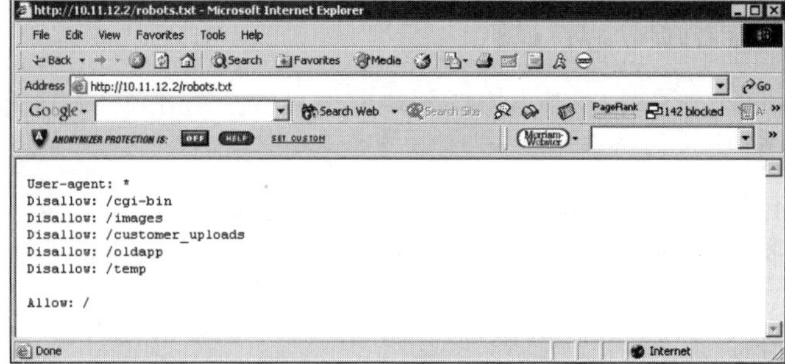

Figure 16-3: A Web server's `robots.txt` listing.

Filenames

Confidential files on a Web server may have names like those of publicly accessible files. For example, if this year's product line is posted as `www.your_Web_app.com/productline2004.pdf`, confidential information about next year's products may be `www.your_Web_app.com/productline2005.pdf`.

A user may place confidential files on the server without realizing that they are accessible without a direct link from the Web site.

Crawlers

A spider program like BlackWidow (`www.softbytelabs.com/BlackWidow`) can crawl your site to look for every publicly accessible file. Figure 16-4 shows the crawl output of a basic Web site.

Complicated sites often reveal more information that should not be there, including old data files and even application scripts and source code.

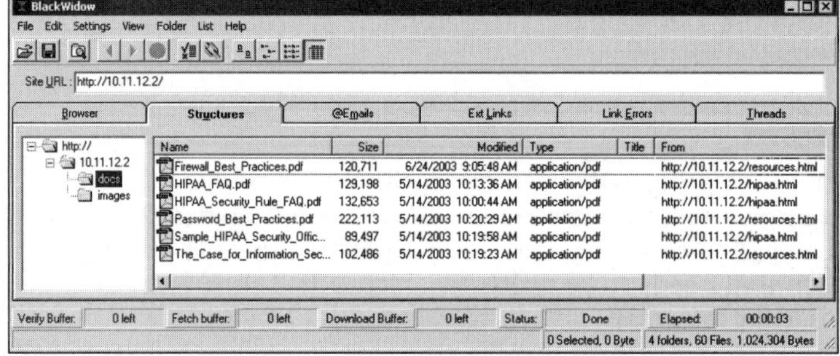

Figure 16-4: Using BlackWidow to crawl a Web site.

Look at the output of your crawling program to see what files are available. Regular HTML and PDF files are probably okay, because they're most likely needed for normal Web-application operation. But it wouldn't hurt to open each file to make sure it belongs.

Countermeasures

You can employ two main countermeasures to having files compromised via malicious directory traversals:

- **Don't store old, sensitive, or otherwise nonpublic files on your Web server.** The only files that should be in your /htdocs or DocumentRoot folder are those that are needed for the site to function properly. These files should not contain confidential information that you don't want the world to see.
- **Ensure that your Web server is properly configured to allow public access only to those directories that are needed for the site to function.** Minimum necessary privileges are key here, so provide access only to the bare-minimum files and directories needed for the Web application to perform properly.

Check your Web server's documentation for instructions to control public access. Depending on your Web-server version, these access controls are set in

  - The httpd.conf file and the .htaccess files for Apache

    Refer to httpd.apache.org/docs/configuring.html for more information.
  - Internet Information Services Manager settings for Home Directory and Directory (IIS 5.1)
  - Internet Information Services Manager settings for Home Directory and Virtual Directory (IIS 6.0)

The latest versions of these Web servers have good directory security by default, so if possible, make sure you're running the latest versions:

- Check for the latest version of Apache at httpd.apache.org.
- The most recent version of IIS (for Windows Server 2003) is 6.0.

Input Filtering

Web applications are notorious for taking practically any type of input, assuming that it's valid, and processing it further. Not validating input is one of the greatest mistakes that Web-application developers can make. This can lead to system crashes, malicious database manipulation, and even database corruption.

Input attacks

Several attacks can be run against a Web application that insert malformed data — often, too much at once — which can confuse, crash, or make the Web application divulge too much information to the attacker.

Buffer overflows

One of the most serious input attacks is a buffer overflow that specifically targets input fields in Web applications.

For instance, a credit-reporting application may authenticate users before they're allowed to submit data or pull reports. The login form uses the following code to grab user IDs with a maximum input of 12 characters, as denoted by the `maxsize` variable:

```
<form name="Webauthenticate" action="www.your_Web_app.com/login.cgi"
            method="POST">
...
<input type="text" name="inputname" maxsize="12">
...
```

A typical login session would be presented a valid login name of 12 characters or less. However, hackers can manipulate the login form to change the `maxsize` parameter to something huge, such as 100 or even 1,000. Then they can enter bogus data in the login field. What happens next is anyone's call — they may lock up the application, overwrite other data in memory, or crash the server.

Automated input

An automated-input attack is when a malicious hacker manipulates a URL and sends it back to the server, directing the Web application to add bogus data to the Web database, which can lead to various DoS conditions.

Suppose, for example, that you have a Web application that produces a form that users fill out to subscribe to a newsletter. The application automatically generates e-mail confirmations that new subscribers must respond to. When users receive their e-mail confirmations, they must click a link to confirm their subscription. Users can tinker with the hyperlink in the e-mail they received — possibly changing the username, e-mail address, or subscription status in the link — and send it back to the server hosting the application. If the Web server doesn't verify that the e-mail address or other account information being submitted has recently subscribed, the server will accept practically anyone's bogus information. The hacker can automate the attack and force the Web application to add thousands of invalid subscribers to its database. This can cause a DoS condition on the server or the server's network due to traffic overload, which can lead to other issues.

I don't necessarily recommend that you carry out this test in an uncontrolled fashion with an automated script you may write or download off the Internet. Instead, you may be better off carrying out this type of attack with an automated testing tool ,such as WebInspect or, or one of its commercial equivalents, such as Sanctum's AppScan (www.sanctuminc.com).

Code injection

In a code-injection attack, hackers modify the URL in their Web browsers or even within the actual Web-page code before the information gets sent back to the server. For example, when you load your Web application from www.your_Web_app.com, it modifies the URL field in the Web browser to something similar to the following:

```
http://www.your_Web_app.com/script.php?info_variable=X
```

Hackers, seeing this variable, can start entering different data into the info_variable field, changing X to something like one of the following lines:

```
http:// www.your_Web_app.com/script.php?info_variable=Y
```

```
http:// www.your_Web_app.com/script.php?info_variable=123XYZ
```

The Web application may respond in a way that gives hackers more information — even if it just returns an error code — such as software version numbers and details on what the input should be. The invalid input may also cause the application or even the server itself to hang. Similar to the case study earlier in the chapter, hackers can use this information to determine more about the Web application and its inner workings, which can ultimately lead to a serious system compromise.

Code injection can also be carried out against back-end SQL databases — an attack known as *SQL injection.* Hackers insert rogue SQL statements to attempt to extract information from the SQL database that the Web application interacts with. Microsoft has a good Web site dedicated to Microsoft SQL Server security, including Slammer prevention and cleanup, at www.microsoft.com/sql/techinfo/administration/2000/security/slammer.asp. Also check out the popular and effective Shadow Database Scanner at www.safety-lab.com/en/products/6.htm.

Hidden field manipulation

Some Web applications embed hidden fields within Web pages to pass state information between the Web server and the browser. Hidden fields are represented in a Web form as <input type="hidden">. Due to poor coding practices, hidden fields often contain confidential information (such as product prices for an e-commerce site) that should be stored only in a back-end database. Users should not be able to see hidden fields — hence, the name — but the curious hacker can discover and exploit them with these steps:

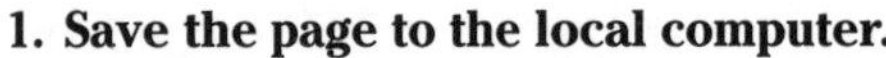

1. **Save the page to the local computer.**

2. **View the HTML source code.**

   To see the source code in Internet Explorer, choose View➪Source.

3. **Change the information stored in these fields.**

   For example, a hacker may change the price from $100 to $10.

4. **Re-post the page back to the server.**

   This allows the hacker to obtain ill-gotten gains, such as a lower price on a Web purchase.

Cross-site scripting

Cross-site scripting (XSS) is a well-known Web application vulnerability that occurs when a Web page displays user input — via JavaScript — that isn't properly validated. A hacker can take advantage of the absence of input filtering and cause a Web site to execute malicious code on any user's computer that views the page.

For example, an XSS attack can display the user ID and password login page from another rogue Web site. If users unknowingly enter their user IDs and passwords in the login page, the user IDs and passwords are entered into the hacker's Web server log file. Other malicious code can be sent to a victim's computer and run with the same security privileges as the Web browser or e-mail application that's viewing it on the system; the malicious code could provide a hacker with full read/write access to the entire hard drive!

A simple test shows whether your Web application is vulnerable to XSS. Look for any parts of the application that accept user input (such as a login field or search field), and enter the following JavaScript statement:

```
<script>alert('You have been scripted')</script>
```

If a window pops up that says `You have been scripted`, as shown in Figure 16-5, the application is vulnerable.

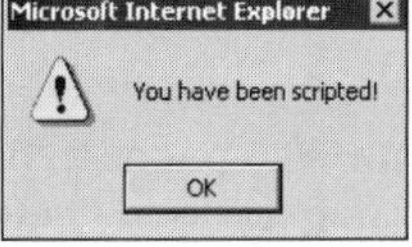

Figure 16-5: A sample JavaScript pop-up window.

Countermeasures

Web applications must filter incoming data. The applications must check and ensure that the data being entered fits within the parameters of what the application is expecting. If the data doesn't match, the application should generate an error and not permit the data to be entered. The first input validation of the form should be matched up with an input validation within the application to ensure that the input parameter meets the requirement.

Developers should know and implement these best practices:

- To reduce hidden-field vulnerabilities, Web applications should never present static values that the Web browser and the user don't need to see. Instead, this data should be implemented within the Web application on the server side and retrieved from a database only when needed.
- To minimize XSS vulnerabilities, the application should filter out `<script>` tags from the input fields.
- You can also disable JavaScript in the Web browser on the client side as an added security precaution.

Some secure software coding practices can eliminate all these issues from the get-go if they're made a critical part of the development process.

Default Scripts

Poorly written Web programs, such as Common Gateway Interface (CGI) and Active Server Pages (ASP) scripts, can allow hackers to view and manipulate files on a Web server that they're not authorized to access, as well as upload tons of files that can eventually fill the Web server's hard drive. Attacks such as the Poison Null attack and Upload Bombing attack against vulnerable CGI scripts written in Perl permit unauthorized access.

Attacks

Default script attacks are common because so many poorly written scripts are floating around the Internet. Hackers can also take advantage of various sample scripts that install on Web servers — especially older versions of Microsoft's IIS Web server.

Many Web developers and Webmasters use these scripts without understanding how they really work or testing them, which can introduce serious security vulnerabilities.

Some poorly written scripts contain confidential information, such as usernames and passwords! To test for this, you can peruse scripts manually or use a text search tool — such as the Search function built into the Windows Start menu or the find program in Linux or UNIX — to find any hard-coded usernames and passwords. Look for such words as *admin, root, user, ID, login, password, pass,* and *pwd.*

Confidential or critical information that's embedded in scripts like this is rarely necessary and is often the result of poor coding practices — convenience over security.

Countermeasures

You can help prevent attacks against default Web scripts:

- Know how scripts work before deploying them within a Web application.
- Make sure that all default or sample scripts are removed from the Web server before using them.

Don't use scripts that have confidential information that's hard coded. They're a security incident in the making.

URL Filter Bypassing

It's possible for internal employees to bypass Web-content filtering applications and logging mechanisms to browse to sites that they shouldn't go to — potentially covering up malicious behavior and Internet usage.

Bypassing filters

Malicious employees bypass URL filtering mechanisms by using proxy servers, tunneling Web traffic over nonstandard ports, spoofing IP addresses, and so on. But an even-easier hack is to exploit the general mechanism built into URL filtering systems that filter Web traffic based on specific URLs and *keywords* (words that match a list or meet a certain criteria). Users take advantage of this practice by converting the URL to an IP address and then to its binary equivalent. The following steps can bypass URL filtering in such browsers as Netscape and Mozilla:

1. **Obtain the IP address for the Web site.**

For example, a gambling Web site (`www.go-gamblin.com`) blocked in Web-content filtering software has this IP address:

```
10.22.33.44
```

This is an invalid public address, but it's okay for this example; you may want to filter out Web addresses on your internal network as well.

2. **Convert each individual number in the IP address to an eight-digit binary number.**

Numbers that may have fewer than eight digits in their binary form must be padded with leading zeroes to fill in the missing digits. For example, the binary number 1 is padded to 00000001 by adding seven zeroes.

The four individual numbers in the IP address in Step 1 have these equivalent eight-digit binary numbers:

```
10 = 00001010
```

```
22 = 00010110
```

```
33 = 00100001
```

```
44 = 00101100
```

The Windows Calculator can automatically convert numbers from decimal to binary notation:

i. Choose View➪Scientific.

ii. Click the Dec option button.

iii. Enter the number in decimal value.

iv. Click the Bin option button to show the number in binary format.

3. **Assemble the four 8-digit binary numbers into one 32-digit binary number.**

For example, the complete 32-digit binary equivalent for 10.22.33.44 is

```
00001010000101100010000100101100
```

Don't add the binary numbers. Just organize them in the same order as the original IP address without the separating periods.

4. **Convert the 32-digit binary number to a decimal number.**

For example, the 32-digit binary number `00001010000101100010000100101100` equals the decimal number 169222444.

The decimal number doesn't need to be padded to a specific length.

5. **Plug the decimal number into the Web browser's address field, like this:**

```
http://169222444
```

The Web page loads easy as pie!

The preceding steps won't bypass URLs in Internet Explorer.

Countermeasures

If the bypassing of certain Web-content filters is an issue for your network, ask your content-filtering vendor if it has a solution.

Automated Scans

Automated application-security-assessment tools can find vulnerabilities within a Web application that are next to impossible to find otherwise.

You can't solely rely on automated tools to test your Web applications. But I can't imagine comprehensive security testing without them.

Nikto

Figure 16-6 shows the partial results of a Nikto scan against a default IIS 5.0 installation. This scan found that the remote scripts directory is browsable and that the server is vulnerable to XSS. It also identified default scripts. Nikto found 16 potential vulnerabilities out of the 2,000 items checked.

WebInspect

Figure 16-7 shows the output of a WebInspect scan against the default IIS 5.0 installation. This scan found XSS vulnerabilities, the IIS-specific Microsoft Data Access Components, and the `null.printer` vulnerabilities. WebInspect found a total of 208 potential vulnerabilities out of the 3,000 items checked.

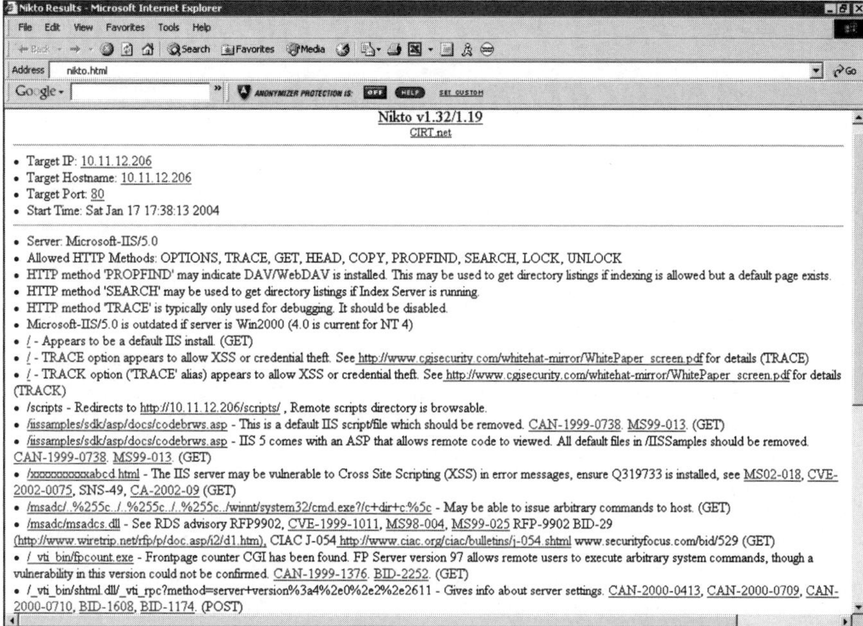

Figure 16-6: The results of a Nikto Web application scan.

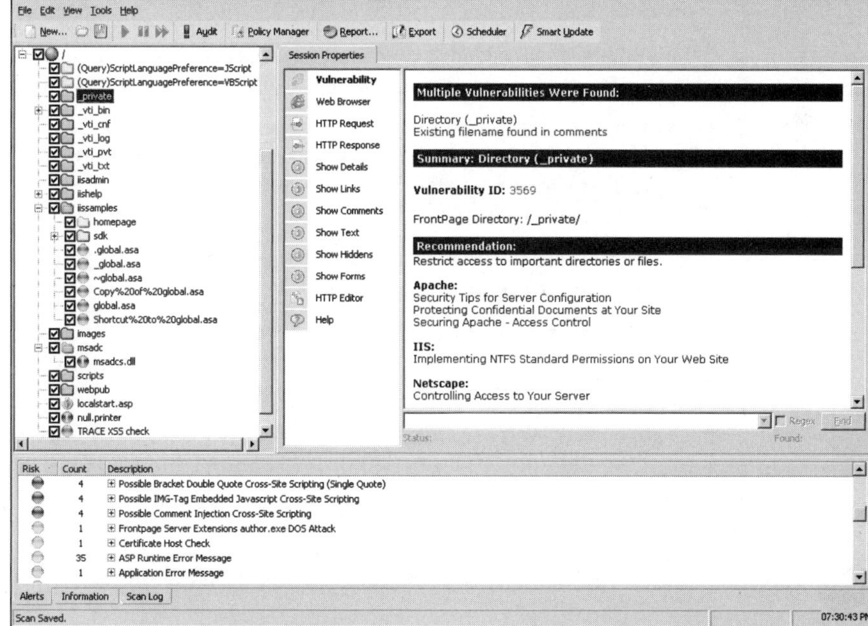

Figure 16-7: The results of a WebInspect Web-application scan.

General Best Practices for Minimizing Web-Application Security Risks

Keeping your Web applications secure requires ongoing vigilance from an ethical hacking perspective and from your Web-application developers and vendors. Keep up with the latest hacks and testing tools and techniques.

Obscurity

The following forms of security by *obscurity* can help prevent automated attacks from worms or scripts that are hard-coded to attack specific script types or default HTTP ports.

- To protect Web applications and related databases, use different machines to run each Web server, application, and database server.

  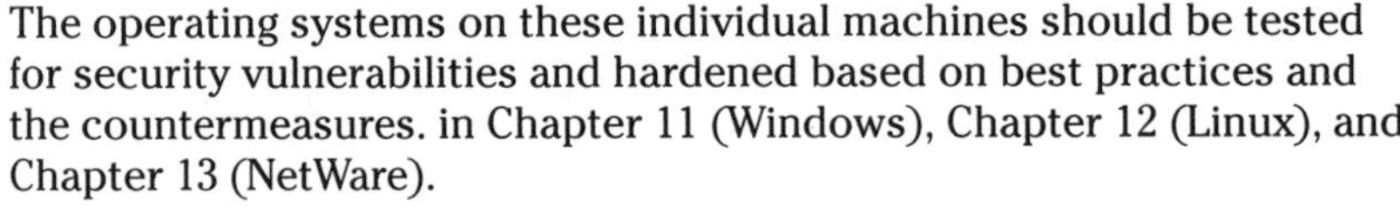

  The operating systems on these individual machines should be tested for security vulnerabilities and hardened based on best practices and the countermeasures. in Chapter 11 (Windows), Chapter 12 (Linux), and Chapter 13 (NetWare).

- Use built-in Web-server security features to handle access controls and process isolation, such as the application-isolation feature in IIS 6.0.

  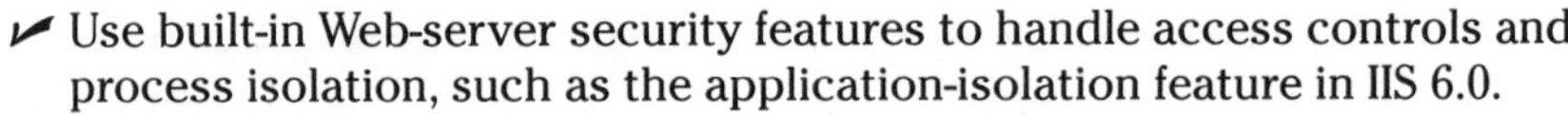

  This helps ensure that if one Web application is attacked, it won't necessarily risk any other applications running on the same server.

- If you're concerned about platform-specific attacks being carried out against your Web application, you can trick the attacker into thinking the Web server or operating system is something completely different. Here are a few examples:
  - If you're running a Microsoft IIS server and applications, you may be able to rename all your ASP scripts to have a `.cgi` extension.
  - If you're running a Linux Web server, use a program such as IP Personality (`ippersonality.sourceforge.net`) to change the OS fingerprint so the system looks like it's running something else.
- Change your Web application to run on a nonstandard port. Change from the default HTTP port 80 or HTTPS port 443 to a high port number, such as 8877.

Don't rely on obscurity alone; it isn't foolproof. A dedicated hacker may be able to determine that the system isn't what it claims to be.

Firewalls

Consider using these Web-application firewalls to protect your systems and information:

- A network-based firewall that can detect and block attacks against Web applications.
  - Commercial firewalls are available from such companies as NetScreen (www.netscreen.com), TippingPoint Technologies (www.tippingpoint.com), and Check Point (www.checkpoint.com).
  - An open-source firewall project called CodeSeeker is maintained by OWASP (www.owasp.org/development/codeseeker).
- Host-based Web-application intrusion-prevention applications such as
  - BlackICE — my all-time-favorite software application
  - Ubizen DMZ/Shield Enterprise (www.ubizen.com)
  - Eeye SecureIIS (www.eeye.com)
  - McAfee Entercept (www.nai.com)

  These programs can detect Web-application attacks in real time and cut them off before they have a chance to do any harm.
- Find security holes in Web applications before they're deployed. Use a third-party code-examiner expert or an automated tool, such as Flawfinder (www.dwheeler.com/flawfinder), ITS4 (www.cigital.com/its4), and RATS (www.securesoftware.com/auditing_tools_download.htm)

Software development is where security holes begin and should end — but rarely do. If you can influence your Web developers, you can really make a difference in the security of your Web applications by encouraging secure development practices from the start. See Appendix A for resources.

Part VI
Ethical Hacking Aftermath

"A centralized security management system sounds fine, but then what would we do with the dogs?"

In this part . . .

Well, now that the hard — or at least technical — stuff is over with, it's time to pull everything together, fix what's broken, and establish some good practices to move forward with.

First off, this part covers reporting the vulnerabilities you discovered to help get upper management buy-in and (more) budget to fix the security problems you've found. This part then covers some good practices on plugging the various security holes within your systems and patching everything up to keep from being hacked. Finally, this part covers what it takes to manage change within your security systems for long-term success, including outsourcing ethical hacking so you can add even *more* projects to your overflowing plate! That's what working in information technology is all about anyway, right?

Chapter 17

Reporting Your Results

In This Chapter

- Bringing your test data together
- Categorizing the vulnerabilities you discovered
- Documenting and presenting the final results

If you're looking for a break after testing, now isn't the time to rest on your laurels. The reporting phase of your ethical hacking is the most critical piece. The last thing you want to do is to run your tests, find security problems, and leave it at that. It's important to make sure that all your time and effort is put to good use by thoroughly analyzing and documenting what you found to ensure that security vulnerabilities are fixed.

Ethical hacking reporting includes debriefing upper management or your client on the various security issues found. You share the information you gathered and give the other parties guidance on where to go from here. Reporting also shows that time, effort, and money are put to good use.

Pulling the Results Together

When you have gobs of test data — from manual observations you documented to detailed reports from the various tools you used — what do you do with it all? The task at hand is to go through your documentation with a fine-tooth comb and highlight with a marker all the areas that stand out. Base your decisions on

- Your knowledge as a security professional
- Vulnerability ratings from your assessment tools

Many feature-rich security tools assign each vulnerability a risk rating, explain the details of the vulnerability and give possible solutions, and even reference a specific link to the Common Vulnerabilities and Exposures (CVE) Web site at `cve.mitre.org` so you can find out more information about the vulnerability. For further research, you may also need to reference the vendor's Web site to find out more and see whether the vulnerability affects your particular system.

You can plug this information into a table in Excel or in Word. I prefer to go through everything in hard-copy form because it's easier for me to read, but your choice may depend on how much data there is. If you think more highly of trees, you may want to just read the results off the computer screen and copy and paste the items that stand out into a new *Vulnerabilities to Address* document.

In your document, you may want to organize the vulnerabilities as shown in the following list:

- Nontechnical Issues
  - Social Engineering Vulnerabilities
  - Physical Security Vulnerabilities
  - Miscellaneous
- Workstations
  - Operating Systems
  - Applications
  - Miscellaneous
- Servers
  - Operating Systems
  - Applications
  - Miscellaneous
- Other Network Hosts
  - Hubs and Switches
  - Routers
  - Firewalls
  - Intrusion-Detection Systems
  - Miscellaneous

Consider creating a couple of separate lists for these security vulnerabilities:

- Internal vulnerabilities, such as internal hosts and organizational issues
- External vulnerabilities, such as public hosts, business-partner network connections, and telecommuters

Prioritizing Vulnerabilities

It's critical to prioritize the security vulnerabilities you've found, because many may not be fixable or not worth fixing. You may not be able to eliminate some vulnerabilities due to various technical reasons, and you may not be able to afford to eliminate others. You need to factor in whether the benefit is worth the effort and cost involved. For instance, if you determine that it will cost $8,000 to encrypt a sales-leads database worth $5,000 to the organization, it may not make sense. You need to study each vulnerability carefully and weigh whether it's worth fixing.

Analyze each vulnerability carefully, and determine your worst-case scenarios. It's not possible — or not worth trying — to fix every vulnerability that you've found.

Here's a quick-and-dirty method you can use when prioritizing your vulnerabilities. You should tweak it based on your needs. You need to consider two major factors for each of the vulnerabilities you've discovered:

- **Likelihood of use:** How likely is it that the specific vulnerability you're analyzing will be taken advantage of in a malicious way by a hacker, a rogue insider, or malware?
- **Impact if exploited:** The impact is rated based on how detrimental it would be to the information systems you're assessing and the organization as a whole.

Rank each vulnerability, using criteria such as High, Medium, and Low or a 1-through-5 rating (where 1 is the lowest and 5 is the highest) for each of the two categories. Table 17-1 shows a sample table and a representative vulnerability for each category.

Table 17-1 Prioritizing Vulnerabilities

Impact	*Likelihood*		
	High	**Medium**	**Low**
High	Unsecured wireless AP	No admin password on SQL server	Unencrypted emails being sent
Medium	End users with Internet-only access having weak login passwords	Unauthorized access when user is away from computer	Tape backups that are not password-protected
Low	Outdated virus signatures on a stand-alone PC dedicated to Internet browsing	Cleaning crew personnel gaining unauthorized network access	Weak encryption being exploited

The vulnerability prioritization shown in Table 17-1 is based on the qualitative method of assessing risks. It's subjective, based on your knowledge of the systems and vulnerabilities, but you can also consider any risk ratings you get from your security tools. Chapter 18 identifies vulnerabilities to focus on.

Reporting Methods

You need to organize your vulnerability information into a nice, pretty document for upper management or your customer. Ferret out the critical findings, and document them in a way that other parties can understand them without having to be security experts.

Graphs and charts are a plus but not required. Screen captures of your findings — especially when it's more difficult to save the data to a file — can add a really nice touch to your reports.

Document the vulnerabilities in a concise, nontechnical manner:

- Every report should contain the following information:
  - Tests that were performed
  - Specific dates and times the testing was carried out
  - Summary of the vulnerabilities discovered
  - Prioritized list of vulnerabilities that need to be addressed (action items)

- If it will add value to upper management or your customer, add this information to your report:
  - Steps on how to plug the security holes found
  - List of general recommendations to improve overall security

Most people want the hard-copy report to include a *summary* of the findings — not everything. The last thing most people want to see is a 5-inch stack of papers to sift through.

Many managers and customers like receiving raw-data reports from the security tools on a CD-ROM. They can reference the data later if they want but don't have to get mired in hundreds of hard-copy pages of technical gobbledygook.

Your list of action items may include something similar to the following:

- Enable Windows auditing on all servers.
- Put lock on server-room door.
- Harden operating systems based on best practices from SANS (`www.sans.org`), NIST (`crsc.nist.gov`), the National Security Agency Security Recommendation Guides (`www.nsa.gov/snac/index.html`), and *Network Security For Dummies*.
- Use a paper shredder for the destruction of confidential hard-copy information.
- Install personal firewall/IDP software on all laptops.
- Apply the latest vendor patches to the Web server.

As part of the final report, you may want to document employee reactions you observed when carrying out your ethical hacking tests. For example, were employees completely oblivious or even belligerent when you carried out an obvious social-engineering attack? Did IT or security staff completely miss technical tip-offs, such as the performance of the network degrading during testing or various attacks listed in system log files? You can also document other security issues you observed, such as how quickly IT or security staff responded to your tests or whether they even responded at all.

If an ethical hacking report and all the associated documentation and files were to fall into the hands of a competitor, hacker, or malicious insider, that could spell disaster for the organization. Here are some ways to prevent this from happening:

- Keep the report and associated documentation and files confidential, and deliver them only to those who need to know.

- Remove these programs and data that a hacker or rogue insider could use from the report in malicious ways:
  - Tools, such as password crackers and network analyzers
  - Log files
  - Test data

I recommend leaving the actual testing steps out of the report. Just answer any questions on that subject as needed.

Chapter 18

Plugging Security Holes

In This Chapter

- Determining which vulnerabilities to address first
- Patching your systems
- Looking at your security in a new light

Now it's time to head down the road to greater security. You've found some security vulnerabilities — ideally, not too many serious ones! These security holes must be plugged before someone exploits them. This is going to require rolling up your sleeves and using a little elbow grease to make things happen. First, you need to come up with your game plan and decide which security vulnerabilities to address first. A few patches may be in order, and possibly even some system hardening. This may be a time to reevaluate your network design and security infrastructure as well. I touch on some of the critical areas here. You may also want to refer to the fine book *Network Security For Dummies,* by Chey Cobb (Wiley Publishing Inc.). Chey does a great job of covering each of these topics in depth.

Turning Your Reports into Action

It may seem obvious which security vulnerabilities to address first, but it's often not that black-and-white. The variables involved with each host that need addressing include

- Whether the vulnerability can be fixed
- How critical the host is
- Whether you can take the system offline to fix the problem
- How easy the vulnerability is to fix
- Costs involved in purchasing new hardware or software to plug the holes

In Chapter 17, I cover the more basic issues of how important and how urgent the security problem is. You should look at this from a time-management perspective and address the issues that are both important (high-impact) and urgent (high-likelihood). You don't want to try to fix the vulnerabilities that are *just* high-impact or *just* high-likelihood. You may have some high-impact vulnerabilities that will likely never be exploited. Likewise, you probably have some vulnerabilities that have a high likelihood of being exploited, yet won't really make a big difference in the future of the company.

Focus on the highest-payoff tasks — those that are both high-impact *and* high-likelihood. Ideally, this will be the minority of your overall number of vulnerabilities. Then you can go after the less important and less urgent tasks, such as a renaming the administrator ID on a handful of noncritical stand-alone workstations, as time and money permit, if that's what you choose to do.

Patching for Perfection

Do you ever feel like all you do is patch your systems to fix security vulnerabilities? If you answer yes to this question, good for you — at least you're doing it! If you constantly feel pressured to patch your systems but can't seem to find time — at least it's on your radar! Many IT and security professionals don't even think about patching their systems until they get hacked. If you're reading this book, you're obviously concerned about security and way past that.

Whatever you do, whatever tool you choose, and whatever procedures work best in your environment — keep your systems patched!

Patching is a necessary evil. The only real solution to eliminating the need for patches is developing secure software in the first place, but that's not going to happen any time soon. The majority of security incidents can be prevented with some good patching practices, so there's simply no reason not to patch.

Patch management

Whether you can keep up with the deluge of security patches for all of your systems, don't despair; there are some ways to get a handle on the problem. Here are my three basic tenets of applying patches to keep your systems secure:

- Make sure all the people and departments that are involved in applying patches in your organization's systems are on the same page and follow the same procedures.

- Have procedures in place for these critical processes:
  - Obtaining patch alerts from your vendors.
  - Assessing which patches affect your systems.
  - Determining when patches are applied.

  Appendix A lists links to patch-notification systems.
- Make it policy and have a procedure in place for testing patches *before* you apply them to your production servers, if that's possible. Many patches have undocumented features and subsequent unintended side effects — believe me, I've experienced this before. An untested patch is an invitation for system termination!

Patch automation

There are various patch-deployment tools you can use to lower the burden of constantly having to keep up with patches, as described in the following sections.

Commercial tools

I recommend a robust patch-automation application — especially if you have

- A large network
- A network with several different operating systems (Windows, Linux, NetWare, and so on)
- More than a dozen or so computers

There are various patch-automation solutions. Be sure to at least check out:

- Patch Manager from BigFix (`www.bigfix.com`)
- HFNetChk Pro from Shavlik Technologies (`www.shavlik.com`)
- Ecora Patch Manager from Ecora (`www.ecora.com`)
- SysUpdate from SecurityProfiling (`www.securityprofiling.com`)

The GFI LANguard Network Scanner product that I use to demonstrate a vulnerability-assessment tool in this book can both check for patches to be applied and deploy the patches.

Watch the other major vulnerability-assessment tool vendors. They are starting to integrate logic in those programs to deploy patches to address the vulnerabilities their products find — a process called vulnerability management.

Free tools

If you're running Windows, use one of these free automated tools:

- Windows Update, which is built into Microsoft Windows systems
- Microsoft Baseline Security Analyzer (MBSA)
- Microsoft Software Update Services (SUS) Server

Hardening Your Systems

Even after you patch your systems, you're still not done. You've got to make sure your systems are hardened from the other security vulnerabilities that patches cannot fix. I've found over the years that many people stop with patching, thinking their systems are secure, but that's just not possible. Throughout the years, I've seen network administrators ignore recommended hardening best practices from organizations such as SANS (`www.sans.org`), NIST (`www.nist.gov`), and the National Security Agency (`www.nsa.gov/snac/index.html`), leaving many security holes wide open.

Network Security For Dummies contains a lot of great resources for hardening various systems on your network.

I was once involved in cleaning up a hack attack on a Windows NT server for a customer of mine. I had been telling them ever since they hired me that they needed to let me harden their network from attack. They basically had a server wide open on the Internet with a public IP address (ouch!) and no firewall installed. They were willing to pay me to patch the server, but that was it. There was only so much that could be done to secure it completely from the elements, given their environment and specific needs. They didn't heed my advice on at least getting the server behind a firewall, if not reconfiguring the way their application worked. Neither of these was an option.

Time passed, and nothing happened until one day, a hacker compromised the server, uploaded FTP server software, and started hosting illegal movies and music — effectively locking everyone out the server. After the downtime, lost business, and cost of paying me to finally fix the problem, it ended up costing them way more than the price of a firewall and a couple of hours of installation time.

This book presents hardening countermeasures that you can implement for your network, computers, and even physical systems and people. These are the ones I've found to work the best for the respective systems.

It's absolutely critical to implement at least the basic security best practices. Whether installing a firewall on the network or requiring users to have strong passwords — you *must* do the basics if you want any modicum of security.

Beyond patching, if you follow the countermeasures I've documented in this book, along with the other well-known security best practices that are freely available on the Internet for such network systems (routers, servers, workstations, and so on), as well as perform ethical hacking tests on an ongoing basis, you can rest assured that you're doing your best to keep your organization's information secure.

Assessing Your Security Infrastructure

A review of your overall security infrastructure can add oomph to your systems.

Look at the big picture. How is your network actually designed? What about your building? You should even consider organizational issues such as whether policies are in place, maintained, or even taken seriously. Does upper management take information security seriously, or do they simply shrug it off as another unnecessary expense?

Using the information you gathered by performing the ethical hacking tests in this book, map your network. Update existing documentation — a major necessity. Outline IP addresses, running services, and whatever else you've found out. Although I prefer Visio or other, more-capable network diagramming tools, you could even draw out your map on a napkin! Just draw it out. Network design and overall security issues are a whole lot easier to assess when you can see them visually.

Are you focusing all your efforts on the perimeter and not on a layered security approach? Think about how most convenience stores and banks are protected. Their security cameras are focused on the cash registers, teller computers, and surrounding areas — not just on the parking lot or entrance areas. Look at security from a *defense in-depth* perspective. Make sure that several layers of security are in place just in case one measure fails, so the malicious user must go through various other barriers and jump through other hoops to carry out a hack attack successfully.

Do the same thing with organizational issues as well. Document what security policies and procedures are in place and how effective they are. Look at the overall security culture within your company, and see what it looks like from an outsider's perspective. What would customers or business partners think about how your organization is treating their confidential information?

Looking at your security from a high-level and nontechnical perspective will give you a new outlook on what else still needs to be done. It takes some time and effort at first, but after you establish a baseline of security, it will be much easier to manage and keep a handle on moving forward as new threats and vulnerabilities emerge.

Chapter 19

Managing Security Changes

In This Chapter

- Automating tasks
- Watching for misbehavior
- Outsourcing testing
- Keeping security on everyone's mind

Information security is an ongoing process that must be managed effectively to be successful. This goes beyond applying patches and hardening systems every so often. Performing your ethical hacking tests again and again is critical; information security threats and vulnerabilities constantly emerge. Combine this with the fact that ethical hacking tests are just a snapshot in time view of your overall information security, so you have to perform your tests on an ongoing basis to keep up with the latest security issues.

You need to consider a few key issues in your ongoing efforts, such as automating some of the testing, monitoring for malicious use, and even outsourcing some or all of your ethical hacking and security services. In this chapter, I cover the critical issues that you can consider to help ensure long-term success in your security efforts.

Automating the Ethical Hacking Process

The ethical hacking tests that can be automated are covered in this book:

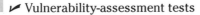

- Port scans
- Password-cracking tests
- Vulnerability-assessment tests

You've got to have the right tools to automate tests:

- Some commercial tools can set up ongoing assessments and create nice reports for you without any hands-on intervention — just a little setup and scheduling time up front. This is why I like many of the commercial security testing tools. This often helps justify the price of the tools — especially if you don't have to be up at 2:00 in the morning or on call 24 hours a day to monitor the testing.

- Stand-alone security tools such as Nmap, John the Ripper, and Nessus aren't enough. You can use the Windows Scheduler and AT commands on Windows systems and cron jobs on UNIX–based systems, but manual steps are still required.

True security isn't possible by automating everything. Certain issues can't be set on autopilot, such as enumeration of new systems, social engineering, and physical-security walk-throughs. Even the smartest computer "expert system" will never be able to accomplish some security tests. Good security requires both technical know-how and good old-fashioned experience.

Monitoring Malicious Use

Monitoring for security events is essential for ongoing security efforts. This can be as basic — and mundane — as monitoring log files on routers, firewalls, and critical servers every day or as advanced — and, often, expensive — as implementing an event-correlation system to keep tabs on every little thing happening on the network. A common method is to deploy an IDS or IDP system and monitor for malicious behavior. The problem with this and most security monitoring solutions is that it can be a very boring yet very difficult task to do effectively.

Consider dedicating a time every day — such as first thing in the morning — to check your critical log files from the previous night or weekend to ferret out intrusions and other computer and network problems that could be security-related. You could also dedicate a person to this task, but do you really want to subject someone to that kind of torture?

- Finding some — much less all — critical security events in system log files is difficult or impossible. It's just too tedious a task for the average human to accomplish effectively.
- Some security events, such as IDS evasion techniques and hacks coming into allowed ports on the network, may not be detected at all, depending on the type of logging and security equipment you have in place.

Enable as much event logging as possible. You don't necessarily need to capture all computer and network events, but you should definitely look for certain obvious ones, such as login failures, packets, and unauthorized file access. The preferable way to log security events is to use a syslog server on your network and not keep logs on the local host, if at all possible. This can help prevent hackers from tampering with log files to cover their tracks. Check out `www.loganalysis.org` for great logging resources.

A couple of good solutions to the security monitoring dilemma are to

- Purchase an event-logging system. A few low-priced yet effective solutions are available, such as GFI's Security Event Log Monitor (`www.gfi.com/lanselm`). Just keep in mind that typically lower-priced event-management systems usually support only one OS platform: Microsoft Windows. Higher-end solutions, such as GuardedNet's neuSECURE (`www.guardednet.net`), offer both basic log management and event correlation to help track down the source of security problems, as well as the various systems that were affected during an incident.
- Outsource security monitoring to a third-party managed security services provider (MSSP). Dozens and dozens of MSSPs were around during the Internet boom days, but only a few strong ones still remain. The value in outsourcing security monitoring is that the MSSP often has facilities and tools that you may not be able to afford. They also have analysts working around the clock and can take the security experiences and knowledge they gain from other customers and share it with your systems.

  When these MSSPs discover a security vulnerability or intrusion, they can usually address the issue immediately often without even getting you involved. I recommend at least checking whether third-party firms and their services can free up some of your time and resources so you can focus on other things. Just don't depend solely on their monitoring efforts; an MSSP can't catch insider abuse or social-engineering attacks. You're still going to have to be involved in a limited capacity.

Outsourcing Ethical Hacking

Outsourcing ethical hacking is very popular. It's a great way for organizations to get an unbiased third-party perspective on their information security.

Outsourcing ethical hacking is expensive. Many organizations will have to spend thousands — often, tens of thousands — of dollars, depending on the testing needed. But it's not cheap to do all of this yourself!

Outsourcing allows you to have a sort of checks-and-balances system.

Outsourcing isn't free or inexpensive. A lot of confidential information is at stake, so you must be able to trust your outside consultants and vendors. Consider the following questions when looking for a vendor to partner with:

- Is your ethical hacking vendor on your side or third-party vendors' side? Is the vendor trying to sell you products, or is it vendor-neutral? Many vendors may try to make a few more dollars off the deal — which may not be necessary for your needs. This may be okay, but just make sure that no major conflicts of interest are making you uncomfortable.

- What other IT or security services does the vendor offer? Does it focus solely on security?

  It can help to find an ethical hacking specialist instead of an IT generalist organization to do this testing for you.

- What are your vendor's hiring/termination policies?

  Look for measures the vendor takes to minimize the chances that an employee will walk off with all of your confidential information.

- Does the vendor understand your business needs behind ethical hacking?

  Have the vendor repeat the list of your needs back to you to make sure you're both on the same page.

- How well does the vendor communicate? Do you trust that the vendor will keep you informed and will follow up with you in a timely manner?
- Do you know exactly who will be performing the tests? Will one person do all the testing, or will subject-matter experts focus on the different areas? This isn't a deal breaker — it's just nice to know.
- Does the vendor have the experience to recommend practical and effective countermeasures to the vulnerabilities found?
- Do you get the impression that the vendor is in this to make a quick buck off the services, with minimal effort and value added, or is the vendor in this to build loyalty with you?

  Find a good organization to work with long-term. That will make your ongoing efforts much simpler.

- Ask for several references, and sample *sanitized* deliverables from your vendor. If the vendor cannot produce these, or it seems overly difficult, look for another vendor.
- Run criminal-background checks on every person involved on the ethical hacking project. It's really cheap. I even slap my own customers' hands when they don't ask for permission to run a background check before hiring me for ethical hacking projects. If criminal-background checks aren't an option, make a thorough Internet search via search engine.

If your vendor won't agree to background checks of everyone involved in the ethical hacking projects, run — fast — to find another vendor. In addition, if the vendor won't disclose the details of what it's going to test for (not necessarily how the testing will be carried out), or won't commit to being available in case problems arise, find another vendor. Also, be wary if your vendor talks openly about the security (or general lack of it) of other clients. The vendor may just do the same for your organization as well!

Your vendor should have its own services agreement for you to sign, which should include a mutual nondisclosure statement. Make sure you both sign off on this to help protect your organization in the future.

Thinking about hiring a *reformed* hacker?

Former hackers — I'm referring to the black-hat hackers who have hacked into computer systems in the past — can be very good at what they do. Many people swear by it. Others compare this to hiring the proverbial fox to guard the chicken house. If you're thinking about bringing in a former unethical hacker to test your systems, consider these issues:

- Do you really want to reward hacker behavior with your organization's business?
- Claiming to be reformed doesn't mean he or she is. There could be deep-rooted personality issues you're going to have to contend with. *Buyer beware!*
- Information gathered during ethical hacking is some of the most sensitive information your organization possesses. This information in the wrong hands — even ten years after being gathered — could be used against your organization. Some hackers hang out in tight social groups. You may not want your information being shared in their circles.

Everyone deserves a chance to explain what happened in the past. Zero tolerance is senseless. Listen to his or her story, and use common-sense discretion as to whether or not you trust this person to help you. The supposed black-hat hacker may have actually just been a gray hat or even a misguided white-hat hacker who makes a good fit in your organization.

Outsourcing ethical hacking may make good business sense for you, especially if you don't have the time or internal resources. Stay educated on the process, and keep tabs on what your vendor is doing during the process.

Instilling a Security-Aware Mindset

Your employees are often your first and last line of defense. Make sure all of your ethical hacking-efforts and money spent on all of your information-security initiatives aren't wasted due to a simple employee slip-up that gives a hacker the keys to the kingdom.

These elements can help establish a security-aware culture in an organization:

- Make employee awareness of security an active and ongoing process.
- Treat awareness and training programs as a long-term business investment.

  It doesn't have to be expensive. You can buy posters to hang up in break rooms, as well as mouse pads, screen savers, pens, and sticky notes to help get the word out and keep security on the top of everyone's mind. Some great vendors are Greenidea, Inc. (`www.greenidea.com`), Security Awareness, Inc. (`www.securityawareness.com`), and Interpact, Inc. (`www.interpactinc.com`).

- Get the word on security out to upper management!
- Align your security message with your audience, and keep it as nontechnical as possible.
- Lead by example. Show that you take this seriously, and offer evidence that helps to prove that everyone else should, too.

If you can get the ear of upper managers *and* end users alike, and put enough effort forth to make security a priority day after day, you may be able to help shape the culture in your organization. This can provide security value beyond your wildest imagination. I've seen the difference it makes!

Keeping Up with Other Security Issues

Ethical hacking isn't the *be all, end all* solution to information security. It cannot even guarantee security, but it's certainly a great start. Ethical hacking must be integrated as part of an overall information-security program that includes

- Higher-level information-risk assessments
- Strong security policies that are enforced
- Solid incident-response and business-continuity plans
- Effective security awareness and training initiatives

This may require hiring more staff or outsourcing more security help as well.

Don't forget about formal training for yourself and any colleagues. You've got to educate yourself consistently to stay on top of this game.

Part VII
The Part of Tens

"Our automated response policy to a large company-wide data crash is to notify management, back up existing data, and sell 90% of my shares in the company."

In this part . . .

Well, here's the end of the road, so to speak. In this part, I've compiled what I believe are the absolute critical success factors to make ethical hacking — and information security in general — work in any organization. Bookmark, dog-ear, or do whatever you need to do with these pages so you can refer to them over and over again. This is the meat of what you need to know about information security — even more so than all of the technical hacks and countermeasures I've covered thus far. Read it, study it, and make it happen. You can do it!

Chapter 20

Ten Tips for Getting Upper Management Buy-In

In This Chapter

- Staying away from fear, uncertainty, and doubt
- Proving yourself
- Communicating on their level
- Highlighting the benefits

Several key steps exist for obtaining the buy-in and sponsorship that you need to support your ethical hacking efforts. In this chapter, I describe the ones that I find to be the most effective.

Cultivate an Ally and Sponsor

Selling ethical hacking and information security to upper managers isn't something you want to tackle alone. Get an ally — preferably, your manager or someone at that level or higher in the organization — who understands the value of ethical hacking. Although this person may not be able to speak for you directly, she can be seen as an unbiased third-party sponsor and can give you more credibility.

Don't Be a FUDdy Duddy

Sherlock Holmes said, "It is a capital offense to theorize before one has data." It's up to you to make a good case and to put information security and the need for ethical hacking on upper management's radar. Just don't blow stuff out of proportion for the sake of stirring up fear, uncertainty, and doubt (FUD). Managers worth their salt see right through that. Focus on educating upper management with practical advice. Rational fears proportional to the threat are fine — just don't take the Chicken Little route, claiming that the sky's falling.

Demonstrate How the Organization Can't Afford to Be Hacked

Show how dependent the organization is on its information systems. Create *what-if* scenarios — kind of a business-impact assessment — to show what can happen and how long the organization can go without using the network, computers, and data. Ask upper-level managers what they would do without their computer systems and IT personnel. Show them real-world anecdotal evidence on hacker attacks, including malware, physical security, and social-engineering issues — but be positive about it. Don't approach this in a negative way with FUD. Rather, keep them informed on serious security happenings in their industry. Find stories related to similar businesses or industries so that they can relate. Clip magazine and newspaper articles.

Google is a great tool to find practically everything you need here.

Show management that the organization has what a hacker wants — a common misconception among those ignorant to the threats and vulnerabilities. And be sure to point out the potential costs from damage caused by hacking:

- Missed opportunity costs
- Loss of intellectual property
- Liability issues
- Legal costs
- Lost productivity
- Clean-up time and costs
- Costs of fixing a tarnished reputation

Outline the General Benefits of Ethical Hacking

In addition to the potential costs listed in the previous section, talk about how ethical hacking can help find security vulnerabilities in information systems that normally may be overlooked. Tell management that ethical hacking is a way of thinking like the bad guys so you can protect yourself from the bad guys — the *Art of War* mindset.

Show How Ethical Hacking Specifically Helps the Organization

Document benefits that support the overall business goals:

- Demonstrate how security doesn't have to be that expensive and can actually save the organization money long-term.
    - Security is much easier and cheaper to build in up front than to add on later.
    - Security doesn't have to be inconvenient and can enable productivity if it's done properly.
- Talk about how new products or services can be offered for a competitive advantage if secure information systems are in place.
    - Certain federal regulations are met.
    - Managers and the company look good to customers.
    - Ethical hacking shows that the organization is protecting customer and other critical information.

Get Involved in the Business

Understand the business — how it operates, who the key players are, and what politics are involved:

- Go to meetings to see and be seen. This can help prove that you're concerned about the business.
- Be a person of value who's interested in contributing to the business.
- Know your opposition. Again, use *The Art of War* and the "know your enemy" mentality — if you understand what you're dealing with, buy-in is *much* easier to get.

Establish Your Credibility

Focus on these three characteristics:

- Be positive about the organization, and prove that you really mean business. Your attitude is critical.
- Empathize with managers, and show them that you understand the business side.

- To create any positive business relationship, you must be trustworthy. Build up that trust over time, and selling security will be *much* easier.

Speak on Their Level

No one is really that impressed with techie talk. Talk in terms of the business. This key element of obtaining buy-in is actually part of establishing your credibility but deserves to be listed by itself.

I've seen countless IT and security professionals lose upper-level managers as soon as they start speaking. A megabyte here; stateful inspection there; packets, packets everywhere! Bad idea! Relate security issues to everyday business processes and job functions. Period.

Show Value in Your Efforts

Here's where the rubber meets the road. If you can demonstrate that what you're doing offers business value on an ongoing basis, you can maintain a good pace and not have to constantly plead to keep your ethical hacking program going. Keep these points in mind:

- Document your involvement in IT and information security, and create ongoing reports for upper-level managers regarding the state of security in the organization. Give them examples of how their systems will be secured from known attacks.
- Outline tangible results as a proof of concept. Show sample vulnerability-assessment reports you've run on your own systems or from the security tool vendors.
- Treat doubts, concerns, and objections by upper management as requests for more information. Find the answers, and go back armed and ready to prove your ethical hacking worthiness.

Be Flexible and Adaptable

Prepare yourself for skepticism and rejection at first — it happens a lot — especially from such upper managers as CFOs and CEOs, who are often completely disconnected from IT and security in the organization.

Don't get defensive. Security is a long-term process, not a short-term product or single assessment. Start small — with a limited amount of such resources as budget, tools, and time — if you must, and then build the program over time.

Chapter 21

Ten Deadly Mistakes

In This Chapter

- Obtaining written approval
- Assuming that you can find and fix everything
- Testing only once
- Having bad timing

Several deadly mistakes — when properly executed — can wreak havoc on your ethical hacking outcomes and even your job or career. In this chapter, I discuss the potential pitfalls that you need to be keenly aware of.

Not Getting Approval in Writing

Getting approval for your ethical hacking efforts — whether it's from upper management or the customer — is an absolute must. It's your *get out of jail free* card.

Obtain documented approval that includes the following:

- Explicitly lay out your plan, your schedule, and the affected systems.
- Get the *authorized* decision-maker to sign off on the plan, agreeing to the terms and agreeing not to hold you liable for malicious use or other bad things that can happen unintentionally.
- Get the signed original copy of the agreement.

No exceptions here!

Assuming That You Can Find All Vulnerabilities During Your Tests

So many security vulnerabilities exist — some known and just as many or more unknown — that you can't find them all during your testing. Don't make any guarantees that you'll find all security vulnerabilities. You'll be starting something that you can't finish.

Stick to the following tenets:

- Be realistic.
- Use good tools.
- Get to know your systems, and practice honing your techniques.

Assuming That You Can Eliminate All Security Vulnerabilities

When it comes to computers, 100 percent security has never been attainable and never will be. You can't possibly prevent all security vulnerabilities. You'll do fine if you

- Follow best practices.
- Harden your systems.
- Apply as many security countermeasures as reasonably possible.

Performing Tests Only Once

Ethical hacking is a snapshot in time of your overall state of security. New threats and vulnerabilities surface continuously, so you must perform these tests regularly to make sure you keep up with the latest security defenses for your systems.

Pretending to Know It All

No one working with computers or information security knows it all. It's basically impossible to keep up with all the software versions, hardware models, and new technologies emerging all the time — not to mention all the associate security vulnerabilities! Good ethical hackers know their limitations — they know what they don't know. However, they certainly know where to go to get the answers (try Google first).

Running Your Tests without Looking at Things from a Hacker's Viewpoint

Think about how an *outside* hacker can attack your network and computers. You may need a little bit of inside information to test some things reasonably, but try to limit that as much as possible. Get a fresh perspective, and think outside that proverbial box. Study hacker behaviors and common hack attacks so you know what to test for.

Ignoring Common Attacks

Focus on the systems and tests that matter the most. You can hack away all day at a stand-alone desktop running MS-DOS from a 5¼-inch floppy disk with no network card and no hard drive, but does that do any good?

Not Using the Right Tools

Without the right tools for the task, it's almost impossible to get anything done — at least not without driving yourself nuts! Download the free tools I mention throughout this book and list in Appendix A. Buy commercial tools if you have the inclination and the budget. No security tool does it all. Build up your toolbox over time, and get to know your tools well. This will save you gobs of effort, plus you can impress others with your results.

Pounding Production Systems at the Wrong Time

One of the best ways to lose your job or customers is to run hack attacks against production systems when everyone and his brother is using them. Mr. Murphy's Law will pay a visit and take down critical systems at the absolute worst time. Make sure you know when the best time is to perform your testing. It may be in the middle of the night. (I never said being an ethical hacker was easy!) This may be reason enough to justify using security tools and other supporting utilities that can help automate certain ethical hacking tasks.

Outsourcing Testing and Not Staying Involved

Outsourcing is great, but you must stay involved. It's a bad idea to hand over the reins to a third party for all your security testing without following up and staying on top of what's taking place. You won't be doing anyone a favor except your outsourced vendors by staying out of their hair. Get in their hair. (But not like gum — that just makes everything more difficult.)

Part VIII
Appendixes

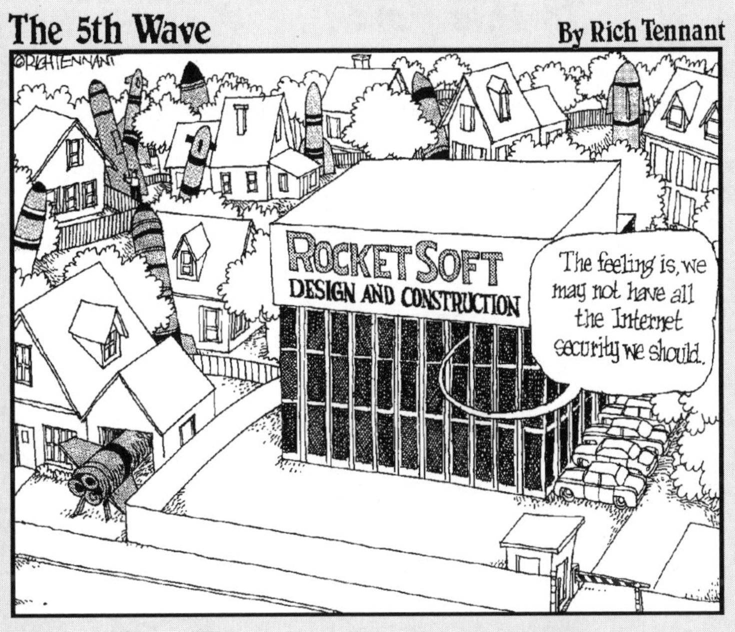
The 5th Wave
By Rich Tennant
©RICHTENNANT
ROCKETSOFT
DESIGN AND CONSTRUCTION
The feeling is, we may not have all the Internet security we should.

In this part . . .

In this final part of the book, Appendix A contains a listing of my favorite ethical hacking tools that I cover throughout this book, broken down into various categories for easy reference. In addition, I list various other ethical hacking resources that I think you'll benefit from in your endeavors. Appendix B talks about the book's companion Web site. Hope it all helps!

Appendix A
Tools and Resources

In order to stay up to date with the latest and great ethical hacking tools and resources, you've got to know where to turn to. This Appendix contains my favorite security sites, tools, resources, and more that you can benefit from too in your ongoing ethical hacking program.

Awareness and Training

Greenidea, Inc. Visible Statement (www.greenidea.com)

Interpact, Inc. Awareness Resources (www.interpactinc.com)

SANS Security Awareness Program (store.sans.org)

Security Awareness, Inc. Awareness Resources (www.securityawareness.com)

Dictionary Files and Word Lists

ftp://ftp.cerias.purdue.edu/pub/dict

ftp://ftp.ox.ac.uk/pub/wordlists

packetstormsecurity.nl/Crackers/wordlists

www.outpost9.com/files/WordLists.html

Default vendor passwords www.cirt.net/cgi-bin/passwd.pl

General Research Tools

CERT/CC Vulnerability Notes Database `www.kb.cert.org/vuls`

ChoicePoint `www.choicepoint.com`

Common Vulnerabilities and Exposures `cve.mitre.org/cve`

Google `www.google.com`

Hoover's business information `www.hoovers.com`

NIST ICAT Metabase `icat.nist.gov/icat.cfm`

Sam Spade `www.samspade.org`

U.S. Securities and Exchange Commission `www.sec.gov/edgar.shtml`

Switchboard.com `www.switchboard.com`

U.S. Patent and Trademark Office `www.uspto.gov`

US Search.com `www.ussearch.com`

Yahoo! Finance site `finance.yahoo.com`

Hacker Stuff

2600 — The Hacker Quarterly magazine `www.2600.com`

Computer Underground Digest `www.soci.niu.edu/~cudigest`

Hackers: Heroes of the Computer Revolution book by Steven Levy

Hacker t-shirts, equipment, and other trinkets `www.thinkgeek.com`

Honeypots: Tracking Hackers `www.tracking-hackers.com`

The Online Hacker Jargon File `www.jargon.8hz.com`

PHRACK `www.phrack.org`

Linux

Bastille Linux hardening utility `www.bastille-linux.org`

Debian Linux Security Alerts `www.debian.org/security`

Linux Administrator's Security Guide `www.seifried.org/lasg`

Linux Kernel Updates `www.linuxhq.com`

Linux Security Auditing Tool (LSAT) `usat.sourceforge.net`

Red Hat Linux Security Alerts `www.redhat.com/support/alerts`

Slackware Linux Security Advisories `www.slackware.com/security`

Suse Linux Security Alerts `www.suse.com/us/business/security.html`

Tiger `ftp.debian.org/debian/pool/main/t/tiger`

VLAD the Scanner `razor.bindview.com/tools/vlad`

Log Analysis

LogAnalysis.org system logging resources `www.loganalysis.org`

Malware

chkrootkit `www.chkrootkit.org`

EICAR testing string `www.eicar.org/anti_virus_test_file.htm`

McAfee AVERT Stinger `vil.nai.com/vil/stinger`

PestPatrol's database of pests `research.pestpatrol.com/PestInfo/pestdatabase.asp`

Rkdet `vancouver-webpages.com/rkdet`

The File Extension Source `filext.com`

Wotsit's Format at `www.wotsit.org`

Messaging

GFI e-mail security test `www.gfi.com/emailsecuritytest`

smtpscan `www.greyhats.org/outils/smtpscan`

How to disable SMTP relay on various e-mail servers `www.mailabuse.org/tsi/ar-fix.html`

mailsnarf `www.monkey.org/~dugsong/dsniff` or `ww.datanerds.net/~mike/dsniff.html` for the Windows version

Rogue Aware by Akonix `www.akonix.com`

NetWare

chknull `www.phreak.org/archives/exploits/novell`

Craig Johnson's BorderManager resources `nscsysop.hypermart.net`

NCPQuery `razor.bindview.com/tools/index.shtml`

Novell Product Updates `support.novell.com/filefinder`

Remote `packetstormsecurity.nl/Netware/penetration`

Rcon program at `packetstormsecurity.nl/Netware/penetration/rcon.zip`

Userdump `www.roy.spang.org/freeware/userdump.html`

Networks

dsniff `www.monkey.org/~dugsong/dsniff`

Ethereal network analyzer `www.ethereal.com`

ettercap `ettercap.sourceforge.net`

Firewalk `www.packetfactory.net/firewalk`

Firewall Informer `www.blade-software.com`

Foundstone FoundScan `www.foundstone.com`

GFI LANguard Network Scanner `www.gfi.com`

MAC address vendor lookup `coffer.com/mac_find`

Nessus vulnerability assessment tool `www.nessus.org`

Netcat `www.atstake.com/research/tools/network_utilities`

NetScanTools Pro all-in-one network testing tool `www.netscantools.com`

Nmap port scanner `www.insecure.org/nmap`

Port number listing `www.iana.org/assignments/port-numbers`

Official Internet Protocol Standards `www.rfc-editor.org/rfcxx00.html`

Qualys QualysGuard vulnerability assessment tool `www.qualys.com`

SuperScan port scanner `www.foundstone.com`

WildPackets EtherPeek `www.wildpackets.com`

Password Cracking

LC4 `www.atstake.com/research/lc`

John the Ripper `www.openwall.com/john`

pwdump2 `razor.bindview.com/tools/desc/pwdump2_readme.html`

NetBIOS Auditing Tool `www.securityfocus.com/tools/543`

Crack `ftp://coast.cs.purdue.edu/pub/tools/unix/pwdutils/crack`

Brutus `www.hoobie.net/brutus`

Pandora `www.nmrc.org/project/Pandora`

Proactive Windows Security Explorer `www.elcomsoft.com/pwsex.html`

NTFSDOS Professional `www.winternals.com`

NTAccess `www.mirider.com/ntaccess.html`

TSCRACK `softlabs.spacebitch.com/tscrack/index.html`

TSGrinder `www.hammerofgod.com/download/tsgrinder-2.03.zip`

War Dialing

Palm ToneLoc Viewer chroot.ath.cx/fade/projects/palm/pTLV.html

PhoneSweep www.sandstorm.net/products/phonesweep

THC-Scan www.thc.org/releases.php

ToneLoc www.securityfocus.com/data/tools/auditing/pstn/tl110.zip

ToneLoc Utilities Phun-Pak www.hackcanada.com/ice3/phreak

Web Applications

2600's Hacked Pages www.2600.com/hacked_pages

Archive of Hacked Websites www.onething.com/archive

App Detective www.appsecinc.com

BlackWidow www.softbytelabs.com/BlackWidow

Flawfinder www.dwheeler.com/flawfinder

ITS4 www.cigital.com/its4

Netcraft www.netcraft.com

Nikto www.cirt.net/code/nikto.shtml

RATS www.securesoftware.com/auditing_tools_download.htm

Sanctum AppScan www.sanctuminc.com

Shadow Database Scanner www.safety-lab.com/en/products/6.htm

SPI Dynamics WebInspect www.spidynamics.com

Windows

Amap www.thc.org/releases.php

DumpSec www.somarsoft.com

Legion packetstormsecurity.nl/groups/rhino9/legionv21.zip

Microsoft Office Patches office.microsoft.com/officeupdate

Microsoft Security Resources `www.microsoft.com/technet/security/Default.asp`

Network Users `www.optimumx.com/download/netusers.zip`

Rpcdump `razor.bindview.com/tools/files/rpctools-1.0.zip`

SMAC MAC address changer `www.klcconsulting.net/smac`

Vision `www.foundstone.com`

Windows Update Utility for Patching `windowsupdate.microsoft.com`

Winfo `www.ntsecurity.nu/toolbox/winfo`

Wireless Networks

AirJack `802.11ninja.net/airjack`

AirMagnet `www.airmagnet.com`

AirSnort `airsnort.schmoo.com`

Cantenna war-driving kit `mywebpages.comcast.net/hughpep`

Fluke WaveRunner `www.flukenetworks.com`

Kismet `www.kismetwireless.net`

Lucent Orinoco Registry Encryption/Decryption program `www.cqure.net/tools.jsp?id=3`

Making a wireless antenna from a Pringles can `www.oreillynet.com/cs/weblog/view/wlg/448`

NetStumbler `www.netstumbler.com`

Pong wireless firmware vulnerability testing program `www.mobileaccess.de/wlan/dl.php/pong_v1.1.zip`

Security of the WEP Algorithm `www.isaac.cs.berkeley.edu/isaac/wep-faq.html`

The Unofficial 802.11 Security Web Page `www.drizzle.com/~aboba/IEEE`

Wellenreiter `www.wellenreiter.net`

WiGLE database of wireless networks at `www.wigle.net`

WildPackets AiroPeek `www.wildpackets.com`

Appendix B

About the Book Web Site

This book's companion Website contains links to all the tools and resources listed in Appendix A. Check it out at `www.dummies.com`.

Index

• Numbers & Symbols •

• A •

• B •

• C •

• G •

• H •

• L •

• M •

• N •

• O •

• P •

• Q •

• R •

• S •

• T •

• Z •

FOR DUMMIES®

Helping you expand your horizons and realize your potential

INTERNET

0-7645-0894-6

0-7645-1659-0

0-7645-1642-6

Also available:

America Online 7.0 For Dummies
(0-7645-1624-8)

Genealogy Online For Dummies
(0-7645-0807-5)

The Internet All-in-One Desk Reference For Dummies
(0-7645-1659-0)

Internet Explorer 6 For Dummies
(0-7645-1344-3)

The Internet For Dummies Quick Reference
(0-7645-1645-0)

Internet Privacy For Dummie
(0-7645-0846-6)

Researching Online For Dummies
(0-7645-0546-7)

Starting an Online Business For Dummies
(0-7645-1655-8)

DIGITAL MEDIA

0-7645-1664-7

0-7645-1675-2

0-7645-0806-7

Also available:

CD and DVD Recording For Dummies
(0-7645-1627-2)

Digital Photography All-in-One Desk Reference For Dummies
(0-7645-1800-3)

Digital Photography For Dummies Quick Reference
(0-7645-0750-8)

Home Recording for Musicians For Dummies
(0-7645-1634-5)

MP3 For Dummies
(0-7645-0858-X)

Paint Shop Pro "X" For Dummies
(0-7645-2440-2)

Photo Retouching & Restoration For Dummies
(0-7645-1662-0)

Scanners For Dummies
(0-7645-0783-4)

GRAPHICS

0-7645-0817-2

0-7645-1651-5

0-7645-0895-4

Also available:

Adobe Acrobat 5 PDF For Dummies
(0-7645-1652-3)

Fireworks 4 For Dummies
(0-7645-0804-0)

Illustrator 10 For Dummies
(0-7645-3636-2)

QuarkXPress 5 For Dummies
(0-7645-0643-9)

Visio 2000 For Dummies
(0-7645-0635-8)

Available wherever books are sold. Go to www.dummies.com or call 1-877-762-2974 to order direct.